Stories for the Homeschool Heart

P9-DFT-130

© 2010 by Bezalel Books

Published by
Bezalel Books
Waterford, MI
www.BezalelBooks.com

Printed in the United States of America

To invite Patti Maguire Armstrong and/or Theresa A. Thomas to speak at your event, visit www.RaisingCatholicKids.com, email Patti at pattiarmstrong@mac.com, email Theresa at TheresaThomasEveryDayCatholic@gmail.com, or contact the publisher at 248-917-3865

Cover image: Purestock/Getty Images

ISBN 978-0-9844864-1-0
Library of Congress Control Number 2010930026

Praise for
Stories for the Homeschool Heart

Patti Armstrong and Theresa A. Thomas have put together an uplifting gem for homeschoolers or parents who want to parent with wisdom and wit. Whether you are discerning becoming a homeschooling family or have already "been there and done that," *Stories for the Homeschool Heart* will inspire about the wonderful world of homeschooling. Through the real-life struggles, joys, and the life-changing lessons in the book, you will come away renewed in your commitment as your children's primary teacher, even if you don't teach full time in the home.

- Matthew Pinto
Author, *Did Adam & Eve Have Belly Buttons?*

A treasure trove of captivating narratives—*Stories for the Homeschool Heart* will inspire your soul and warm you to the core! From angel stories to "Peanut Butter from Heaven," this distinctive collection dips into matters of struggle, faith, triumph, fear, betrayal, renewal, prayer, and the ultimate discovery of God's compelling lessons abounding in everyday family life.

-Donna-Marie Cooper O'Boyle
Catholic author
EWTN host "Everyday Blessings for Catholic Moms"

This book is a beautiful sharing of life experiences and lessons learned. Through personal stories, it provides encouragement to all parents as we make the journey together, helping each other to lead our children to God. Through humor, love, trials and triumph, this book will touch your heart and lift you up.

- Jeff Cavins
Author *The Great Adventure Bible Study*
and Emily Cavins
Author *The Great Adventure Bible Study for Kids*

Stories for the Homeschool Heart

Heavenly Stories of Inspiration, Hope and Joy

compiled and edited by
Patti Maguire Armstrong
and Theresa A. Thomas

Bezalel Books
Waterford, Michigan

"Teaching Madonna" depicts Jesus and his holy mother, studying a very significant map...that of Jerusalem, where He will one day offer His life for us. It is the hope of the artist, Nellie Edwards, that this may inspire all Christian parents to be docile to learning from their children, as Mary learned from Jesus—even as He, in His humanity, learned from her. Nellie was blessed with eight children to learn at home with. Just three years ago she received an inspiration to do sacred art, which may be seen at www.ImmaculataArt.com. She can be reached by email: mo8@srt.com

To my dear husband Mark and my children that have taken me on a journey I never could have imagined: Aaron, Luke, Calvin, Tyler, Joash, Jacob, Mary, Teresa, John and Isaac. I love you with all my heart and pray that through God's grace, we will be united always.

-Patti

To my best friend and husband: David. I love you more than you will ever know. To my wonderful children: David, Michael, Caroline, Matthew, Melissa, Rachel, Grace, Theresa, and Angela and our five blessings in heaven. You mean everything to me. To my parents, Bonnie and Irv Kloska, who encouraged me to write from the time I learned to hold a pencil.

-Theresa

TABLE OF CONTENTS

INTRODUCTION

Families can have one child or many; school at home for just a season or through high school; keep kids at home because they are so advanced or because they struggle, and for many other reasons. It is rarely a choice made lightly. While parents choose homeschooling for any number of reasons, those who have shared their stories in this book ultimately do so for one reason: love--both of God and of their children.

We know that there are many parents who love God and their children with equal passion but who have not been led to homeschool. God's ways are wise and mysterious. He has a different mission and call for each family so this book's audience is not limited to those who exclusively homeschool full-time. Rather, it is a sharing of the love, inspiration and support for families who wish to teach their children to live for God and reach for eternity.

It is a book for those who take seriously the awesome responsibility as primary educators of their children, regardless of their academic choices for them. It is for families with a 'homeschool heart'. It includes all dedicated parents; those that teach their kids at home from birth through high school and those such as humor writer Tim Bete, (who generously shared two of his stories) who seriously considered homeschooling but did not ultimately feel called to do so.

Within these pages are the experiences of many but each story is a slice of life. They are not presented necessarily as the model or ideal since we are all unique children of God. Some have had unfortunate experiences in classrooms be it from the needs of their child, the situation created by other students, or due to something on the part of teachers or administrators. This is not a condemnation but rather personal experiences being shared. Homeschooling is an avenue for many to create solutions and answer fully God's call to us.

We, (Patti and Theresa) met one another through the "Amazing Grace" book series, where Patti was an editor/author and Theresa was a story contributor. In working together, one email led to another, and we found that like many homeschooling moms, we had many things in common. In addition to our writing and dedication to our husbands and large families, we shared a desire to raise Godly children for the Lord. It turned out that our hectic, happy, laundry and love-filled lives meshed perfectly while working on the book. Both understood the priority of motherhood alongside the work and deadlines demanded in publishing a book. Yes, we did miss our original deadline, but we were blessed with a wonderful publisher, Cheryl Dickow, who shares our homeschool heart and vision for this book.

Our goal was to assemble stories to uplift, inspire, and demonstrate instances of God's grace in everyday family life. We know well that choosing the homeschool path is laden not just with blessings, but often many challenges from both inside and outside our families. Not everyone understands our calling so it is always a comfort to be surrounded with like-minded souls. Through connecting homeschoolers into a virtual neighborhood of love and support, we can lean on one another and grow stronger.

As the editors for this blessed work, we put ourselves in God's hands and were led to a number of parents with varied experiences; some confronting a number of issues—abandonment, abortion, abuse, infertility, depression and just everyday struggles. But through it all there was also peace and joy; the kind that comes from serving God.

Through it all, God's amazing grace brought them through their challenges and they willingly offer their stories for your own journey—you may be experiencing something similar or may simply need to be reminded that God is always present.

And we promise that you'll laugh as well—because laugher truly is the best medicine!

We also found delightful recollections of everyday instances where God's care was made present sometimes through the ordinary in surprising ways—through coincidences, through little events, and even through a family's hamster and a duck. And of course, God's grace was also demonstrated every day through a mom's own little ones, tugging on her shirtsleeve and looking to her for guidance.

A very talented mother of eight, Nellie Edwards, was willing to share her hand-created "Teaching Madonna" artwork with us...and you.

We were also blessed to be able to include the cartoons of two very talented teenagers, Melissa Thomas and Sarah Storick—whose biographies are found in the back of the book. Both girls have both been homeschooled and we imagine that their fun artwork will be unique and yet somehow familiar because in so many ways our journeys are always unique and yet familiar with one another's.

When we (Patti and Theresa) chatted on the phone over some writing detail, it was like we had known each other for years. What's more, the conversations were punctuated with occasional interruptions, "Would you please get off of there?", "Can you ask Dad instead of me right now?" or SLAM! "Whoa,whoa, whoa!" Then turning back to the phone, "Hey, can you hang on a second? Something just dropped and I don't know what...." We don't have to explain such conversations to you, our readers, because you've had the same ones.

We imagine this book was written much the way it will be read, at the ball park; in the waiting area of a dance studio where little students take class; in the old, but comfortable rocker late at night and early in the morning before the family is up; at the kitchen table with a cup of coffee. Some contributors offered more than one story. In those cases, only one biography will appear with additional stories simply having the contributor's name.

This entire effort has been covered in prayer from start to finish; and even now, as we go to press, we have begun praying for each person who will hold and read a copy this book. You are important to us! We hope that God has allowed us to fill your "homeschool heart" with stories you really will find humorous, inspirational and filled with hope.

We've also included some pages in the back of the book that might be the perfect place to record some of your own "homeschool heart" experiences that will quickly become treasures! Not that we want to give you additional work—we're just offering the space!

Or you can contact us with your own stories on the Internet

TheresaThomasEveryDayCatholic@gmail.com

pattiarmstrong@mac.com

We're on Facebook at: http://www.facebook.com/pages/Stories-for-the-Homeschool-Heart/112387948799115?ref=sgm

And we have a blog that you might enjoy visiting: http://storiesforthehomeschoolheart.wordpress.com/

So, sit back, relax and enjoy these pages.....until the baby wakes, phone rings or the dryer buzzer goes off....Then you can stop and come back to it. We understand.

Chapter One

IT'S ABOUT THE LOVE

"You shall love your neighbor as yourself." (Matthew 22:38)

"Love is patient. Love is kind. Love is not jealous, it does not put on airs."
(1 Corinthians 13:4)

BEATING THE LABELS

After only one year of marriage and both in their early twenties, Donna and Calvin Bader were told it that conceiving children was unlikely for them without some kind of fertility treatments. Since they wanted children right away, this was a big disappointment. Both agreed, however, to skip the specialists. "I knew of other couples who had paid thousands of dollars to fertility specialists," said Donna. "Calvin and I both agreed it would be better to spend our money on adoption. It was Wednesday. By Monday we were the parents to four-month-old Samuel."

Although adoption does not usually work that quickly, Donna's mother-in-law had been caring for Samuel as a foster mother. The original family backed out. He was a mixed-race baby and the parents were concerned his skin was too light compared with their other adopted children.

The Baders were already licensed foster parents in Indiana. "I received a phone call from Adoptions of Kentucky on Monday morning informing us that we could have Samuel right away since we had a foster care license," Donna explained.

She called Calvin at work, unable to contain her excitement. "Calvin," she cried, "we're parents!" He came home right away and they hugged and cried tears of joy. God had answered their prayer for a child with amazing speed. But God was not done answering their prayer yet. And again, things would happen quickly.

Calvin and Donna had applied to work as house parents with Noah's Ark Children's Village. This is a specialized Christian foster care agency. While they waited for an opening, they had contacted the couple to help out one of their foster families by taking over for the weekend.

When Donna walked into the door and into the gaze of five children of varying ages, Dylan grabbed her attention immediately. The little guy in diapers appeared much younger than his three years. Instead of the eager and curious young face he should have worn, Dylan looked deeply sad. In his short little life, he had already experienced so much pain. This was his fourth foster home. Dylan and Donna cared for the kids for about two hours that day. In Dylan's case, Donna said their attempts at interaction were rebuffed. "He did not talk much, instead using grunts and his fists to communicate," Donna said. "Dylan's verbal ability was poor but he excelled at hitting the other children."

Although Dylan wanted nothing to do with Donna, she was captivated with him. "I thought about him all the way home. A few days later, the agency asked Calvin and me to baby-sit the entire weekend for the same family." It was the perfect way for them to determine if they wanted to work at this eighty-eight acre village where homes, support, and other amenities were provided to the on-site foster families.

Donna and Calvin loved the experience and wanted to do it full time. Dylan was no more interested in them than he had been the first time. On top of that, he had diarrhea all weekend. But Donna was drawn to him even more. "I cried all the way home for Dylan," Donna recalled. "I told Calvin that I felt he was supposed to be our son."

Calvin warned Donna not to get her hopes up since parental rights had not even been terminated in his case so he was not available for adoption. "It did not seem to make sense but I've learned to trust my instincts as long as I stay close to God in prayer," said Donna. She could not get Dylan out of her mind and kept praying that God would lead the way concerning him.

A couple months later, Donna and Calvin moved into a Noah's Ark home to work as foster parents. Dylan was in another home on the premises but when that family felt he was too much for them due to his violence with other children, Donna and Calvin took him in. They had other small children and he was very violent. Even though Dylan was three-years-old, he could only say "truck" and "blue" and kept repeating those words. He had been diagnosed as autistic and would often rock back and forth among other repetitive behaviors. Regardless, Donna still wanted to be his mom.

"A few months after he was in our home, parental rights were terminated," Donna said. They immediately filled out the paperwork to begin the adoption process. Dylan's violent behavior continued unabated, however. Often, he would not respond to anyone. When Donna tried to soothe him and told him: "Mommy is here," a typical response was for him was to scream at her. But Donna would not give up. She kept showering him with love and patience and little by little, he started responding. The first time Dylan crawled up on her lap on his own, her spirit soared. "I looked over at Calvin and caught his eye with the unspoken message: 'Are you seeing this?'

"Thank you, thank you, God," she joyfully prayed.

It would be many more months before Dylan allowed Calvin to have anything to do with him. He did not even want to get into the car if Calvin was there. Calvin did not force himself on Dylan but he tried playing toys and games with him. Dylan would have none of it.

One day, Donna took Dylan to the playground. Then, while Dylan warmed up and began having fun, Calvin joined them and took Dylan horseback riding. "Look at you," Donna gushed with tears in her eyes. Dylan grinned. He really looked happy and Calvin was trotting along beside him.

But Dylan's pain would not let go. For the first four months, not a day went by that he did not hit others or act out in some way. One day, Donna put him in the corner for time out. He began screaming and banging his head against the wall. She wrapped her arms around this broken little boy. "I love you Dylan," she cried. "You're safe now. Daddy and I are never going to leave you." Dylan kept swinging his arms so she held him tight and tried not to get hit.

Then, Donna prayed: "God should we be doing this? Help this to stop. Help Dylan not to hurt and be afraid anymore. Lord, whatever his frustration and anger is please take it away."

They sat there for a good thirty to forty minutes. At that point, she wondered if she had been wrong. Maybe she was not supposed to be his Mommy. "God, are we in over our heads?" she asked. "Can we help this poor dear boy?" Finally, Dylan calmed down. He was crying and Donna was crying. She was scared that she might not be able to help Dylan. But then she recalled all the promises she had made to love him forever. "If we did not keep Dylan, who would?" she thought. "I realized he needed us so we could not give up on him."

Calvin and Donna prayed hard for Dylan's healing. They did not want him to hurt anymore, but felt powerless to stop it. It was in God's hands. They and their families and some of the members of their church began adding fasting to their prayers. "We were going to do everything possible to fight for our little boy," Donna said.

The first year was rough but after six months, they began seeing improvements. Through speech therapy, Dylan's speech was getting better and it became obvious that he was not autistic. The pain from his past often came out, but Calvin and Donna kept reassuring Dylan with their love. He also had the love and security of their extended families.

By the time his adoption became final, he was four years old and still lagging behind in some areas, but his progress was incredible. Instead of being trapped by his pain, a happy little boy was emerging. Dylan was bonding with his family and had begun to play with other children without the violence. Once the progress began, it never stopped. There were still bad days and struggles, but Dylan had let Donna, Calvin and little brother Samuel into his heart and he was firmly in theirs.

In spite of his rapid improvement, by the time Dylan approached school age, Calvin and Donna feared sending him into a situation that would label him. To them, labels meant limits. Calvin's mother had mentioned the idea of homeschooling. "I think I said more than once, 'Over my dead body' when the subject was brought up," Donna laughed. But Donna would often marvel at Dylan's progress and then be reminded that the "experts" had said he was going to be very low functioning. "We believed that our God is bigger than that," Donna said. "Then, we realized that once he was labeled, it would follow him.

In the end, it was the fear of labeling that convinced them to teach Dylan at home. "We wanted to push him and challenge him and not to use labels as a crutch." She added, "My hats are off to the teachers; they have many challenges but we thought we could do a better job just one-on-one. That was our main reasoning, but now we just love it."

Dylan did continue to prove the labels wrong. Today, at age thirteen, he does well with school and is just a little behind grade level. He is also outgoing and a very affectionate, son. Often, Dylan will give his parents a hug and say, "I love you Mama, I love you Dad." He and Samuel are typical brothers. They love to wrestle and sometimes fight, but are fiercely loyal to one another. They will even make excuses for each other if one gets into trouble.

Samuel, age ten, is also thriving at home. "I love them being who they are without the pressure of peers to be cool and pressured to do things based on what other kids are doing. Right now, Samuel is a grade ahead of where he should be. School is easy for him. Dylan takes longer to memorize but I'm able to tailor both boy's education."

The boys get plenty of socialization through field trips and get-togethers with other families. Both are on a competitive gymnastic team, which means practicing as much as four hours a day, four days a week. Donna pointed out that some of the other children on the team who don't homeschool, barely get to see their families since practices are from 4 to 8 p.m. during the school year.

A couple years ago, Donna and Calvin decided it was time to move out of the foster care facility into their own home. They bought seven acres in the country where they now raise chickens for the eggs and meat and goats for the milk. On the day they signed the papers for the property, Donna and Calvin had another big surprise to add to their lives. Donna was pregnant! Emma Grace—her name means "absolute faith"—was born in 2009 to the waiting arms of her big brothers.

Donna added that having the boys home to share in the joy of watching their little sister grow, is yet one more benefit of schooling at home.

THE TRICK OF BECOMING A SAINT

I admit it was a dirty trick. As I walked into the playroom with an armful of towels and other clean clothes, I enthusiastically asked three of my little girls, ages eight, six and three, "Who wants to be a saint?!"

"I do!" they all shouted, before they saw my unfolded linens. By then they were trapped. Their little faces sunk when they saw what I had in store — the scrunched up towels, underwear and socks.

"No fair, mommy," whined Grace, the six-year-old. "You said we get to be saints!"

"You *do*," I explained, as I dumped my armload at their feet. "Becoming a saint, like St. Thérese said, is doing little things with great love. By offering up your time and helping when you don't want to, you have the opportunity to do something saintly. Now, let's fold!"

Lucky for me, they bought it, and scrambled for the pieces of laundry, getting right to work. After awhile, though, the novelty wore off. A couple of the girls meandered to another room, undoubtedly looking for something more "fun." I pulled them back a couple times to finish the laundry task, and sat down with them to help and make it a little more endurable. When the last sock was matched and the stacks stood tall, I hugged them and told them how proud I was of them. "Look what a fine job you did," I praised.

OK, I was sneaky, but God is sneaky too, I thought. Drawn in by great aspirations of being His saints, we enthusiastically pray, "I want to be a saint. Show me how!" and then we are frustrated when He sends a million little discomforts or setbacks or work in our daily lives, not realizing that these are the hills He sets before us to climb, to build up our strength and purify our wills. In doing what is necessary but what we don't want, we can mortify ourselves and become holy. Jesus said, "If a man wishes to come after Me, he must deny his very self, take up his cross, and follow in My steps" (Mk 8:34). That means every day, from breakfast through bedtime, no matter what our vocations, we have "yeses" to say. Washing dishes can be a means to sanctification. Reaching out to others can make us holy. Getting up early to go to work can help us on our path to heaven.

Listening intently to our child when our minds want to rush into other thoughts can help us become saints.

Father Paul O'Sullivan O.P., who wrote the classic book, *An Easy Way to Become a Saint*, suggested that any ordinary Catholic can become a great saint without doing anything extraordinary. Just by living out one's vocation to the best of one's ability, and utilizing the opportunities that unfold each day, one can become holy and attain heaven.

A perfect example of this ordinary sanctity would be dear Mrs. Corey, a retired second-grade teacher, a member of our parish, who brought sunshine to everyone she met. I was amazed and humbled the day she stopped me after church and offered to come to my home and read to the children (at that time we had seven). Who was this person? Did she have nothing better to do? Why would she want to come to my home and read to my offspring? I'm so glad I let her come. The calming lilt of her voice mesmerized my children. Did I ever speak that way to them? I resolved then and there that I would from now on. She demonstrated a little thing done with great love.

Three months later it was Christmastime, and Mrs. Corey again stopped me after Mass. "Here is a bit of home-made cookie dough," she said, pushing bowl of the sweet-smelling dough into my hands. "With so many children I'm sure you won't have time to make it from scratch this year." How did she know? I accepted with gratitude another little thing done with great love.

God does invite us all to become saints, and we may heartily reply "Yes" before we know what we're in for. But we needn't be afraid that He'll ask too much. Ordinary tasks done with extraordinary love will do the trick — simple, mundane, non-spectacular tasks, like reaching out to others, doing our daily duties well, going to work and yes, simply helping to fold a pile of laundry.

Theresa A. Thomas

BETTER THAN I PLANNED

My husband David and I reached six years of marriage on the sixteenth of April. I love him more than ever, and he is still the answer to my prayers. However, our anniversary evening did not start out well, nothing like I had planned. Since I had experienced two days of migraines my house was a disaster. My poor children were neglected and bored so they decided to turn into Tasmanian devils, destroying the calm I had tried to create by staying up much of the previous night, cleaning. Their behavior should not have been a surprise though. Mother was self-absorbed, tired, and cranky, still with a headache.

That night of our anniversary I was going to go pick up a griddle and get dinner going. (Iron is the traditional sixth anniversary item, so we were buying each other a cast iron griddle.) Then my thoughts got in the way.

Who wants a nice dinner when the house is falling apart? How am I going to find time to make this nice dinner, and shower and look decent with the children constantly needing my attention?"

As I was growing more and more frustrated, I called the store where I planned to go to get the griddle. It was not in stock. I called another store. I had no luck there either. With this news my mood continued to plummet. I let my children run around without structure. They asked if they could make their own lunch and I agreed. This was not a good idea as it contributed more to the mess.

My mind was busy dwelling on my 'ruined' anniversary. I went shopping finally around 6 P.M. to get a few necessities and a prescription. On the way, I made a decision. "I am not going to try to plan anything special anymore," I thought, "Every time I do, it gets ruined. I just have to come to grips with my mundane life." I decided just to make a quick dinner and then go to bed early.

At the store, the pharmacy was closed. My kids continued to cause a commotion so I bribed them with renting a movie and buying them candy. I finished shopping and then went to pick up corndogs for the children so I could quickly feed them and put them right to bed.

When I walked into the house, however, I found an amazing surprise waiting. My husband had run a bath for me! Candles were flickering and lavender oil was waiting! My stresses started to dissolve as I soaked in the tub. I came out of the bath to see the children watching "Dora" (the movie they picked) but they were not eating candy. On the clean table were the wine glasses from our wedding, two salads, two potpies, two candles, and a gift bag. I sat down to dinner feeling pampered and loved. David and I exchanged cards (I had remembered to get a card), and he gave me a foot soak and scrub with a pedicure promise. What a wonderful anniversary after all.

My point is simple. At first, nothing went the way I wanted. I threw a little pity party and temper tantrum, and my children felt my attitude and reacted. This created a negative spiral effect. My attitude got worse. And it became a scene for my husband to 'save' me. God gave me many chances throughout the day to see my anniversary blessings-my loving husband, my wonderful children, but I didn't notice them. I learned an important lesson: sometimes, my expectations are too high. I don't necessarily need to pull off an amazing dinner and evening. My husband is content just to hold my hand, and maybe, sometimes, he wants to pull something off for me. Also, my children, despite being occasionally rambunctious, are actually very wonderful.

No, my anniversary was not what I had imagined at all. Like most of God's blessings, it was much, much better than I planned.

Written by Melissa White-Contreras & edited by another homeschooling mom,
her best friend Mary Saltzmann

Melissa lives in Lake Forest, CA with her husband and four children. When she is not working as CEO, CFO, Head Chef, Cleaning Lady, and Referee Extraordinaire at home, she is living a serene life as her alter ego, scrapbook-hero, saving the world from lost memories as a Creative Memories Consultant. She can be reached at scrapbookhero@hotmail.com

WITH LOVE, FROM RUSSIA

I met Jamie, the best friend of my best friend's brother when I was fifteen. He had beautiful brown eyes and curly eyelashes, and he looked and acted older and more mature than my friends and me. I liked that he was funny and seemed very sure of himself. I also liked the fact that he could drive and had a lot more freedom than anyone I knew.

When I was sixteen my parents allowed me to see him once a week, so long as we were in a group. Quickly, Jamie and I became best friends. When I was seventeen and graduated from high school, I was finally allowed to date him one-on-one. I can't say there was one single moment when we knew we would always be together; it just seemed like we always would. We got married when I was eighteen and he was nineteen, imagining our future together with a houseful of children. That was "the plan".

Fourteen years into our marriage, "the plan" was not working out entirely. We had two healthy children for whom I was grateful, but had also lost three babies to miscarriage and one to stillbirth. I had a huge empty spot in my heart, grieving for our losses and longing for more children to love. As time went on I was not able to get pregnant again, which deepened my sadness.

Jamie is in the military, and this career led us to many places overseas. While we were stationed in Europe, I started thinking about international adoption. Two other families on our base had recently adopted from Eastern Europe, and it seemed like a solution to my yearning for more children. Jamie understood how I felt about wanting to grow our family but he was negative about the idea of adoption, because of the cost. I wasn't happy with his conclusion, but I tried to turn the situation over to God and to accept it. The matter seemed settled until Jamie went on a field exercise in the Czech Republic. The soldiers were invited to visit an orphanage in the town in which they were stationed, and Jamie was one of a few officers who went on this visit. In the orphanage the soldiers witnessed toddlers and infants who simply yearned to be loved and held. Jamie was so moved by the children he saw there that he left his scapular with a little girl who wanted it. Later, soldiers in his unit took donations

from military families and supplies back to this orphanage. The experience stuck with Jamie and he felt financial concerns could be worked out. When he came back from this trip, he told me he felt we should adopt!

Jamie and I decided on Russia. After we did the necessary paperwork and home visit, we waited. Months passed. Then, right before we were to travel to a new destination for a military assignment, adoption officials from one agency called and told us it would take much longer than expected for us to adopt a child because my husband was getting ready to deploy. My heart sank, and my mind was filled with desperate questions. Should we cancel the whole thing until after the deployment? Should we proceed at all? We were trying to be open to God's will, but there was suddenly all this red tape. The older children had been praying every night for their new sibling. The exact prayer during our family Rosary was "for an addition to our family according to God's will".

God's will was made immediate and clear. On the same day that we received the news from one agency that the adoption was going to be stalled, we got a call from another agency that had several sibling pairs available. Were we interested? Yes, we were interested! The representative from the agency told us that they had three sets of toddler siblings: a boy and girl set, another boy and girl set, and a two boy set. We were told that the boy/girl pairs were easier to find families for, because everyone wanted either two girls or one of each sex.

When I told Jamie about the options, he didn't hesitate. "We want whoever has the least chance of being adopted", he said. I told the agency worker this and she immediately tried to send me pictures. For some reason her email would not come through on my computer, so she sent the pictures to Jamie's military email account instead. Jamie had to go to Belgium as his unit was deploying to Kuwait in preparation for the invasion of Iraq. On his way out, he stopped at his work office to open his email. He called me, laughing, saying he was looking at a picture of his new little sons, two and three years old. I cried. Jamie then sent the pictures to my email. While connected by the phone, we looked at the boys together!

After we agreed to go and meet the boys (Russian requirements a trip to meet the to-be-adopted children and then a separate one to pick them up), the agency worker asked us to name them. We had never discussed this. I panicked. Jamie just calmly said, "When I count to three we will each write a name down. I chose "Noah" and he chose "Jon" and that was that! We decided to keep their Russian names as their middle names to preserve their heritage.

The circumstances surrounding our planned trip to Russia were very stressful. Jamie had only a few days to spend with us before deployment. He had to go through a lot of red tape to get his visa. As a United States service member, he was grilled with questions, and Russian officials were not particularly sympathetic to Americans. In fact, before we went to Russia, Jamie was asked to let his hair grow so that he would not look so "military."

Meanwhile, I was a nervous wreck planning our first trip to Russia, having cold feet about even getting on the plane. I was very anxious about leaving our two older children, Emma and Shane, at home. Jamie's mother agreed to come to Germany to stay with them, but Shane, who has high functioning autism, was not a particularly easy child to baby-sit, so I worried how my mother-in-law and he would get along. Also, I had never left my kids for more than a day. How would they do without me?

Jamie, unlike me, was Mr. Relaxed. He handled the people and the paperwork with confidence and ease. Soon we were sitting in the orphanage visitor's room in Russia, waiting for someone to bring us our children. I looked around the simple room, which had a couch and a couple of chairs. The walls were painted with scenes from children's fairy stories, and there was a shelf with toddler's toys for prospective parents to use to play with the children. The building was clean but old and somewhat deteriorated. I found it odd that seventy babies aged three and younger lived in this building but not a sound could be heard. It seemed like an eternity before the door swung open and the orphanage director, a tall, serious-looking woman in her mid-fifties, brought in our little boys. They were pale but not thin, and like tiny old men with white-blonde hair. They were beautiful.

I was so excited I started crying. Jamie immediately got on the floor and started playing cars with them. I still just sat there bawling my eyes out. The funny thing is that I've always been good with babies and children.

My whole life I've worked with them, loved them, and children have seemed to respond well to me. But there I was, with my own children, unable to move and Jamie was on the floor with them making them laugh. He was even using the language book I had been studying. The boys had clearly defined personalities from the beginning. Jon, the oldest, was shy and very cautious. Noah was very active, funny, and into everything.

After this first trip to meet the boys, we had to agree formally to the adoption. We filled out more paperwork and then flew back to Germany. Ten days later, the day before our daughter Emma's eleventh birthday, we went to court in Moscow. Again, I was petrified. We were in a foreign land with a foreign language. All I wanted to do was collect our sons and go home. Jamie, calm as usual, did all the talking in court. The judge seemed to love him and probably thought I was an idiot as again all I could do was nod and cry. Apparently the judge didn't hold my demeanor against me, though. We received permission to take our children home. At last! We rushed out of the courtroom and we drove around the city, getting the necessary passports for our trip home and the last bit of paperwork finished.

The following day Jamie and I went back to the orphanage to pick up Jon and Noah. The orphanage workers matter-of-factly gave the boys to us with nothing--no clothes, no toys, no blanket, not even the things we had brought for them ten days earlier. We changed them into clothes we had brought for them and took them. It was so sad to me that nobody so much as kissed my boys good bye. It was almost like nobody really cared about them. This just broke my heart, and Jamie and I were so relieved to take them out of there. At the hotel, we ordered room service, fed them and gave them lots to drink. They were very dehydrated and all of the sudden very hyper! They loved their first bath, brushing their teeth, and all the toys we brought them. And so, two months and two trips after we first received the call from the adoption agency, we brought our boys home to our quarters in Germany.

The first few months home with the boys were scary and a roller coaster of emotions for us all. Jamie deployed, which was very, very hard on all of us. Suddenly, I had doubled the amount of children, a husband in a war zone, and we were in a foreign country with no extended family anywhere near us. The little ones, who didn't understand us at all, were into everything. Also, our oldest son was having a particularly hard time. He missed his dad, experienced typical autistic frustrations, and didn't like the fact that I was suddenly so much busier.

I think our weakest point was after three weeks of things going wrong. A friend's helicopter was shot down in Iraq and he died. Our dog of thirteen years also died. Our car broke down and we did without it for a few days. Finally, due to a careless mistake on my part we had a huge fire in our kitchen. I cried myself to sleep that night. Our oldest, Emma, really grew up and matured almost overnight. She became my right hand in helping with the house and her three younger brothers, and somehow, with God's grace, we made it. Our older children had been homeschooling for four years when we brought Jon and Noah home. Keeping them all home helped so much in the little boys' bonding to us, and the older kids' development.

I cocooned myself and the children during the deployment so we got very close to each other. We relied on one another because we had no other choice. I am positive that the boys made the transition to us and our culture so well because of the fact that we homeschooled and kept outside distractions to a minimum. They received unconditional love, and quality and quantity time.

I am surprised at how quickly Jon and Noah blended in with our family, and how fast they learned. Within a week from the adoption our three year old could say the grace before meals all by himself. I know that the boys' development was enhanced by their older brother and sister. Their patience with and kindness towards their new brothers offered Jon and Noah something priceless. This was something that Jamie and I could not give them alone—the love of siblings.

This adoption was absolutely meant to be, of that we are sure. Our little boys "feel" just like our biological kids do—totally ours. They have blended in perfectly and it is so funny to see how much they act like us. About ten months after the adoption an acquaintance said to me, "You know, it seems like the boys have always been with you. I can hardly remember your family without them." It felt so great to hear that. We are so blessed.

We tell Jon and Noah how much we prayed for them, how much we wanted them and how much we have loved them since the first day we set eyes on them. We hope to one day travel back to Russia with all the children and show them the place where we went to get Jon and Noah. We have made adoption albums for the boys and now, at ages six and a half and five and a half, they look at them often. We have told them their adoption story many times but right now I don't think it is entirely real to them. Jon and Noah are not our "adopted sons" they are simply our sons, who just happen to be adopted. Our family story was God's plan all along, and we are grateful for His amazing grace and for the houseful of children we always wanted.

Mary Ann Kavanagh

The Kavanagh's are now stationed in Savannah, and Jamie is currently deployed, again, to Afghanistan. The children are growing and thriving. Jon and Noah are doing fifth and fourth grade work now and are very bright and happy little boys.

SET TO SAIL

It hit me last night. We have only two weeks until the two oldest boys head back to college. I was in the Target store, picking up a couple pairs of shorts for my ninth grader, and I witnessed an influx of moms with their presumably college-aged kids, buying extra long twin bedding, wastebaskets and such. That's when it occurred to me. I've been ignoring the inevitable. My boys are leaving soon.

Oh sure they'll be home for visits at Thanksgiving, and Christmas, but likely those will be whirlwind trips during those busy times of year. In and out, they'll come. They'll cram in visits to high school friends. They'll squeeze in work on weekends so they can make it financially through the next semester. It won't be until next summer again that they are really back here under our roof.

I know. Some moms have sent sons their age off to war, and my boys will be in the seemingly safe environment of a Catholic campus and in a network of friends I like and approve of. But they won't be here, and that's why this mother's heart aches.

I like being with them. I like the full house and the noise. The boys' bedroom is directly below my husband's and mine, and many a night after telling one another good night, I can hear their voices talking and laughing (or a guitar strumming) as I fall asleep. I love the activity in the morning as I ready the younger ones for swim team and the older ones head off to work. "What time will you be home?" "Will you be eating dinner with us?" I try not to be bossy as I ask them these questions, careful not to word it in a too controlling way because they are, after all, not little children any more. I even like that. They are growing into fine young men.

Often this summer I knocked on their door. I planted myself on the little loveseat in the middle of their room and just sat and talked with them. Fortunately they didn't seem to mind. I got in my lecturing mode a couple times, hoping to implant one more virtuous idea in their heads before they leave, hoping to make one more impression on them before college life again engulfs them. Will they keep their Catholic faith? Will they remember the daily catechism we taught them as little children? Do they call to mind the Sunday night 'family meetings' of their youth? Have I done enough? Did I nag too much? Can we make that transition from hovering and doting parent to adult mentor and friend? I wondered.

Father John Hardon, S.J. once wrote of three ways to keep kids Catholic: be a channel of grace to them; pray with and for them every day; train them to understand what they believe. Being a channel of grace is trying to be an authentic Catholic myself. It is modeling behavior and attitudes which I hope to see in them. Praying *with* them may be tougher when they are at school, but praying *for* them is not. I can encourage my sons to call, email or text when they need extra prayers. I can find out ahead of time the Mass and confession schedule and venue on campus to make it easier for them. I can make contact with some good priests and introduce them so they will have allies there. I can encourage involvement in Catholic clubs and organizations. I might even send some money to support the dues. Finally, I can encourage them to share their experiences and ask questions to help them discern how to put their faith in action. I will acknowledge the difficulty of living for Christ on a college campus and let them know I will always be here to support them.

"A ship is safe in a harbor, but that is not where ships are meant to go." I saw this on a poster. Yes, boys are destined to be men. And mothers are supposed to help them reach their potential, not wistfully pine for their ever-presence. So, in a couple weeks I will help them pack their J.C. Penny sheets and Target fan, and Wal-Mart notebooks and pens into their car heading for campus. With a hug and a kiss and I will release them to God and let them sail. I'll also let them know I'll be in the port, waiting, whenever they come home.

Theresa A. Thomas

MOM'S DAY OFF

It was barely mid-September and the kids and I were cramming our studies in anticipation of a December due date for my eighth child, Bernadette! I was quickly becoming overwhelmed; no one was listening, my expectations were seemingly impossible, and the sky had been covered with a thick, grey mantle for over a week. I was sinking further and further into a gloom of self-pity. I just needed to get away from the schoolroom before I cracked!

Tears welled up in my eyes but I fought them back. I looked out the window at the dark, dismal, rainy day. Then I looked at the sun-catcher of the "Good Shepherd" in the middle of the window. I imagined Jesus holding me instead of that sheep. A Bible verse came to me. "Come to me all you who labor and are heavy laden, and I will refresh you." I closed my eyes. Those words were so sweet!

"Refresh me, then," I whispered.

No sooner did those words escape my lips than the phone rang. It was my father.

"Hi, Lisa! How's my little girl?" he said cheerfully. (I am thirty-something, but he still calls me his little girl)

"Fine." I lied.

"Say, I'll be in your area this afternoon! Do you need any help with schooling?" he offered. It was as if lightning just struck.

"Yes! Please come!" I said.

"Great. See you later. I love you!" he said, clueless of the magnitude of need he had just filled.

"I love you, too!" I squeaked.

After hanging up, I ran to the picture of the Good Shepherd, and said through a river of tears, "You don't waste time, do you?" It was no coincidence!

My father was such a great teacher. Not only was he a wellspring of wisdom and knowledge both with academics and life in general; but also he continually teaches me to be a better parent through his eternal patience. After he left, my house was at peace once again. God bless my father! I thanked the Lord a million times. But still, I was struggling.

A few days later, my Mom called and asked me what I wanted for my birthday.

"I just want a day off; nothing else, just a day off," I said.

Well, my Mom loves special requests. She secretly collaborated with my husband. What fun they had, presenting a scroll on my birthday which read:

Mom's Day Off
No kids. No Phone. No School!
You will be swept off to a Bed and Breakfast with your Knight in Shining Armor
(John with aluminum foil on his head)

John and I went to stay at an inn up in the Northwest corner of Connecticut. I was so excited, that I couldn't wait to leave. Suddenly, schooling didn't seem so bad with a beautiful vacation ahead.

Finally, the day arrived. I said my good-byes, gave my blessings, and turned around to go to the car. That's when it hit me. *We'll be two hours away from them. What if the baby starts choking? What if the toddlers sneak outside? What if they don't understand?* We barely left the driveway, and my heart inside was screaming, *We can't go, they need me!*

John squeezed my hand. "They'll be fine, Honey. Relax."

I hid my tears and picked up my knitting. My fingers flew through the stitches. The second we arrived at the inn, I called home.

"Is everything all right?" I asked.

"Everything is fine! Why are you calling? Go have fun. Enjoy your weekend," Mom reassured me.

"Just relax," John encouraged me. With a little wine, a bubble bath and of course, chocolate, I was finally able to do just that.

The next morning we were like newlyweds again! We walked hand in hand all over the beautiful grounds, chatting the day away--about the children, of course. On Sunday, when it was time to leave, I started to miss the children terribly. I couldn't wait to get home. We didn't seem to be going fast enough.

When we finally arrived, I ran in to greet them, waiting for them to all scream with delight and jump into my arms!

"Hi kids! We're HOME!!!" I hollered. I waited. Then, I walked upstairs. The kids were all busy with various activities.

"Oh hi, Mom!" they said, and went immediately back to their playing. I ran upstairs to see my baby, Becky.

She looked so sweet, sound asleep in her crib. I couldn't resist. I picked her up and squeezed her tight!

"Oh my precious angel! I missed you so much!" I said, as she cried and wiggled to get back into the crib because I had disturbed her nap.

It had been a wonderful weekend but it was so good to be home where I belonged.

My poor Mother and Sister were exhausted. They could not hide their relief that we were finally home. I was finally at peace. My heart was now in the proper disposition, and it made me look at everything in a new perspective.

For the rest of the day, we just cuddled and played with the children!

I guess sometimes we just need a day off!

Thank you, Lord for that wonderful gift! Especially for the gift of appreciating my family!

Lisa Marie Duda

Lisa is a homeschooling Mom of 10. She lives in Connecticut with her husband of 23 years, and 9 of her children. She currently has 3 sons in college, with the twins graduating with a dual major (criminology and accounting) in May 2010 with honors. Her oldest daughter is now married and working as an RN supervisor. Lisa is a freelance writer and loves to write about her family.

OUR FAITH: SMALL BUT MIGHTY

During the summer of 2002 we had seven children; the youngest was six months of age. My husband, Greg, and I decided that, although our youngest was still a baby, we wanted to continue to be open to receiving more children if God willed it. We felt very happy and blessed to discover that September we were expecting another one in May of 2003.

The soul, like the body, lives on what it feeds on.
~J. Gilbert Holland

It was during that summer also that I happened to be reading a biography of St. Catherine Laboure and the Miraculous Medal. I had heard the story of this saint briefly before but I became enthralled when I read that during one of her visions of Mary, St. Catherine was able to rest her head on the Blessed Mother's lap. How comforted and loved she must have felt! I was drawn to the Miraculous Medal and decided to buy one for every member of my family. On November 27th, St. Catherine's feast day, I read the story of the Miraculous Medal to my husband and children and then presented them each with their own medal. They were very excited and wore them immediately.

Imagine my joy when I called for my first ultrasound appointment and was given the date of the Feast of the Immaculate Conception! I believed this was a wonderful sign from God and I looked forward to seeing my baby for the first time.

Armed with a blank videotape so that the ultrasound technician could record the scan for my children, I arrived very excited at my ultrasound appointment. The technician was very quiet as I exclaimed over every picture of my baby. I noticed she was not recording the images and I inquired about it. She replied that she would record them later after she talked with the radiologist. She left to develop the film and returned with the radiologist who spent considerable time looking at my baby's images on the screen. Finally the radiologist turned to me and said, "I'm not seeing normal development of the baby's skull."

Confused, I asked, "Is there anything that can be done for my baby? Will my baby be able to live with such a defect?"

She looked at me and just said, "This is an abnormal baby. You need to go see your doctor." Before the technician left the room she turned to me and said, "Your baby is a girl." She then returned my blank videotape to me, left the room, and I clutched my Miraculous Medal and sobbed.

That evening my husband and I sat down and told our children about their baby sister. We explained her birth defect the best we could and told them she would not live for very long once born. Their collective cry was the saddest sound I have ever heard.

From that day on we prayed ceaselessly for a miracle. Our wonderful network of homeschooling friends and our extended families prayed with us. Every night at the conclusion of our family prayers, the children would line up and take turns blessing my belly with holy water, hugs, and kisses. Their baby sister responded with kicks and rolls and turns. Together we decided to name her Faith Bernadette. Faith would be for the faith we knew we would need desperately to live through this sadness and Bernadette in honor of Mary as the Immaculate Conception.

Needless to say, each day we felt the heavy burden of our sadness. We plugged along with our schoolwork as best we could but our hearts lay elsewhere. We all struggled with our faith in God and wondered where He would be with us during our family's greatest sorrow. We begged Him for strength to get through our studies, to face the criticisms and opinions of those in the medical community who told us that abortion was the easiest answer since our baby was not a true human being without complete development of her brain, and our fears of seeing our fragile daughter for the first time. With my doctor's support, I had chosen to give birth to Faith by C-section so that the birth would be easier on her. I spent many nights praying that I would make it through the surgery safely, that my choice would be the right one, and that I would have the courage to see it through.

Faith

I treat myself
To thoughts of you
When the house sleeps
In a pillow of silence

Reliving the moment
I saw your face
And wings of joy
Suspended my heart

Was it only eight months
Our hearts shared space?
I recognized you
One that I love

A tiny pocket of time
Held so precious a life
Hello barely touching
The lips of good-bye

Life suddenly becomes long
When waiting for forever
Your little face echoes
In the ones that remain

Each morning we stare
At the gaping wound
Deciding today to keep it covered
Or expose it to the air of others

God pours out His medicine
And gratefully we drink in
The drops that sustain us
In the largeness of the day

Sweet faces to be washed
Large questions from small mouths
His previous gifts
Reopened and savored

Scars begin to take shape
The wound less naked
We are so thankful to wear them
You were here, yes, you were here

I treat myself
To thoughts of you
A glimpse of grace
From the One I love

–Stephanie Hubbel

I went into labor with Faith three weeks prior to my scheduled C-section date. Once I realized I would be unable to put off this day any longer I sat down and cried. This would be the hardest thing I had ever done. I had always left for the hospital in labor knowing I would be working hard but overjoyed because I would be bringing a baby home. This time giving birth would mean my baby would die. My womb suddenly seemed like the safest place in the world for this baby and I wanted to stay pregnant with her forever.

My children cried when we left that day. They said they would say a Rosary during the surgery and pray for a miracle. My sister was with them and planned to bring them to the hospital to meet their new sister as soon as she was born. We needed to be a family with her for as long as we could. I hugged each one of them and blessed them before I left that day. It was those faces that kept me moving.

I called my obstetrician, Dr. Marc Eigg, and told him I thought I was in labor, and he had me come to his office. Throughout my pregnancy he was a blessing, supporting my decisions and helping me plan Faith's birth. He examined me and said I was already in labor and that I had to go to the hospital. He said one of his partners was on call for the day and would be there to meet me when I got there.

My husband and I had also been trying to reach our parish priests so one of them could be in the operating room to baptize Faith. Neither of them was at the rectory. I began to get anxious facing the surgery without my doctor and our priests. I felt very alone and very, very scared.

At the hospital we soon found out where God would be that day. He would be in the hands of those who took care of us. The nurse who prepared me for surgery sat next to me on my hospital bed and gently told me the story of her granddaughter, Angelica, who had been born with the same birth defect a couple of years earlier. She talked about her precious granddaughter, with such joy and peace. I was grateful that she would be by my side during the surgery.

The door to my room then opened and in came my very fantastic doctor who left his patients and came to do my surgery. I knew he would be gentle and careful with my daughter and I will always be forever grateful to him for his big heart on that day. As he opened the door to leave, another amazing surprise waited outside the door. Both our parish priests were waiting in the hallway! They just happened to be at the hospital that morning, filling in for another priest. My doctor walked me to the operating room and, even though I was so scared, I felt surrounded by kindness and love. As the surgery began, I repeated the prayer of the Miraculous Medal over and over again, "Oh Mary, conceived without sin, pray for us who have recourse to thee."

When Faith was born there was no cry of a newborn. The room was amazingly quiet. My husband saw her first and I will never forget the look of happiness on his face when he first laid eyes on her. With tears pouring down his face he looked at me and said, "Oh, Stephanie, you did the right thing." Our pastor, Father Erdle, quietly baptized Faith. The nurse handed Greg our daughter and he brought her to me and I looked into the beautiful, open eyes of our fragile little girl. It was so wonderful to finally see her face! She had pudgy cheeks and blue eyes and my mouth and looked just like her brothers and sisters. Despite her birth defect, she even had locks of dark brown hair.

For three hours our family gathered around Faith and loved her. The children all held her and kissed her, checked out her baby fingers and toes, and took in that wonderful baby smell. The nurses were kind and loving towards the children and made them as comfortable as possible. The kids argued over whose turn it was to hold her and marveled at how tiny she was. And, I finally filled that blank videotape with images of our family loving our daughter. Whenever I am missing Faith terribly, I watch that videotape so I can see her face again and relive that day for just a little while.

My daughter's funeral was a hard day for our family. But, once again, we were surrounded by love and kindness. The church was filled with family, friends, neighbors, and so many of our fellow homeschooling families. The Mass was celebrated by our three parish priests, Father Erdle, Father Bush, and Father Nolan and our parish deacon, Jim Chatterton. The choir sang our favorite hymns. Because she had been baptized and lived without sin, our pastor preached on the sainthood of our daughter. This tiny, fragile little baby girl could now intercede for us with God!

I buried my daughter with a Rosary in her hands and a Miraculous Medal tied to a pink ribbon and sewn on a soft little cotton hat for her head. I dressed her for the Blessed Mother. I wanted her to rest in the arms of Mary as St. Catherine once did. My children put letters and pictures in her casket and our entire family carried it down the aisle in the processional at her funeral Mass.

My children didn't have the best school year that year, academically speaking. We did very few extracurricular activities and we spent most of that summer catching up on work we had fallen behind on. But this was the year we learned the most. This was the year we learned about perseverance during suffering, about the value of life and our time here on earth. We witnessed how Christ touches us through the hands and hearts of others and how God pours out His mercy when we can no longer stand on our own. And all of this came to us through the life of one tiny baby-- small but mighty, our Faith Bernadette.

Stephanie Hubbel

Stephanie gave birth to a healthy baby girl, Grace, on March 10, 2004, two weeks prior to the one year anniversary of Faith's birth. Another daughter, Lily, followed 14 months later. Stephanie and her husband, Greg, homeschool their 9 living gifts from heaven in Rochester, NY

Chapter Two

HOMESCHOOLING?

"It was not you who chose me, it was I who chose you to go forth and bear fruit."
(John 15:16)

A 'Least-Likely-To' Mother

"If we have children, I will take no more than four weeks off work and put them in daycare immediately. No child will interfere with my life. I will never be financially dependent on anyone, and certainly not a husband."

"I don't bake, I don't iron to your standards, I won't make sack lunches, and I sew with a staple gun."

"The kids may go to private schools. I will never, ever homeschool."

Those were some of the sweet nothings I told Richard while we were dating, before we married. He still proposed. Nineteen years after we married, I've broken every one of those pledges except two. I still sew with a staple gun or pass the mending to my daughter, who learned from Grandma the seamstress (his mother, not mine). He still irons better than I.

My friends at the time would have voted me least likely to marry, to mother, or to ever settle down. When my path occasionally crosses old pals who knew me back when, they are always shocked. "You're *still* on marriage number one? *You* had children? *You* quit working to raise them? *You* homeschool?" A couple still don't believe it and assume I'm joking.

Homeschooling begins... Now!

County Hospital Obstetrics

Life of a homeschooling mother...

Sometimes they ask, "What happened to you?"

The answer is simple: the grace of God changes everything.

Despite my protests, I knew that when I became a parent, my kids would be a top priority. God used some pretty direct methods to help me realize what that meant. First, we lost our first baby. After that, we didn't know if I would ever be able to carry a baby to term, and I resolved if it did happen I would give my life to those children.

We had two children after that. It is only by the grace of God that my children and I survived those pregnancies. When I was pregnant with my son, I underwent four in-utero platelet transfusions, five weeks of high dose intravenous immunoglobulin treatments, and a four-week bed rest in a high risk unit of a hospital one-hundred miles from home. I learned very quickly how suffering distills the fluff from life and leaves the real stuff.

When my daughter was a toddler, my desires turned a complete 360 degrees from my earlier attitude. I wanted to homeschool her, but ironically at this point I was afraid I couldn't teach her to read. It's funny that somehow she learned on her own. When our son needed extra help with speech therapy and language skills, home seemed the natural place to get him that help.

Yes, the grace of God changes everything, and so do great kids. As we parent our children, our kids inspire us to grow up, straighten up, and become better people. Whatever I give them, do for them, or teach them will never measure up to what they give me, do for me, teach me. They got a mother, yes — but it was a process in which I had to become one.

Whenever someone tells me, "I don't have the patience to mother, to school my children, or to do x, y, or z," I always answer, "Neither did I. I still wouldn't by myself. Whatever good I give my kids is simply by the grace of God."

Our children are now winding down their homeschool years and branching into a broader world. Next year, both will be teens in high school. My role as a mom changes but is as important now as it was when they were younger. I hope when they are grown, they will be prepared to discern and follow God's call for their lives.

Once, when David was a young boy, God helped him kill Goliath. That same God can take someone like me and help me parent and teach my children. He fills in my gaps — and God only knows how expansive those gaps really are. The God who helped Saul become Paul helped a mom like me grow to become a mother. If He can take me and help me be a better person, wife, and parent, He can help anyone.

I love this Bible quote: "*I can do all things through Him who gives me strength*" (Phil 4:1). Paul told us earlier in Philippians what to do if we worry about problems or our own inadequacies: "*Have no anxiety at all, but in everything, by prayer and petition, with thanksgiving, make your requests known to God. Then the peace of God that surpasses all understanding will guard your hearts and minds in Christ Jesus. Finally, brothers, whatever is true, whatever is honorable, whatever is just, whatever is pure, whatever is lovely, whatever is gracious, if there is any excellence and if there is anything worthy of praise, think about these things. Keep on doing what you have learned and received and heard and seen in me. Then the God of peace will be with you."* (4:6-9)

The same person, who 20 years ago preferred software to children because she thought software was easier to handle, now enjoys software *with* her children. "Least likely to" moms can become "most grateful for the chance to" mothers. And thank God for that.

Mary Biever

Mary and her husband, Richard, homeschool their two teens in Evansville, Indiana. Mary teaches continuing education computer classes for Henderson Community College and works as a social media strategist. As a 4-H leader, she helped found a Tech Club to provide science and engineering training to area 4-H members. She also helps with the family home business, The Copper Lion, Inc.

A FORMER HOMESCHOOLER STOPS RUNNING

Angela Roller and her three siblings were given input about whether to stay in school or homeschool in 1991. They all opted to homeschool. Angela was going into seventh grade at the time. Her parents were already teaching her lessons at home in the evenings when they saw that some of the schools methods or academic content was misleading or incomplete. With very little effort in the classroom, Angela was a straight "A" student. In addition, her parents did not feel the schools needed to be teaching sex education in school.

Although Angela was not challenged academically, her faith and morals were—in a bad way. In her Iowa Catholic school, Angela was seen as "too religious". Fortunately, she was not fazed by peer pressure. "I knew that I was doing what was right and I kept going back to that Bible verse, 'Blessed are you who are persecuted for my sake....' It didn't matter how much they made fun of me, I was going to do what was right."

So, while her mom was pregnant with a fifth child, she began homeschooling in 1991 using a correspondence school. Angela did not miss the peer pressure and was finally challenged academically but grew weary of homeschool because her family put in long hours; sometimes even weekends and summertime for school. She received an excellent education but decided it was not something she would ever do if she became a parent.

When Angela and Dennis married on Oct. 30, 1999, they already knew that they could not conceive children. In spite of her strong maternal instinct,

Angela was undeterred. Her practical personality determined that she and Dennis should become foster parents right away. On Dennis's birthday, August 28, 2000, the phone call came informing them that Thomas, a one-year-old foster boy, needed a home and that his parents' rights would likely be terminated. That meant it was likely that Angela and Dennis would be able to adopt him. They said "yes" immediately.

"I loved having him around even though he was already hyper and oppositional right away," Angela explained. She went into it thinking that all he needed was time and love. Only gradually, did Dennis and Angela begin accepting outside assistance. "I learned it was okay to admit we needed help," she explained. "At first, I felt like we'd be failing if we didn't do it on our own. After he was four and the adoption was final, I think I stopped being afraid we would be judged and finally gave in to taking him to a family therapist." This provided some support and guidance for the challenges of raising a child with early deprivations.

If you think you don't have any time for prayer, and can't find any time, then ask God to forgive you. The Pope isn't too busy for his daily Rosary. If you're busier than the Pope, you're too busy.
~Fr. James Peterson

Angela and Dennis continued to do foster care until they took a break in October of 2003 when they adopted an African American baby, Xavier. At this time, Thomas was enrolled in pre-school. The idea was that outside activity and structure would do their very active little boy some good. Instead, Angela came to dread picking him up from school only to hear yet another report of how Thomas had disrupted the classroom that day.

"I began wondering how kindergarten was going to work for Thomas," said Angela. She feared for his future, envisioning a kid pegged as a troublemaker and made fun of by others. In spite of being homeschooled herself, she pushed such a possibility out of her mind. After all, that subject had been decided long ago; it was never going to happen.

Then, while talking with a casual friend from church one day, she expressed her concerns for Thomas. "Why don't you just homeschool him?" the friend suggested. The question suddenly brought the idea up out of the unthinkable. "I don't know anyone around here that homeschools," Angela said, her brain on fast-forward. Even if she did break her vow, she quickly envisioned the loneliness of going it alone—*no thanks.*

"Well, I homeschool," the friend announced. "And so do a lot of other families in town." Angela had no idea there were homeschooling families in the area. In an instant, a whole new world opened up to her. Suddenly, the near-certain future of Thomas being labeled a problem child, melted away. At that moment, the wall came down and Angela knew that homeschooling was really the *only* option for Thomas.

Angela continued the conversation a little longer, feeling a sudden sense of peace at the answer that was so obvious to her now. "The truth just hit me and I stopped running." As the friend began to explain the benefits of homeschooling, Angela smiled and interrupted. "Yeah, I know all about it," she announced. "I was homeschooled." Yes, the benefits all came to the forefront now—education at his own pace, according to his needs and without peer pressure. That evening at home, Dennis needed no convincing.

Thomas did learn in his own way—sometimes standing up instead of sitting down for lessons—sometimes getting through things quickly and at other times, fighting distractions. Angela's mother even had many suggestions that were a big help. For instance, rather than writing out spelling words on paper, he delighted in using a dry-erase marker on the floor to spell words and then wiping it clean with a baby wipe. Thomas learned to read around five years old and by the time he was in second grade, enjoyed reading Angela's old high school biology books, just for fun. He loves science but is bored with fiction stories.

Thomas participated in a library reading program. Much to the surprise of the librarian, Thomas read for an extensive amount of time despite his Attention Deficit Hyperactivity Disorder (ADHD) diagnosis. Angela explained that his reading continues to be a lifesaver for us, keeping him entertained, especially on car rides.

Thomas benefited from a customized academic plan. For instance, he has no sequential memory so in spite of his advanced reading ability, math is a challenge and he is not at grade level. With an additional four children in the family, Angela admitted that homeschooling has not always been easy. "Actually, I thought I was going to lose my mind that first year."

In 2007, Dennis and Angela traveled to Ethiopia and on March 17, adopted Asamenew, age four and his little sister Rebekah, fourteen months. They have also become legal guardians to Heather who is now seventeen and attends public high school while the younger ones all homeschool.

Dennis and Angela are also currently fostering another teen girl and still hoping to add to their family so Angela says she must always carefully assess everyone's needs in the family. For Thomas, who has done well at homeschool, the plan is for him to attend the local public school on a limited basis in the upcoming school year to provide additional structure along with extracurricular opportunities. "He'll do music and some other extras at school but still do math, religion and science at home," she explained.

It's no surprise that people are often in awe at Angela's willingness to homeschool amid adoption and foster parenting—even referring to her as a saint. However, she rejects such a notion. "I'm not a saint," she laughs. "I can scream with the best of them, but I'm willing to do it and stick with it. I'm willing to accept that I'm not perfect and not let it stop me from doing this."

Angela lives with her husband Dennis and their children in North Dakota. She enjoys stamping, reading, and sewing. Much of her time is spent advocating for her own children and those who are still in need of permanency through adoption. She can be contacted at arroller@q.com.

I JUST NEEDED TO LISTEN!

Sitting in my backyard on a warm, sunny, spring day and watching my son contentedly flip through an encyclopedia, stopping to read anything that catches his eye, I am filled with an inner peace and joy. I marvel at the fact that we are at a point in our lives where I can let him leisurely enjoy this book, and know that eventually he will finish his research paper and do a great job of it. I still can't believe that this is school. It certainly wasn't always like this for us.

Before we started homeschooling, Nickolas went to school (both public and private) for six years. From kindergarten to fourth grade, he was in a public school. I agreed to be a volunteer and a "learning leader" so I was at the school a lot. Even my husband Kenny was recruited from time to time. We could see clearly that our son was frequently bored.

Then, the school began its push to "teach to the test;" which meant the students would study and practice almost exclusively the subject of the upcoming standardized test. When that one was done, they would then focus on the next subject to be tested. Only the questions to be covered on the test were studied and huge packets of practice work were given on weekends and vacations. Simultaneously, recess was phased out. The students went to lunch at their assigned tables and were forbidden to get up from the table. They were allowed to talk quietly. No exercise was provided, and they then went back up to the classrooms to work. When my husband approached the principal about at least letting them do a bit of exercise before returning to their classrooms, he was told the kids could exercise when they got home. Of course, that was after completing the homework they received. We felt that this was no life for a child.

Added to this was the fact that after all those years, the school was insensitive to my son's medical issues. He has a life-threatening allergy to dairy. One teacher, who knew about his allergy, based one of her lessons around milk chocolate candy bars. The children ate them, and then voted on which variety they preferred to be made into a graph. For over an hour, my son sat there surrounded by a food that could harm him, unable to participate. Another time, he was rewarded as the top fundraiser (everyone was expected to sell the products) by being given a pizza party for his class. When we reminded them that he could not eat pizza, it changed nothing. The pizza was served, and we scrambled to get a dairy-free pizza there and keep him safe from the surrounding cheese. This was his reward?

I prayed daily for direction because I knew this was not the best life for my son. Frequently, the idea of homeschooling popped up, either on TV or in a magazine or from snippets of conversations I would overhear. Although the idea intrigued me, I paid little attention to it. The idea seemed too foreign for us.

The disciple simply burns his boats and goes ahead. He is called out. The old life is left behind, and completely surrendered. The disciple is dragged out of his relative security into a life of absolute insecurity... out of the realm of the finite... into the realm of infinite possibilities.
~ Dietrich Bonhoeffer

By fourth grade, we had enough of the public school and, along with a friend of his whose mom felt as we did, we switched him to a local parochial school. We were hoping for a more varied and well-rounded education and they did offer a better curriculum at the new school. There was a wonderful principal and she insisted on recess almost every day, as well as providing chorus, music and art. Nickolas made new friends quickly and was less bored, but the new school presented a new set of problems. Homework took hours. There were a variety of teachers, and each gave their own assignments. Most of it was busy work, and seemed pointless. They were at school early in the morning until 3:00, and then spent most of their after-school time doing homework, studying for multiple tests and doing projects. We then had to squeeze in dinner and sleep so they could start it all over the next day.

There were some rules at this school that seemed a bit unreasonable also. One teacher in particular seemed to thrive on humiliating the children. She was a very angry person, and more than once, I personally witnessed her unpleasant treatment of a child.

Many of the parents I spoke with were unhappy with the situation as well, but they all felt they had no better options. I began pleading to God for an answer. I often stopped into Church and sat with my eyes closed, desiring to hear God's answer. I actually felt annoyed at times because my thoughts were distracted with the thought of home education.

Two weeks before his sixth grade classes were about to begin, I met with the new principal. The previous one had retired that summer. The changes she told me she was planning, from simple things such as eliminating chorus and music to more extreme ideas, shocked me. I knew it was not something that I wanted for my son anymore.

I left the school practically in tears. I stopped at the neighborhood bookstore, bought a cup of tea, and sat down at a table. There was a book on the table. I pushed it around for a while not paying much attention but then I took a look at it. It was a book on homeschooling. It was my "a-ha" moment. It was then that I realized I had gotten an answer from God a long time ago. I just needed the courage to do what I knew was right for our son, and have the faith that God would help us on this journey.

I was doubly blessed because that afternoon I received a call from an old friend who knew a homeschooler. She gave me the woman's phone number, and that call led to so many others, which started us on a new way of life. It was frightening and a bit strange at first. And then there was the reaction from other people. Many were supportive but the negative reactions from some didn't make things easy. It varied from fear that we had joined a cult of sorts to anger. It took me awhile to understand the anger. It seems that some felt 'betrayed' by us because we left them and the system behind, and others were annoyed because their children were then asking to be homeschooled as well. Yet as the year passed, more and more were asking me question about how to start and if we could help them as well. Sometimes it just takes time to get used to an idea.

Homeschooling has been a blessing for us. During the past nineteen months, my son has met many wonderful people and made new friends. I have seen him maturing into a confident young man who is starting to love learning just for the fun of it. Nickolas was always a good student with a quick mind and a sweet sympathetic nature, but since we began homeschooling, I have noticed there is a level of contentment.

The energy I once put into his school now goes towards his homeschooling. We started a parents' support group and for kids, a Clubhouse on Friday, 4-H group, and other weekly activities. My son is thrilled to resume his music and to be involved with many sports including new ones such as fencing, archery and cycling. These activities had to take a backseat before due to lack of time.

In the process of understanding our new journey and helping others follow that path, I have come to know more about myself as well. I realize that I must trust my instincts and open up my mind and heart to God. He was giving me the answer all along. I just wasn't paying attention.

Annette Dubin

Annette is a CCD teacher in a local parochial school and has started up a tween/teen homeschooling group that is AHEAD-NY@yahoogroups.com. She is also the owner of Enchanted Notions which sells handmade items.

IT WAS THE SNOW

Homeschooling is something that my husband and I had talked about, but then I put it out of my mind. Before my oldest son started kindergarten, I thought about it some more, but instead put him into public school. Then, when our next son had problems in school, I thought about it briefly before setting it aside.

It was brought to mind again when a woman that I did not even know at church turned around at the end of Mass and said, "I know this might sound funny, but do you homeschool or have you considered it?" Seriously, right there in church. Years later, she told me that she had never done that before or since but just felt called to ask at that moment.

She got me on an email list for a group of Catholic homeschoolers, but I soon changed email addresses and forgot to grab her contact information before deleting it. Then, a chance discussion with her sister-in-law (whom I didn't know at that time, but she is now one of my best friends) ended up getting me back on the emailing list.

There were many other "signs" that drew me to homeschooling, but I resisted. Despite having two current teaching licenses, I told my husband one night, "I just don't feel qualified." He laughed. At Mass that week, our associate pastor's homily hit home. He said that even if we don't feel qualified for what God is calling us to do, if God is calling us, then it is what He wants for us. I almost wanted to stand up and say, "Okay, God, I get it." Instead, I prayed to God asking for a clear sign. (This is the point at which my husband and I joked that Jesus might have to come to our front door and say, "Really, Angie, I think I have been clear enough, haven't I?")

Then, one day, I opened the blinds as I put away dishes. There was snow on the ground, but there was no snow coming down. It was crystal clear outside.

I was thinking about what my boys had shared with me the day before about their discussion with the school's occupational therapist, telling her that we might homeschool. I thought, *I just don't know. What should I do?*

At that moment, I looked up and snow was everywhere. It was coming down in huge snowflakes that were quickly swirling all around as far as I could see. I took a deep breath at that moment and had an argument of sorts with God.

"I'm just not sure. I don't know if I can do a good job. Will it work out if I do it?" I told God.

In my heart, I felt God's gentle urging, "Just a year. Commit to a year for now. I'll be with you." All the while, the snow was flying through the air at a breakneck speed.

"Okay!" I shouted, all alone in the kitchen, but with my eyes gazed upward, knowing that I wasn't really alone. "One year. I promise You, unless something happens between now and next school year that makes it impossible, I'll commit to the year and see where it goes from there."

And then, the snow stopped, immediately and completely. I held my breath a moment. Somehow, I felt a strong connection with God--a sign of His presence with me in my kitchen. I said aloud, "You think you're pretty funny, don't you?"

I continued to put away my dishes and then thought to myself, "Huh. So, am I really going to do this?"

I looked up at the window, and then snowflakes started to fall again where there had been none just a moment before. I laughed and shook my head. "Okay, okay. I get it. No more doubts for now," I announced, standing at the sink, with a calm submission. The snow, again, stopped.

Some might say that it was just a matter of the weather coincidentally acting in union with my prayers. My faith, however, tells me otherwise. I know that I was not alone in the kitchen that afternoon—or with my homeschooling since.

Angie Kauffman

Angie is a university trained elementary and special education teacher turned stay-at-home mom who began homeschooling two years ago. She lives in the Midwest with her husband and their three children who were all received into the Church in April 2007. Angie is the founder of ManyLittleBlessings.com, HSClassroom.net, CatholicMothersOnline.com, and CatholicGadget.com.

HOMESCHOOLING, THE LORD'S IDEA

My eldest daughter was halfway through first grade when I finally was at my wit's end and turned to the Lord for help. My husband and I had struggled ever since she entered kindergarten with the immoral behaviors we saw her being exposed to, the inconsistency of school rules, the political correctness being taught, and how all of this was affecting our precious little girl. We saw this once happy and beautiful little six year old turn daily into a puddle of tears and fits of anger when she came off the bus after her nine and half hour day.

I talked until I was blue in the face to school officials about changes. I complained to my family and friends. Everyone told me that we needed to get over it, that this was life and she would be fine. I just was not convinced by that. My mom finally told me to do something about it or stop complaining. So I joined a school improvement group that ended up bringing me home in tears. Why did it have to be so complicated? I just wanted my daughter to have a good education in a morally sound environment. I just dreaded the thought of sending my other three girls to school ever.

So on a cold January day, I just sat down and asked the Lord what I was supposed to do about school. I prayed for peace and knowledge to make the right decision. I prayed this everyday several times a day for two months. Then one night in March, I was washing supper dishes. I heard the word homeschool. I paused and I wondered where that had come from. I went back to my dishes. Again, I heard the word homeschool.

"Lord, is that you? I asked you what I was supposed to do about school. I did not say anything about homeschooling. That is a different kind of people. I do not have the patience for that. I am not going to do that!"

A second later, homeschool, there was that word again.

I dismissed it instantly. But the next day and the day after that and the day after that for about week I would hear that same word again and again and again. I finally relented and decided to look into it. I made some phone calls and searched the Internet. It was amazing the information I found. I shared this all with my husband. After much discussion, we decided to try it for one year. If it did not work, we would then try to figure out what we would do next.

We are now on our fourth year of homeschooling. The graces that have flowed from following the Lord have been too numerous to count. The amazing change that came over my eldest daughter once she was home full time brought so much peace to our home. My husband and I see our four girls now enjoying life, wanting to learn, being each other's best friends, not afraid to try new things, and the best of all being raised in solid Catholic values. Maybe the most amazing grace was bestowed on me though. I have learned to turn to the Lord in every situation; trusting in him even when he brings unusual ideas to the equation. In doing so I gained the greatest friend and counselor anyone could have.

Amy Pautsch

Amy and her husband Kurt have been married for twelve years and have four daughters Elizabeth (11), Laura (9), Katherine (6), and Anna (4) whom they have homeschooled for four years. They live on five acres in Iowa strive everyday to be more self-sufficient, committed to organically, locally grown foods and sustainable agriculture.

Motor-Homeschooling with Cat.Chat

When Denise Montpetit began teaching French and religion in grades four through twelve at a Catholic school in Alberta, Canada, she was on fire for her faith and wanted to ignite the same flame in her students. This, she strived to do for two years until another desire caught hold of her— something she did not even know existed at that point. She had never heard of homeschooling until "Jesus" walked down the school hallway one day. Actually, he was the man who played Jesus in the annual Passion play titled, *Love According to John*. She had watched him act in the play for almost fifteen years, so to her, he was a celebrity.

The actor was at the school to visit his sister that taught there, but Denise started up a conversation with him and learned he homeschooled his family. It was a lifestyle that she previously, never knew existed. "My first thought was, 'Are their kids normal?'" Denise recalled.

She did not have to wait long to find out. The actor invited Denise and her newlywed husband Gerald, to dinner in his home to meet his wife and six children. "We were amazed at the family dynamics," said Denise. "The kids were fun, respectful and creative. They gave us a tour of their home and what they do."

It was an impression that never left Denise and Gerald. The family befriended the young couple and a few weeks later, Gerald and Denise babysat five of the kids—minus the nursing baby—for a weekend. Again, Denise reported that the impression was surprising and lasting. "We worried about being able to handle five kids but they totally inspired us. We thought, if our future kids could be half of this, we'd be so blessed. By the end of the weekend, we wanted to adopt them all."

Back in the classroom, Denise's students began to look different to her. She saw how bad influences spread and that the culture was very different at school than from within the family of their homeschooling friends. "There wasn't the respect. It seemed like kids that were not respectful were closed to what God wants to do with them. The ones that were respectful were not so caught up in themselves and they were open to God," Denise said. She noted that at parent/teacher meetings that the disrespectful kids came from homes where the faith wasn't being lived out. "It was allowing me to evaluate why that homeschooling family was so amazing," she said.

Once their daughter Reanne was born, there was no question that Denise would stay home and eventually homeschool. "I like to give 110 percent to whatever I'm doing," said Denise, "and I knew I could not split myself 50-50 between work and motherhood."

Gerald and Denise were one in this decision but there came a time to try their financial security and ability to keep Denise at home. Gerald was working as an audio systems technician to support the family. He enjoyed playing the guitar and singing and even wrote a few songs just for fun. As his song writing developed and began to center around God, he connected with "Life-Vision" a speaking and music ministry group in Canada. Denise said that she could see that music was Gerald's passion.

There were so many requests for recordings of their Sunday night music, that Gerald began producing CD's. Janelle, a singer with the group, caught the attention of the world in 2002 when she sang at World Youth Day in Toronto before Pope John Paul II. The core team of "Life-Vision" consisted of Gerald, who was writing and performing music for children; Janelle and her husband Jason, who attracted teens and young adults; and John

Connelly, who was primarily doing speaking and some music for adults. The group came to the unanimous decision that they should part ways into their various ministries. The pooled income resulted in only $1,000 a month for Gerald to support his family of four. Denise recalled feeling scared.

It was "do or die" time; either Gerald would be able to live his dream and write and perform music for a living or he would need to find another way to take care of his family. It boiled down to everything depending on the Cat. Chat—albums of stories and music for children that Gerald and Denise had created together. "Cat." signified both an abbreviation for Catholic and also represented Moses, the talking Cat that is the program mascot. Drawing on Denise's teaching and writing skills, stories about Moses and his family became entertaining ways to teach children about their Catholic faith. Gerald wrote music to complement the lessons of each story.

As a teacher and parent, Denise knew that there was nothing like this for Catholic children. There was plenty of Christian children's music by Protestants but nothing that sang of the core Catholic teachings  in ways to both entertain and teach. But would there be enough interest that they could support their family on this?

The first album was dedicated to Mary. Eventually, the interactive stories and music albums became a six-part series on Mary, Jesus, the Angels and Saints, Mass, Christmas and Advent, and Lent and Easter. Initially, there was no way the family could have made it with just Cat.Chat. Denise credits the support of their families with making it possible for them to get started. The rest was God's graces.

Word of mouth advertising began buzzing and soon Cat.Chat exploded onto the Catholic World. The family is now totally supported through the Cat.Chat ministry through music, books, t-shirts, saint cards and also the recently created Vacation Bible school (VBS) programs. It was another area where Catholics were borrowing from Protestant's since there was nothing purely Catholic available. The first VBS program is about how Mary leads us closer to Jesus and the second is on the Mass. Wilderness Adventure, on the sacraments, is the third.

Six years ago, they took the Cat.Chat concert on tour through Canada and the United States. Gerald, known as the Cat.Chat man, sings and interacts with his children through dancing, playing a variety of instruments, juggling and unicyling—entertaining and reinforcing the faith at the same time. Denise works the soundboard and the appearance of Moses the Cat thrills his young audience. Their next tour—the seventh—will include time at the Eternal Word Network (EWTN) studio to do a 10-part children's concert series for television.

A 31-foot motor home is now Denise's classroom. "I love the simple way of life on the road," she said. Denise credits their daily Rosary with making everything work for nine people with one bathroom in a motor home. They travel with their five children and two other adults that help by playing Moses the Cat and set up. "I physically sense the graces when we travel in all the miles we cover—over 50,000 and forty states in last three years."

School takes place on the road. Kids take turns sitting next to Denise for help and the other two adults participate including playing fun learning games while they travel. "The kids love it," Denise said. "Usually in the last week as we get closer to home, the kids get antsy to get back but then when it's time to go again, they are excited." There is no school during the summer and concert tours take place during fall and spring. During the last five years, Denise estimates that they have reached over 50,000 kids with their concerts.

Denise said God was preparing her family for this back when she met her first homeschool family. Without homeschooling, she said none of this would have been possible. "No school would allow our kids to be gone for two or more months," she said. "I see God's hand in every aspect of our lives. It feels like an amazing grace for us to keep wanting to travel. We can't wait for the next tour."

Gerald and Denise Montpetit live with their kids Reanne, 14, Dominic 12, Jerome 9, Luc, 6, Vanessa 18 months in the small town of Bruno in Saskatchewan, Canada. You can visit the Cat.Chat website to win a monthly CD and to see when a concert will be in your area.
www.catchat.ca

MISSIONARIES AND A FLIGHT PLAN CHANGE

Tim and I were married almost a year when we went on a missionary trip to Jamaica. Tim's friend from medical school had gone down to an orphanage in the middle of the island the year before and volunteered. He asked us to accompany him on a trip back. Young and eager, we jumped at the opportunity.

It was an exciting two weeks. I never knew what to expect each day, and the landscape was breathtaking. In contrast to the beautiful countryside, though, I saw many people suffering and in need. Looking out the window in the morning, I could see dozens of people lined up waiting for a doctor or dentist, likely the only one they had seen in many years. On several days I assisted one dentist by suctioning saliva while he extracted black, rotting teeth from villagers, some of whom were not any older than me. He did dental work on many, and it made me sad when he had to take out decayed teeth from some of the children, who hardly had adequate food, much less fluoridated toothpaste with extra whiteners. Other days I worked in the primitive pharmacy, handing out medicine for eliminating worms and infections, as well as lots of pain reliever.

In this atmosphere, inspiration abounded. An elderly Baptist couple from Florida, for example, had given up the easy retiree's life to minister to orphan children, who were bright, happy, and well-fed because of them. Volunteers banded together all around us to make people's living conditions better. They helped the local people obtain healthy foods and receive medical care for conditions which had been long left untreated.

Most remarkable were our volunteer friends' two girls (ages six and nine), who fit in with everyone around them quite naturally. They spent the two weeks in happy spirits, despite the lack of modern luxuries and comforts of home. They played, read, ate exotic things like pig's feet without complaining, and were just generally all-around good sports. . I mentally took note of these girls and decided I wanted my future children to be like them.

After a very full two weeks, Tim and I, along with our friends and their little daughters, were dropped off at the airport to return to the United States. We busied ourselves taking care of typical flying details until we discovered that the plane was broken. A team of Jamaican men were out on the tarmac, scurrying about with tools and frowns. Hour after hour dragged on and eventually we were all put up in a cheap hotel with pink walls and smelly bedspreads.

Early the next morning, we returned to the airport and resumed our wait. During this time our friends' girls were still unfazed by the inconveniences and continued to be content and cooperative. They happily drew pictures, played UNO, and were upbeat and polite. This was in sharp contrast to some other travelers who had been staying in the resorts and who were supposed to be flying on the same plane with us. These people roughly complained, argued with each other, and yelled at the ladies at the airline counter because they had to wait. They shouted into their cell phones and acted like, well, children. The irony was that the only children waiting to board were acting much more mature.

I began to chat with their mother. While we talked, I learned that the children of this missionary couple were homeschooled. Wow. I was impressed.

By that afternoon, it was evident that the plane was permanently broken. There was no replacement coming, and all the passengers would have to be put on other flights. It looked like we were stuck for the day, even though all of us had jobs to return to the following day.

In a lovely twist of fate, the girls of our missionary friend marvelously saved the day. They had drawn pictures for the ladies at the counter during our lengthy wait, and the girls' model behavior had caught the attention of everyone. One of the representatives from the airline beckoned us over after the "permanently broken" plane announcement and whispered, "There are six seats on this next flight, on another plane, leaving in an hour– I saved them for you. Thank you for being so patient and having such nice children." Those little ambassadors for goodness had secured us a speedy flight home! What an amazing blessing!

> *To see the miraculous within the ordinary is the mark of highest wisdom.*
>
> *~Ralph Waldo Emerson*

Actually, it was more of a blessing than I could ever have imagined then, for because of this incident I spent the flight back to the United States asking the girls' mother about her daughters, how she educated and trained them so well. The topic led to an in-depth discussion of homeschooling. I had always assumed without much thinking that when Tim and I had children we would just move into the 'default' mode of sending them to traditional school. In listening to this mother's simple and direct answers, however, I started to think, "Maybe I could do this! Maybe I could homeschool!" I certainly liked the result I saw in the children of our friends.

When the plane landed and we parted, a seed had been planted in my mind. It took root shortly thereafter when Tim and I started having children of our own. I absolutely knew how I wanted to educate our little ones.

Four years later, we are still happily educating our children at home. I can't claim that my children are always the most patient or would eat pig's feet willingly, but they are happy, loving, helpful children, much like the two little 'missionary' children on our trip to Jamaica.

My adventure in Jamaica sent me in a direction with a happy destination that I would never have known otherwise. In looking back I now see that the adults who came to serve the people of Jamaica were not the only missionaries on that fateful trip.

Katherine Collins

Katherine is the mom of six beautiful and smart children and Navy wife.
Her former life includes stints as a landscape architect and teacher.
She is currently a homeschooler and homemaker.
Soon she and her husband will retire to their farm in Maine
where they plan to raise sheep, chickens, and children.

Chapter Three

SURPRISES AROUND EVERY CORNER

"Give thanks to the Lord for He is good." (Psalm 136:1)

A WAYWARD DUCK LEADS THE WAY

"Dad, can I just peek inside?" our ten-year-old son Luke asked, holding a cardboard box.

"Wait until we get home," my husband, Mark, answered.

This was a day Luke had dreamed of for weeks. Finally, ducks! Our move out into the country two months earlier coincided with our plan to embark on our first year of homeschooling in the fall. Somehow, the two seemed meant to be experienced together—country life and homeschooling.

Even though we had dogs, cats and an assortment of reptiles and amphibians, Luke was impatient for some kind of farm animal. His five brothers and sisters were mildly interested in the ducklings, but not like Luke. He was the one who had pleaded mercilessly for them.

Luke had been the one that begged us for the ducks but it was the grasshoppers that clinched it. There was a serious invasion of them that summer of 1996, inflicting major damage on Mark's first country garden.

"They eat grasshoppers?" Mark had asked with sudden interest. That's when Luke knew his dad would relent.

Luke barely waited until the engine turned off before he bounced out of the car with his box. As if unwrapping a precious treasure, Luke gingerly lifted the lid. Once by one, the ducklings jumped out into a blinding August sun. Never content just to watch critters, he cornered and scooped up the ducklings one by one. As he held them securely and talked softly, each one relaxed in this hand until he slowly put it down and lifted another.

"I'm going to name this one Quacks," Luke decided, holding the littlest one. As Quacks calmed down, Luke held him gently against his chest and stroked his fluffy down.

The remainder of the day was spent with my kids and neighbors coming in and out of the yard to watch the peeping little flock. Luke never left the brood except to eat dinner. Throughout the day he herded them in and out of Mark's garden for several periods of grasshopper patrol.

As the sun began to set, Luke steered his ducklings into the garden for one last snack. When he attempted to return the flock to their pen, however, he accidentally stepped into their huddle and scattered them. The other ducks drew back together but Quacks ran off. Luke hurriedly got the flock into the pen and then chased Quacks where he had scampered behind a storage chest in the garage.

"Good, I've got him cornered," Luke thought. When he moved the chest aside, he heard little peeps but Quacks was nowhere in sight. Taking a closer look, Luke gasped. Quacks had fallen down a small drainage pipe. The opening was golf-ball sized. Luke ran into the house for a flashlight. The deep hole only swallowed up his light. Stricken, he walked into the house to find me.

"Mom, something bad has happened," Luke said. He explained the situation. "Is there anything we can do?" he asked doubtfully.

I went with him to the hole. "I can't think of anything," I told him helplessly.

"That's what I thought," he said and sadly turned to the house. "And he was my favorite one too—Quacks." The day, which had started with such promise, had turned sour. Bedtime was quiet except for the heartbreaking peeps that drifted into my second-floor bedroom from the garage underneath.

There were still eleven ducklings left but the little lost one broke our hearts. The parable of the Good Shepherd suddenly took on a new relevance. Quack's frantic cries continued through the night. When I awoke to his peeps early the next morning, I wondered how long before lack of food and water would finally quiet him.

"Food," I thought. "That's it!" Luke, the first one up, was just coming out of his room. "Luke," I whispered," I have an idea. "What if you used a piece of fishing line and tied a grasshopper to the end of it? If Quacks is hungry enough, maybe he'll swallow it and you can pull him up. Then we can cut the end of the fishing line off." I admitted I had no idea if he could survive swallowing the fishing line.

"It's worth a try," Luke said, bounding out the door. He returned a short time later.

"Mom," Luke called excitedly. "Can you pray that Quacks bites the grasshopper but when I pull up the line, he lets go?"

I was surprised by the question. Pray for a duck? Luke looked at me hopefully, so of course I told him yes.

As he left to try again, Luke's request suddenly made perfect sense. God made animals with feelings. They got cold, scared, lonely, tired, and hungry. I sat down in the living room and prayed for God to guide Quacks up out of the hole. In minutes, Luke returned with a big smiles and a little duckling.

"He bit the grasshopper and I was able to pull him all the way up," he explained breathlessly. "When I grabbed him, he just let the grasshopper drop out of his mouth."

By now the other kids were coming downstairs. As we filled them in on the rescue, I could not get over the fact that Quacks had actually made it out of the hole.

"Didn't you all think it was impossible that we'd ever see Quacks again?" I asked.

The kids looked at me surprised. "I knew God could do anything so I prayed to Him last night to save Quacks," seven-year-old Tyler said, nonchalantly.

"That's what I did too," agreed Luke.

Now, I was really impressed. Through their unwavering faith, I learned my first real lesson as their homeschool teacher—that sometimes it's the students that lead the way.

Patti Maguire Armstrong

"HOMESCHOOLING WILL BE THE SALVATION OF THE CHURCH"

When my husband, Francisco first mentioned his desire to homeschool, I froze. I had no desire to do something like that...something so weird. We were in a prayer group with another couple that had shared with us their plans to homeschool. On the ride home that evening, I sent up a quick prayer, "Oh Lord, please change his mind."

Then, I let the subject drop. It was 1992 and Francisco and I were newlyweds. I did not want to argue about homeschooling since we did not even have children yet. *This will pass*, I told myself.

Instead, as I watched our friends in their homeschool endeavor, I was impressed. When I tuned into EWTN Catholic television one day and saw a group of homeschoolers as guests on Mother Angelica's program, I was again impressed. The kids seemed to know and love their faith. What a different learning environment compared to my own school years.

By 1994, I was convinced that homeschooling was the best option for our one-year old daughter, Gabriela. It would be a natural as extension of my motherhood to be her primary educator. I wanted her to have like-minded friends that would reinforce her faith and morality—a community where the Catholic faith was loved and followed with enthusiasm.

There was one thing, however, that marred my enthusiasm—my parents. Suddenly, it seemed we were opponents. They feared their grandchildren would be isolated and unable to socialize with their peers. They kept asking me if it was legal and whether my daughter would grow up 'normal.' Given my own school experience and the fact that my parents and I were always close, I was frustrated that they could not see the beauty in homeschooling.

Growing up in the seventies (I graduated from high school in 1980) my parents made sure I knew my faith. Mom taught CCD classes in our home for years, and our home was filled with Sacramentals and wonderful Catholic books. We attended Mass as a family on Sunday, attended in the March for Life, and began praying a daily Rosary when I was in high school. I didn't just know the faith, but I loved it too. So when history and social studies teachers would disparage it and teach falsehoods about our Church, I spoke out. There were times when entire class periods were debate matches between the teachers and me. This was especially true when we studied European history.

As a result of my frequent debates, I became pegged as strange by my peers and felt very isolated in the midst of many. There were other Catholics in my classes, but no one ever came to my defense. Still, I did not back down. Often, my beloved parish priest, Fr. Fagan, a Jesuit, armed me for these battles. He provided me with explanations and gave me books to read on the topics of debate.

During my adolescence, a time when kids sometimes rebel or distance themselves from their parents, my parents and I were on the same team. There were many open school nights where my father, a lawyer, would challenge the teachers, especially in regards to sex education. "Whose values are you teaching?" he would demand. "You are a science teacher (or history, or social studies, etc.) but you have no business teaching your values to our children."

Finally, for my junior and senior years, my parents transferred me to an all-girl's Catholic high school. I loved it. I was able to leave my reputation as an oddball behind. I quickly made friends and fit in—sort of. I fit in because I decided to keep my mouth shut. Remember, this was the 70s. Everything was not as it should have been at this school. There were nuns, but they did not always teach us right. The Pope was referred to as 'the old man in Rome' that was out of touch, and in theology class miracles were taught to have scientific explanations attached to them. I knew better but his time, I kept quiet. I liked having friends and fitting in and wanted to keep it that way. My silence came at a price. Instead of debating, I listened and even started believing false teachings.

My love for my Catholic faith never wavered, however, and in time, I was back to the truth. Through my studies at a strongly Catholic college, watching EWTN, a strong prayer life and Catholic reading, I came to an understanding and orthodoxy in my faith. It was a blessing that I found a husband that shared my faith. Francisco had been the one that led the way to homeschooling and soon I shared his desire. I wanted my kids to be raised in an atmosphere of love and truth for their religion and I also wanted it to be present in every aspect of their lives.

But my parents' negative opinion of homeschooling hurt. I explained to them that even though I had gone to public and Catholic school, I had actually been very isolated, but still, they did not get it. Finally, I just kept quiet on the subject rather than argue. I asked God to help them come around. For two years, this was a heartfelt intention.

Then, one day, I went with my parents to listen to a talk by Fr Joseph Fessio SJ. His purpose was to give an address to a group of families who were intent on obtaining the EWTN signal on Long Island, NY. Unfortunately, Gabriela, then a toddler, was not interested in Fr. Fessio, so instead of listening, I had to chase her through the building lobby, with other mothers of toddlers. I was in good company. I sensed camaraderie about the group, and looking back fifteen years, I realize that these are my homeschooling friends today. My night out had a benefit after all, but I was soon to learn the blessing was far more than I ever expected.

After Fr. Fessio's talk, the doors to the auditorium opened and people slowly filed out into the hallway. I spotted my parents coming towards me, but there was something different; a look in their eyes. My dad approached me, grabbed both my hands, looked into my face and said, "You MUST homeschool Gabriela!"

His words took my breath away. I was grateful for my Dad's approval, but totally mystified. What just happened? My parents explained that during

Fr. Fessio's talk, he had stated, "Homeschooling will be the salvation of the Church." In an instant, my parents had gone from anti-homeschooling to embracing it. I appreciated their endorsement, but I was also a little shocked. It seemed they even surpassed me with their enthusiasm.

I had a lot to learn in the next fifteen years but it has been a true blessing. As I observe the uniquely gifted, poised, and faithful young ladies and gentlemen who are emerging from the chrysalis of homeschool to leadership in the world, I am beginning to grasp Fr Fessio's vision. Two years ago, while waiting for a shuttle bus that would transport my daughter Gabriela and me to St Joseph's Seminary in Dunwoodie to a youth rally with Pope Benedict that I was covering as a writer for the *National Catholic Register* (The Pope of the Young), we interviewed several teenagers among our homeschooling community on Long Island. They had grown into mature Catholics, brimming with joy and zeal for the New Evangelization, thrilled to be able to greet Pope Benedict that lovely spring morning.

I noticed with a small amount of pride that many of teens who seemed the most excited to see the Pope, the ones who knew the most about him and were most on fire with the mission of the New Springtime of Evangelization, were those who were homeschooled. They had a clear appreciation of their role in that New Springtime, and were consciously preparing for it. These young men and women are indeed bolstering the Church, by sharing the abundance of faith with their peers: following the call to vocations to religious life in great numbers, and giving vibrant examples of Catholic faith joyfully lived.

After ten years of homeschooling, led by prayer, our family of five moved from Long Island to the eastern area of Connecticut where there is a strong Catholic community. My need to work part-time and our family's changing needs, led me to solid Catholic schools to place them in. My daughter Gabriela, 16, is a junior in the Academy of the Holy Family, Isabella age 12 is in seventh grade in St Joseph School and my little one with Down syndrome, Christina age 8, is in first grade in Canterbury Elementary School.

Recently, Isabella commented to me, "Mom, you made learning our Catholic faith so much fun." My girls have become strong leaders in the teen pro-life movement and are living their faith publicly in many ways. I treasure the years we homeschooled not only for what they learned, but *how* they learned; bonded as sisters under our roof. We still feel that extraordinary closeness even as we face the challenges of the teen years. Another precious legacy from our decade of homeschooling is that learning at home with Christina exerted a profound influence on them, teaching them patience, self-sacrifice, and how to love others for whom they are, not how they look. That is the basis of their deep pro-life commitment; in fact they are both considering careers in the health field because of their years spent at home watching Christina's therapies. We attend Mass together with their schools on First Fridays and holy days. I have taught in their schools and shared with the students our family traditions celebrating the Liturgical year. Their teachers consider their leadership an asset to their schools. I am convinced that homeschooling put my children on solid ground in just the way that Fr. Fessio's vision had predicted.

Leticia Velasquez

Leticia Velasquez's is a Catholic journalist. She reviews films and books at Catholic Media Review and has won the 2009 American Life League's Pro-life Blog Award for Causa Nostrae Laetitiae. Her debut book is A Special Mother is Born. *She is available as a Culture of Life speaker and can be reached at marysjoys@yahoo.com*

LOST AND FOUND

Academics are important but we know it is the souls of our children that matters most. In the 90s when all eight of my children were still living at home, our family joined weekly with other home-ed families to pray the Rosary—a wonderful meditation on the life, death and resurrection of Our Lord, Jesus Christ. Our dear friend, Anna, often hosted this prayer time in her home.

One time, she lamented that she had lost her favorite Rosary. It was the one she'd been given for her First Holy Communion. I had never paid attention to the Rosary Anna used when we prayed. She told us it was of sturdy construction, though delicate looking and recounted to us the story of how she pulled it out of her pocket on her first date with Jerry, her future husband and suggested they pray together. (When he did pray with her, she knew in her heart he was the right man for her.) Anna had looked everywhere for her Rosary but finally gave it up for lost, feeling as though she had lost a dear friend. We called on St. Anthony to also pray for this intention since he is known as the patron of lost articles.

Some days later, Anna and I made our monthly visit to the local St. Vincent de Paul thrift store. As mothers of large families, we enjoyed looking for bargains together. Our custom was to go around together, so as to share the excitement of our great finds! However, on this certain day, I felt compelled to go the opposite direction and promptly found myself in front of the clear glass counter. My eyes fell immediately to a pearl beaded Rosary, which I promptly claimed for my own.

The cashier said, "This would not have lasted another five minutes; Rosaries go out as fast as we put them in the case!"

I paid for the little treasure and quickly found Anna, to show her my great buy! As I held it up before her, her eyes opened wide. "My Rosary!" she exclaimed.

Laughing, I drew it away from her and said, "No, mine!"

With tears now running over her cheeks, she explained that this was indeed, her First Communion Rosary! The crucifix was truly unique from any others I'd ever seen and so, was quite identifiable. Realizing what had just happened, we looked at each other in silent awe. I praised God that I was given the blessing of restoring such a precious treasure to her. Anna said she must have had it in the pocket of a coat she recently donated to St. Vincent's.

Before we took another step, we thanked God and St. Anthony too, for his prayers and the anticipated the joy of sharing this lesson on the power of intercessory prayer with our children.

Nellie Edwards

Nellie is the mother of eight, grandmother of eleven. After raising their eight children, Nellie realized her lifelong dream of doing fine art painting with no previous ability. She believes Our Lady's intercession made this possible and that the art is for helping to build the Culture of Life.
www.ImmaculataArt.com

THE SIGN

It was the late 70s and I was still in high school. One day during summer vacation, I happened to watch a daytime talk show that featured a family with four darling little girls. Their mother had been a teacher in Japan before coming to the United States with her American husband. She had schooled the girls herself and their education and maturity far surpassed their peers. Even though marriage and family were a long way off for me, I stored the idea in the back of my mind.

A few years later, I married and started a family. My husband, Steve, was in graduate school and I worked full-time. Our two daughters were in daycare. We needed the income from my job and since I had bought into the idea that I needed a career in order to be fulfilled, I knew I didn't want to give it up. When I became pregnant with our third child within five years things began to look different. We couldn't afford to have three kids in daycare. Steve finished his graduate school classes, got a job in his field of study, and I found a part-time job in the evenings when he could be home with the children.

A year later, when our oldest daughter went to kindergarten, I decided I should go back to working full-time. I had just begun my job search when I learned I was pregnant again. Disappointment does not adequately describe my reaction. I had never planned on having a big family and already felt overwhelmed with three.

I was not prepared when our second son turned out to be a very high-needs child. He was fussy and unsettled and rarely slept for longer than two hours at a time.

One particularly dreadful night, my sleep-deprived self knelt down next to his bassinet and cried out to God for help. I looked at my son's red face. His piercing screams pierced my heart and shattered my nerves. "Dear God, please help my son," I pleaded as tears streamed down my face. "Please heal him from whatever is making him so unhappy."

God did not delay. When I woke up the next morning I could tell my son was different. Not perfect, but a definite improvement. But more importantly, I was different. God had used the greatest difficulty of my life up until that point to convert my heart. I had converted to Catholicism after Steve and I married thinking it would be better for our family to be of one faith. But we were not really "one" because I was Catholic in name only. Now, I was compelled to learn and understand everything about the Catholic faith. I needed it and wanted to make it my own.

It was through learning about the Blessed Mother that I found inspiration in my vocation of motherhood. Mary became my helpmate. Who better could help me teach my children to know, love and serve her Son? The thought of homeschooling started to surface in my thoughts, but I was filled with doubts. Did I have what it would take?

The girls were in Catholic school and our older son was to enter in the fall. The thought of him being in a classroom made my stomach tight. He was an active boy and hard to keep on task. I knew he would suffer at the teasing of his peers and the rebukes of teachers. Even though there wasn't a mean bone in his body, I could already see the label of "troublemaker" in his file.

The North Dakota Homeschooling Conference was held in Bismarck that year. Steve and I decided to go to learn more about homeschooling. I attended workshops, looked at books, and observed the families. A talent show was held at the end of the first day. I was impressed as student after student performed with aptitude and confidence in front of the crowd. After the weekend, Steve and I decided homeschooling was for us and the decision was met with enthusiasm from our children.

I'll help you learn to read! You'll see, it's easy!

Starting out with three grades to teach was daunting, but little by little over the summer, I selected curriculum to begin the school year. I had only one big dilemma—I needed a reading program. I had my heart set on the Fast Track Action Reading program that a friend had lent to me. I tried it with my son and really liked the program, but my friend needed it back. The cost was too much for our family budget. Besides, I was still hoping that somehow I would get a sign from above that this was really what God wanted for us.

There was a daily call-in talk show on a local radio station. Guests were often invited to participate on the show on a variety of subjects. I was so excited when I heard that the author of my desired reading program, Jeanie Eller, was the guest. I also found out that she was giving away a free copy of Fast Track Action Reading to a predetermined caller during the show. Even though I was very nervous at the thought of talking on the radio, I decided that this was my chance. Maybe it would be the sign I had waited for.

My call was accepted and I told the author how much I liked the program. I related to her that my hard-to-sit-still son enjoyed the pace of the lessons and the learning games. My four-year-old son had been observing what his older brother was doing. Pretty soon, he was learning his sounds, as well. She was amused by my story and thanked me for calling. When I hung up, I knew everything was now in God's hands. I had prayed for a sign and now I waited on the Lord.

My heart jumped every time the phone rang the rest of the day. Each time the call wasn't from the radio station, I grew more anxious. Finally, I answered the phone and heard, "You won the reading program!" I thanked the caller and told her that I really wanted to win it because I was going to start homeschooling. Surprised, she told me that the radio host had inadvertently taken my call out of order making it the one they had chosen before the show started.

God had given me the sign I needed. We have enjoyed this homeschooling adventure for fifteen years. During this time I have been guided, challenged, and pushed far beyond my comfort zone. We have received blessings on a daily basis and enough struggles to keep us reliant on Him. As I look back, I can see how God was lovingly leading me to this endeavor before I could even recognize where it was going.

Susan Braun

Susan and Steve have been homeschooling for fifteen years. They have eight children and have taught them all to read with Fast Track Action Reading.

NOT TOO BUSY FOR GOD'S BLESSINGS

When my husband and I were asked to take in a boy from Kenya, between time and money, I thought it was more than we could handle. I had one in college, two at the Catholic high school and five schooling at home. Homeschooling can make for a full schedule and I felt I was already at capacity.

It began one evening when our friend, Evan Beauchamp, paid Mark and me a visit. He was in town on sabbatical from his work as a missionary in Kisii, Kenya. We were expecting just to have dinner with him, but he was hoping for something more.

"Is there anything we can do for you?" I asked, thinking along the lines of a comfortable pair of shoes or some other donation.

A sly grin crossed his face. "Well," he began, "I have a bright young student who desperately wants to go to school in the United States. Would you consider taking him in?"

While Mark and I were recovering from the shock of what was being asked of us, Evan elaborated. "Calvin is a very good boy. His parents both died of AIDS and he was living with his two brothers. I found out he often went hungry and walked an hour and a half each way to school." Evan had our attention so he continued. "I invited him to stay at the school with me during the week so he can eat properly. He wanted me to bring him back with me, but I am seventy now so that would be impossible. I've been asking around in Bismarck to see if there is a family who might be willing to take him in."

Calvin had our sympathy, but we already had eight children ranging from one to nineteen; six boys and two girls. "Even if we wanted," I ventured, "we cannot afford one more."

Evan shrugged. "I know. That's why I was not planning to ask you. But after a few families suggested the Armstrongs, I thought I had to at least bring it up. One person thought that since you had so many kids already, maybe one more would not make much of a difference!'" Mark and I looked at each other and smiled. Then, Evan suddenly brightened. "What if I got a family or two to help with the financial expenses?" The idea of becoming a parents to an orphan intrigued us but still, there we many reservations "We'll pray about it," was all we would commit to. Still, our hearts had opened just a crack.

In reality, no one really believed that Calvin would really get permission to leave the country. At fourteen, he had no birth certificate. But when Evan emailed us that Calvin had successfully gotten a birth certificate, the wheels were set in motion. There were still a lot of hoops to get through including becoming his legal guardians but hurdle after hurdle was overcome. Calvin joined us in July of 2002. He easily became a part of our family. My son Tyler and he were only a month apart in age and became especially close.

We thought we were being good Christians to take Calvin in but when we heard the rest of the story, we realized it was we who had been blessed. God had chosen us to answer a special prayer that bordered on the miraculous.

Years earlier, Calvin gently closed his paperback novel as he lay in his mud hut. It was getting dark in the one-room home he shared with his two brothers. There was no money for oil to burn in their kerosene lantern, so reading needed to stop at sunset.

Ignoring the rumbling coming from his empty stomach, Calvin thought about the main character in his novel; a boy who left Africa to live with relatives in the United States and go to school there. "Maybe I could go there someday," Calvin dreamed.

"Dear God," he began praying, "Please let me go to school in the United States." Although it seemed that God had not answered so many of his prayers before, Calvin prayed with the trust of a child, even though at thirteen, his childhood seemed to have been lost long ago. Both his parents had died of AIDS, leaving Rogers, 15, Calvin, 11, and Joash, 9, among

Kenya's 650,000 AIDS orphans. Charles had been away from home, working to earn money for the family. There was no AIDS education and people lacked understanding as to how it spread. Teenage girls and young women, needing money for their own families, often gathered around male work crews offering their services as prostitutes. Although Christianity is spreading, the Kenyan culture traditionally has not been strict about sexual fidelity in marriage. Charles died of AIDS on December 14, 1996. Fourteen months later, Yovencia followed. The boys had loved their parents deeply. The ache caused by their absence overshadowed each day.

Relatives helped out a little, but as time went on, the assistance was gradually withdrawn. An uncle continued to pay the fees for him to attend school, but it was a long walk for Calvin from his hut to St. Patrick's Elementary School. Since he rarely had dinner the night before, his feet felt heavy as he trudged along. "If only I could go to school in the United States," Calvin began thinking on these long walks. And again, he would pray.

When Calvin revealed his prayer to his older brother and an aunt, he was laughed at. "You only own two pairs of pants and have no money," his aunt had laughed. "How do you think you are going to get to the United States?"

Rogers was no more encouraging. "Why don't you pray for something more practical like a bigger garden?" he had asked. The boys' only reliable source of food was a garden. It was not very big, but it provided vegetables around occasional donations of food from others.

Then, Evan Beauchamp came to work at the school as a missionary for the diocese of Bismarck, North Dakota. When he noticed that Calvin had a sore on his foot for several weeks that was not healing, he knew it must be the effects of malnutrition. He learned of the boy's hardships and invited Calvin to live with him during the school week and then return to help his brothers on the weekends. Calvin overflowed with appreciation. Not only would he receive better nutrition but perhaps God was answering his prayer to eventually go to school in the United States.

It was not long before Calvin asked if perhaps Evan could take him back to the United States with him one day. Evan told him that would never be possible. Calvin smiled as if he understood but he kept praying and he kept asking. Finally, Evan told Calvin he would ask his friends when he returned to the United States for his mid-service sabbatical the next year. You know the rest of the story.

It was two weeks after Calvin joined us that we learned of his prayer. We were truly in awe at such faithfulness and felt it was an honor to be picked by God to answer a young boy's prayers. But, there was yet another boy in Kenya praying hard, Joash, his younger brother.

Almost two years after we accepted Calvin, Evan emailed us. "I know you are going to think this is crazy, but would you consider taking in Joash too?"

Could I handle one more? I wondered. *No*, I determined. Even though Calvin was good kid, I felt too busy to add another. I found another family willing to take him in. Mark insisted that Joash belonged with his brother and told me he was going to pray about it. "Go ahead," I said, "but I'm not going to change my mind."

A few days later, I changed my mind. One morning, I read an email Mark had stayed up late to write, full of reasons why we should take Joash in. "If we died, wouldn't we want *our* kids to stay together," Mark argued. I called him at work.

"Okay, Mark. He can come." I said to his happy surprise. Then, I hurried off to morning Mass, as was my custom. I was not really paying attention to the reading, when the words from Hosea 14:4 penetrated my reverie: "In you the orphan finds compassion." I was in awe at the timing.

A few months later, Josh arrived. We assumed the loss he had experienced was much the same as Calvin's. Only later did we gradually learn that his pain cut deeper and affected how he encountered the world. Joash was only eight when he sat desperately by his mother's side as she lay dying. Joash adored his mother, Yovencia. She always loved and protected him— her youngest. The older boys had grown more independent, but Joash usually preferred to be at his mother's side.

When she was taken to a separate hut, Joash was told to keep away but he would sneak through the window at night just to sit by her side. Joash had been at his mother's side only moments before she died. Someone told him to go take a shower but then he heard loud weeping. He ran back towards the hut and forced his way in to see his mother. In horror, Joash realized she was gone.

Joash ran to the river to be alone. There, his body shook as he cried out in anguish. How could he go on? Now there was no one to love him and care for him. *God must be punishing me*, he thought, *He has taken my mother and left me all alone.* Joash sobbed for hours before a cousin came for him. His grandfather took him in for a time, but the gruff old man resented the responsibility. Joash bounced back between relatives and his brother

Rogers. Since Rogers began attending school for masonry, he could not adequately supervise his younger brother and was just a teenager himself. Often in frustration, he disciplined Joash harshly. *If my mother was still alive, they would not be treating me this way,* Joash often thought. He built a wall around his emotions. His angry defenses became ingrained.

At the airport, five years after his mother died, Joash again broke down and cried when Calvin left for the United States. Calvin had always been kind to him and he loved his brother very much. Now, he would not even have him. One evening, after Rogers had been angry, Joash grumbled, "I wish Calvin were here."

"Then you better start praying if you want to go to the United States and see Calvin again," Roger had answered. That night, before bed, Joash said the first prayer he had ever said on his own. He prayed the "Our Father," a prayer he had learned in school. And every night after that, he said an "Our Father" before going to sleep.

About six months later, Rogers revealed to Joash that he was going to join Calvin. Initially, Joash could not believe it was true, fearing it was some kind of a joke. For the first time since his mother's death seven years earlier, he had something to look forward to.

But Joash's defensiveness and pain stayed with him and soon after his arrival in July of 2005, struggles began. I knew his negative behaviors were born of pain, but I could not seem to make things better. Tyler and Calvin were seniors, both doing very well. Joash and my son Jacob were both in ninth grade and were like oil and water. Joash's defensiveness often caused conflict throughout the family. To make matters worse, he struggled in school. His English aptitude scores ranged from first to seventh grade ability.

After about seven months, Mark and I decided the situation was more than we could handle. Joash knew he had crossed a line one day, and for a couple of days, we were all pretty quiet around each other. On the evening Mark and I planned to reveal our plans to find another placement for him, Joash approached us first.

"I know I've messed up," he said, with pleading eyes. "I stopped at the chapel at school today and prayed. I've asked God to help me. Please give me another chance. I promise I will try harder."

His pledge was salve to my heart. I did not want him to go away, I just wanted a manageable family life. Right away, things did start getting better. We could see Joash actually trying although sometimes, situations were beyond him. But I also noticed something Joash had no idea I was aware of. When one of the younger children was upset about something or sullen over getting punished, Joash comforted them. He would try to stop the tears or just talk with them. I knew this boy, who had built a wall around his heart, had a big one indeed.

Then, while taking each day at a time and putting his best foot forward, Joash made an amazing discovery that changed his life dramatically. After lackluster seasons in soccer and basketball, track season began. Joash had once tried to run a race in sixth grade but quit when people laughed after he tripped. In eighth grade, he entered a race and seemed to be off to a good start; running past everyone. Unfortunately, he was quickly pulled out and disqualified. He had no idea it was a walking—not a running—race.

As a freshman at St. Mary's he decided to try track one more time. His first track meet competing with nine schools for the western region of North Dakota, was almost a comedy of errors. He took off like a rabbit and kept turning around to see the runners behind him. Still, Joash managed to cross the finish line at 5:07, nine seconds behind first place. With practice, Joash became unbeatable. During junior and senior year of cross-country, he broke every course record and placed first. Spring of his senior year he had placed third in the entire country at the Nike Cross Nationals cross-country meet and also took firsts at the State Track Meet in the 3200 meter (9:12.49) and 1600 meter (4:16.41).

Running brought Joash great joy and self-confidence. He became respectful, happy and developed a zest for life. Even his schoolwork improved as he grew comfortable in his new home. During the first few months, I had wondered if Joash would even graduate from high school. By senior year, he was regularly on the honor roll and colleges throughout the country were offering him full running scholarships. He accepted a five-year scholarship from the University of Portland. Joash did exceptionally well his college freshman year, but is taking a season off to recover from injuries. In the meantime, he is also excelling in school, getting good grades.

Our family misses him very much. The boy that struggled to adjust to our family, became a much loved member that we hated to see leave the nest. In the meantime, Calvin has graduated from the University of Mary with a degree in respiratory therapy. He will work for a few months before entering medical school. His dream is to become a doctor and one day return to Kenya to help the poor. Both our sons from Kenya have expanded the love and adventure in our family beyond anything possible without them.

Honestly, homeschooling had made me feel so busy, on top of my other kids in high school that I never imagined we could have added to our family in this way. Thanks be to God that He let us know that we were not too busy for more blessings.

Patti Maguire Armstrong

AND THEN SHE SMILED

It probably will not surprise you to hear that as Catholic homeschoolers, our family has a special devotion to Mary. We even named our little school after her: Our Lady of the Angels Academy.

Mary keeps us on track throughout our school day. No matter where we might be gathered, the presence of our Blessed Mother is felt. Over the mantle in our family room is a framed image of the Holy Family: inspiration to the many wrestling children and DVD-viewers that tumble through that room. By the kitchen sink is a small porcelain statue: my kitchen Madonna. Perhaps unnerving to the casual visitor, there is a life-sized statue of Maria Rosa Mystica in our sitting room. She is lovely and is a gift that I treasure from my mom and dad. And finally, in our bedroom, which is home-base for evening prayer, daily read-a-louds for the children and many moments of folding laundry, is a statue of Our Lady of Fatima. We really do like Mary around here.

So when the opportunity came to see the International Pilgrim Virgin Statue of Our Lady of Fatima, we jumped on the chance. This statue of Mary is sent out to bring the message of Fatima to the world. It has traveled to over one-hundred countries including China and Russia, and is known for its many miraculous occurrences and graces.

Our family entered the cathedral to attend Mass and then afterwards see the statue. The cathedral was full-to-bursting with hundreds of Catholic school kids from the Twin Cities and surrounding areas—all assembled to pray, sing, and peer curiously at the mystical, miraculous presence at the front of the church.

After the liturgy we were invited to move closer, and so my own little group approached the statue. We waited quietly while a little girl in a blue uniform got her picture taken with Mary. All of a sudden, I saw the somber expression on Our Blessed Mother's face become a broad, beaming smile. I assure you that I did! And then, in the midst of this surreal, is-this-really-happening moment, my oldest son grabbed my arm and exclaimed,

"Mommy! Do you see? The statue of Mary is smiling!" He had seen it too! To their dismay, however, none of my other children saw this. The story, though, is retold often—and is a reminder of the power of Mary's intercession and of her love, and of God's amazing grace poured out to His children through His mother.

Margaret Berns

Margaret Berns is a Catholic homeschooling wife, mother, and writer. (In that order? She hopes so.) She is the author of the popular blog, Minnesota Mom, (www.patentsgirl.blogspot.com) where she chronicles the joys, sorrows and laughable mishaps of her vocation.

YOUR MOTHER IS CALLING

When I was in the second grade at Holy Cross School next to the brewery of-all-things, my teacher, Sister Teresa Marie, used to give out prizes for exceptional work. Amazingly, each week every child was exceptional. Usually the prizes bestowed were holy cards. But one Friday, Sister walked up and down the rows of desks and allowed everyone to pick a book from her box. The books were withdrawn from the school library, and were old, but to us they were treasures. This was not the time of Scholastic book fairs or super bookstores where one can simultaneously enjoy cool beverages while browsing in a text complex the size of a football field. Back then, one could not select reading material with a simple click of the mouse, and expect it in the mailbox in five to seven working days. No, this was a simpler time. Books were sparser and I think, a little more cherished.

As Sister approached me, I decided to close my eyes and let fate decide my selection. Looking the other way, I thrust my hand into the box and grabbed a tattered book with a maroon linen binding. The name of the book was not readily seen, and at first I wanted to throw it back and have a "do-over." But I didn't. Rummaging through the pages I finally found the title: *A Story of Our Lady of Fatima.*

The book began, "On a hot May day in 1917, three little shepherds were watching their sheep....." and it proceeded to tell the beautiful story of the Blessed Mother who came to three poor peasant children as Our Lady of Fatima. Only years later did I learn that that "hot day in May" spoke of in the book was May 13, my birthday.

In 1981, the day before my high school graduation, I heard the pope had been shot. The bullet passed through him but did not hurt vital organs.

Since I had gone to see him when he visited Chicago, I felt a special kinship with him. I really liked this young pope, John Paul II, who was Polish like me. Later, the pope credited the Blessed Mother, as Our Lady of Fatima, with sparing his life on that fateful day. He felt it was her hand that guided the bullet to a safe destination. The day of the shooting and Mary's protection: May 13.

Fast forward to 1998. I was married, and had 6 children. I had been considering the purchase of a statue of the Blessed Mother for our little schoolroom. I was drawn to Our Lady of Grace because her image was in all the Catholic school classrooms of my youth. I also felt drawn to Our Lady of Guadalupe, who is the patroness of Americas and the unborn. During this time, my husband's grandmother moved out of her home because of failing health. We were given boxes and boxes of her old things. "Take what you want and get rid of the rest," she told us, and we started the daunting task of going through boxes. Guess what I found while rummaging through one box, right next to a crocheted hot pad holder and a package of unused drinking straws? Yup, you guessed it....A statue of our Lady of Fatima. She was definitely trying to stay in touch with me.

I dusted her off and put her in a position of prominence. Then, I laughed at myself for taking twenty-five-plus years to figure out that she was reaching out to me and that I should pay attention. I finally realized the Blessed Mother was there when I was eight. She was there when I was 18. She was there when I was 28, 38, and is here right now. Like the gentle mother that she is, she quietly knocks on the doors of our hearts, waiting for us to respond, but never forcefully entering.

Our heavenly mother who loves us completely beckons us all to her love and protection as she intercedes for us before her Son. I imagine she has blessings like delicate fragrant flowers she wishes to bestow on all mothers whose hearts are open. Consider this article your dusty maroon book, your realization of a hand of protection, your found statue in a box of useless things. Your mother is calling. Go to her. She loves you and she's waiting.

Theresa A. Thomas

A LUNCH AT A LAKE CHANGED MY LIFE

Twelve years ago I was a full-time microbiologist, living in Missouri with a hard working husband and two public schooling children. We were making decent money and while we were not wealthy, we were able to enjoy some modest luxuries now and then. One particularly gorgeous spring afternoon, my husband and I met on our lunch break at a nearby lake. We tried to meet at the lake as often as the weather and our schedules would allow, which was infrequent enough to make it a special occasion. During the work week, the lake was normally very private except for the geese and an occasional hum of a fishing boat. It was a great place to relax, rejuvenate and enjoy each other's company before going back to work for the rest of the afternoon.

While we were picnicking, I noticed a woman, sitting at a picnic table, talking to a high school aged girl. They seemed to be working from a book together. What's more, they seemed relaxed and cheerful, and enjoying one another's company very much. As I continued to watch them, I realized that this was a mother, teaching her daughter from a math text--right there at a picnic table during the middle of the day! I was dumbfounded. I didn't know people did that. It looked so enjoyable. It seemed to be productive. I curiously walked up to the woman and politely asked what she was doing. She didn't seem to mind my question in the least.

"I'm homeschooling my daughter," she said, "When the weather gets nice like this, we like to do our schooling outdoors."

I was so curious. Homeschooling? That was a totally unknown concept to me or anyone in my circles. The woman and I conversed for brief time. She introduced me to her daughter and she shared with me that they had just moved to Missouri from Ohio and that her husband was a Charismatic Episcopal Church minister. Too soon, the lunch hour was over, and both my husband and I had to get back to work. The woman and I parted ways without ever exchanging names.

Later that afternoon, my husband phoned me and told me he felt that homeschooling was something I should look into for our daughters, ages nine and seven. I could have literally fallen out of my chair when he said this. It was most definitely not something I would have ever dreamed would come out of his mouth. He is not one to be influenced on a whim or by a single picturesque scene at a park in an afternoon. His sudden and emphatic suggestion was a miracle to me in and of itself. I don't know how I knew, but I just *knew*, in an instant, that this was entirely the work of the Holy Spirit.

Once my husband suggested I research homeschooling, I could think of nothing else. Not that afternoon. Not the rest of the week, or the week after. I had a one-track mind totally consumed with educating myself on homeschooling.

After devouring every published book on homeschooling that we could lay our hands on, my husband and I decided I would quit my job and start educating our children. I notified my employer, stating I would leave on my children's last day of school. I was scared. We would be cutting our income nearly in half. We were used to purchasing what we wanted when we wanted it. At the time, we didn't necessarily think of ourselves as being well off, but looking back I have to laugh at what we thought were necessities. Despite being afraid of losing my income, both my husband and I were convinced that quitting my job and homeschooling our children was definitely in our children's best interest. We knew we would never regret quitting for our children but we would always regret NOT quitting for our children.

Two weeks after putting in my notice, I found out I was expecting our third child. This threw a mental wrench into the equation and put my husband over the top for awhile. Cutting our income was one thing but adding another dependent after seven years had not been figured into the calculation. We felt overwhelmed and had second thoughts. But still,we pressed on with the plan.

The rewards came. We had good days and bad in our journey of homeschooling, but the good far outweighed the challenges. I wasn't using my skills for the outside world so much anymore. Instead, I was using them to benefit my own children, and it felt great. I was so grateful to be able to teach my children and learn with them. It brought us together in a closeness I never thought was possible.

Over the years, as I reaped great joy and deep satisfaction for the privilege of being able to do this, I thought of the woman in the park. Many times I wished she could know how her example one spring afternoon had changed my family's lives profoundly, instantly, positively, in ways that we could never have imagined.

Six years passed, and I had three more daughters. We continued to homeschool and our family life was good. One weekend, my daughter and I went on a camping trip with her Girl Scout troop. After the trip, my daughter and I attended the Sunday evening Mass in a church across town because we had missed the morning Mass at our own parish. Much to my delight, I encountered a fellow homeschooling friend there. After the usual chit-chat, she said she wanted to introduce us to another Catholic homeschooling friend of hers.

"Cheryl," she called to her friend, "Come here and meet Joan....Cheryl, this is Joan. Joan this is Cheryl."

I looked at the woman and had a strange sensation. Had I met her before? I couldn't recall doing so yet there was something vaguely familiar about her. We exchanged pleasantries. Suddenly, it all came back—it was the woman from the park, so many years ago! Yes, it had to be her! She felt it, too. "Are you......" She was! Cheryl was the woman at the lake that had started me on my homeschool journey! We both remembered. I hugged her and cried.

Wasn't her husband some type of minister? Yes, they had been Episcopal, she said, but she and her whole family were getting ready to enter the Catholic Church that coming Easter. She was excited and quite alive with her love of the beauty and truths of the Catholic Church. I couldn't believe it. This was all too amazing. It was just by chance that I happened to attend that church this morning and just by chance that I happened to run into my friend

God gave me the opportunity I had longed for, right there in His very own house. I was finally able to tell Cheryl the affect her example had on my family and how grateful I have been ever since. Best of all, Cheryl's entire family was coming into the Catholic Church that Easter. We were truly one big homeschooling Catholic family--God's family. It was a great surprise and delight, and Cheryl and I have been friends ever since.

Joan Gilmore

Joan has been married to Greg for 22 years and is the mother of 5 daughters. She has homeschooled for 11 years. With the youngest being just 2 years old, she figures she has 17 years to go. She is also a consultant for Mother of Divine Grace School.

GRACE THROUGH A HAMSTER

At 2:36 a.m., (I know because I looked at the clock), I awoke to the pitter patter of little feet. They were not human feet. They were little, tiny animal feet, and they were....in my bed. Startled, I flipped on the light, and found Hammy, our pet hamster, scampering across my covers. The little fellow seemed as surprised as I was. He wriggled and scurried back and forth on the cool white sheets. *How on earth did he get in my bed?* I wondered. I was afraid if I picked him up, he might bite me, and so I called for my pet rescuer extraordinaire, my 11 year-old son Jared.

Upon my beckoning, Jared came into my room right away, scooped up the little critter and put him in his cage. I still was wondering how Hammy could have gotten in my bed. Our bed had no bed skirt. There were no covers hanging over the edge. It was puzzling.

"Thank you Jared, for helping me get Hammy," I said as I walked him back to his room, "I'm so sorry I had to wake you up."

"Oh, you didn't wake me up," replied my son, "I've been awake a long time. My back itches so badly, Mom."

I lifted Jared's pajama top, expecting to see some mosquito bites, but instead I found that his entire back was angry red, swollen and inflamed. These were not mosquito bites. They were not bites at all. Something serious was going on with my son. The area seemed to be increasing in redness, and welts were forming even as I watched. Quickly I woke my husband.

"Honey, wake up! Something's wrong with Jared! His back is swollen and red and it's spreading!"

My husband woke up right away.

What do you think it is?" I asked.

He didn't know but suggested giving Jared some Benadryl, which I quickly retrieved from the cabinet. As we were administering the medication to Jared I actually watched the rash spread down his arms and legs. Everywhere on my son was puffing up fast. Even his lips began to swell, and alarmed, I asked how his breathing was.

"Fine...." He started, "I... just... have...this... clump... in my... throat...."

At that point we instinctively knew he needed medical help. Within just a few minutes we whisked him away to the hospital emergency room. When the staff saw what Jared was dealing with, he was seen immediately. The doctors diagnosed Jared with an extremely aggressive allergic reaction, and told us that because of it his throat had been swelling shut. Without treatment and immediate attention, the reaction could easily have been fatal.

The hospital personnel treated Jared with adrenalin and steroids, and when his reaction had calmed, they sent us on our way with an epi-pen and oral steroids for him to use for five full days. We were not sure what the reaction was from--perhaps new mustard that we had had for dinner? We may never know.

At 4 a.m. that same night, less than two hours from when Hammy scampered up my arm, I sat by my sweet boy's bedside, watching him sleep, and praying and thanking the dear Lord for sending angels to put a silly hamster in my bed. I have no doubts that the timing was not a coincidence. I looked at my bed this morning, still puzzled, and tried to figure out how a creature as small as Hammy could climb up so high into my bed without the aid of a bed skirt or even blankets hanging over the edge. I still can't figure it out logically, but in my heart I do know how Hammy got there. God used an animal to help my son. God showed His grace...through a hamster.

Chris Armshaw

Chris and her husband Kevin live in Tennessee with their seven children. Their family is entering their 12th year of homeschooling. Jared is almost 16 and has never had another severe allergic reaction. The family continues to see God's grace in the "little" things.

Chapter Four

BY THE GRACE OF GOD

"I will lead the blind on their journey; by paths unknown I will guide them. I will turn darkness into light." (Isaiah 42:16)

"My grace is enough for you..." (2 Corinthians:12:9)

A HOME FULL OF LIFE

When people rediscover their faith and learn what it truly means to be Catholic, going from point A to point Z does not happen all in one step. Thus, we must not judge others but rather pray for them if it seems they are not always on the right course. I can attest to the fact that it takes time to learn all that the Church has to give and some of us our slow learners.

My husband and I began our journey of faith back in Kalispell, MT when he was laid off work at the radio station where he worked as a reporter. We put our lives in God's hands, prayed and trusted and soon moved to Bismarck, ND when Mark was offered a new job there. That is where the adventure of living a Catholic life began. But along the way, after learning to pray the Rosary and not skipping Sunday Mass anymore, we still were in the dark about many Catholic teachings--including the teaching on birth control. After all, the message from society and even in Catholic circles was that using contraception was not just okay, but actually expected at some point in a married couple's life. So, in spite of my love of babies, after having four of them, I pressured my husband Mark to have a vasectomy.

First, a little background. I was one of those little girls that hovered around babies waiting for a chance to hold them. So when my first son, Aaron, was born, my heart brimmed with happiness. As he grew, I thrilled at his quick mind and curiosity for the world. Son number two, Luke, was a cute, cuddly little blonde with a sweet disposition. Our third boy, Tyler, showed his lively personality and athletic prowess early. I loved my little boys with all my heart, but were three little bundles of joy enough? I decided they were. Or rather, I was influenced by the world around me that three was plenty.

My husband, Mark, was not so sure. I knew the Catholic Church taught that artificial birth control was against God's plan, but being surrounded by Catholics who had no qualms with it, I comfortably ignored that teaching. I decided to have surgery for a tubal ligation. Two days prior to surgery, during the pre-op exam, the doctor explained the failure rate was only 1 in 500. Those odds were unsettling. Not bad odds for the lottery, I thought. A failure could result in a tubal pregnancy which could result in death. I canceled.

The next line of attack was birth control pills--prescribed to me by my parish priest. Yes, you read that right. At our church was a priest that was also a doctor. I had a friend that recommended him as a great doctor. He became my doctor too and told me that it was not reasonable for couples to have to follow the Catholic teaching on *Humanea Vitae*. This was the encyclical in which Pope Paul VI clarified the constant teaching that artificial birth control is contrary to God's plan. I had a priest/doctor telling me birth control pills were okay so I looked no further.

I took the pills for a short time but there were problems so I discontinued. I became pregnant the following month. When Mark heard the news, he announced, "I've been praying for this." I wanted to know if he meant that figuratively or had he prayed behind my back? It turned out he had been praying on the sly. Regardless, I could not help but rejoice that another little baby was joining our family.

Jacob was born on May 13, the anniversary date of Our Lady of Fatima's first appearance in Fatima, Portugal. It was also Mark's birthday and Mother's Day. Mark too had been born on Mother's Day thirty-three years earlier. Happy Birthday Mark—from God.

During this time in our lives, we had begun reading about various Marian apparitions and were inspired for the first time, to pray the Rosary. We stopped missing Sunday Mass and started to learn more about our faith. Still, we were not fully converted yet--particularly when it came to family planning. I had insisted Mark have a vasectomy. He finally relented.

Initially, I was oblivious that we had done anything wrong. But gradually, as I grew to desire God's will in my life, started making visits to the tabernacle and continued praying the Rosary, a feeling grew in me. I realized that the Church, which Christ had founded to guide us until the end of time, had authority to teach on spiritual matters, including procreation. This Catholic teaching on this issue had remained constant since the beginning.

I shared my feelings with Mark. He was less than thrilled since he never really wanted the vasectomy to begin with. As a matter of fact, he accused me of being like Eve. "You are right," I agreed. "But remember, Adam was kicked out of the garden too." We began praying that God's will would be done in our lives, including whether we would have more children. Our thinking was that if it was God's will, Mark's vasectomy would fail.

Then, one night, I had a dream in which I saw two babies; one blonde and one dark-haired. I felt an intense love for these babies as if they were my own. At the end of the dream I was made known that these were children God had planned for us, but now they would never be born. I woke up feeling like a mother who just lost her babies. I knew the only way to get to them was to convince Mark to have a reversal of his vasectomy.

When Mark came home from work the next day, I approached him with the idea for a reversal. But I barely got two sentences out of my mouth before he announced the subject was officially closed. Now, it was my turn to pray behind Mark's back. "Okay God," I prayed. "I want to do Your will but I am powerless to change Mark's mind. I'm putting everything in Your hands." Then, I just kept praying, often before the Blessed Sacrament at church.

Several months passed when one morning after Mass, Mark casually wondered out loud how much a reversal operation would cost. "I know," I announced. I had called the doctor's office to get all the information months earlier when I had tried to talk to Mark about it.

"Well, I can't get off from work this month," Mark said, "but next month I could go in and get it done." I was shocked and thrilled. We did not have the money to pay for it, but we determined we could probably make payments to the hospital.

"But, what changed your mind?" I finally asked, wondering what had caused such a drastic change of heart. His answer took my breath away.

"I had a dream last night," Mark said. "I saw two babies that God had planned for us." I had never told a single soul about my dream.

Three months later we were expecting a baby. I had a strong feeling that it would be our first girl and God wanted us to name her Mary after the Blessed Mother who had intervened for us. We had never considered the name with any previous pregnancy. I wrote on a slip of paper, "Yes, I think Mary would be a good name," and tucked it in my wallet. I figured that when God let Mark in on the plan, I would pull out the slip and show him.

Our blond-haired baby girl, Mary, was born on December 22, 1993. A few months before her birth, we inherited the exact amount of money we needed to pay Mark's reversal surgery in full. (As an aside, we had started a family prayer group with two other couples, to say the Rosary together once a week. Within the year, the other couples also had babies; another Mary and a Maria. When we began meeting, not one of us planned to have more children.)

Dark-haired Teresa was born on my birthday, April 18, 1996. I thought we must be done now that we had the babies from our dream. Mark, as usual, said he thought ten would be a good number of children. While praying about it, I recalled that when St. Maximilian Kolbe was young, he had received a vision of Our Blessed Mother. She had shown him two wreaths of roses; one of red representing martyrdom, and one of white, representing purity. She asked him which he would like to choose. He chose both. I wondered, if like St. Maximilian, we should volunteer to take on more than God asked? We prayed for guidance.

John was born on August 31, 1999 and Isaac was born on his sister Mary's birthday, December 22, 2001. There could be no greater blessing on our family than our precious children. The kids' love for each other runs deep. The younger boys are a big draw to have my older children come home more often.

We began homeschooling a year after Mary, our fifth child was born. She was two when I became pregnant with Teresa during our first year. Having babies while homeschooling does require some flexibility, but God gives us the grace to do what he asks of us. This year, I had only the three youngest children still homeschooling. It occurred to me one day that having three did not seem any easier than when I had six at home. I pondered the situation and wondered, *How on earth did I manage with double that amount of kids?* That's when it hit me that God had given me the graces I needed back then.

Eventually, Mark and I became legal guardians of two orphaned boys from Kenya. So, we really did end up with ten children. I will not say that life has always been easy under our roof, but I will say that all my children are a blessing and I am so thankful for all ten of them. Had we stopped at three or four, we'd be empty nesters right now and never would have known what we missed out on. Instead, our house is still busy and full of the life that God had to give us once we opened ourselves up to his will.

Patti Maguire Armstrong

EVEN IN DEATH, THE POWER OF ONE LIFE

We had been married six years, had three beautiful, healthy children and were expecting our fourth. A doctor's visit the week before told us everything was fine. Then, at just ten weeks along, I started bleeding. We soon found out our baby Seth, had died. It was a devastating blow that we did not see coming.

There was no question that we were going to have a funeral mass for our baby. We made the preparations, got a death certificate from our doctor, talked to our priest and made all the necessary arrangements. The funeral service turned out beautifully. Many people came and our baby was buried with the dignity he deserved.

During the whirlwind of events that were going on, I slipped away for a few moments to spend time with God. My journal was in my hands as my head spun with a myriad of thoughts. I could only write just a few sentences, one of which read: "This baby will help to bring abortion to an end."

I did not even think about what I had written. I just wrote it down, and closed my journal. Two years later, I was sitting in my living room with a dear friend from church. My husband was out in the driveway fixing her car as we sat chatting on the couch. From out of nowhere she began to share a part of her life that I had never known.

"I once worked at an abortion clinic," she revealed, looking pained. "Sometimes I'd even laugh with other workers and make jokes about the tiny body parts that were being sucked from the mother's womb." It was hard to listen as she explained how she could see the parts as they would travel down the transparent vacuum tube. My friend confessed that she herself had two abortions and was teaching her daughters that they had the right to do the same. "But one day, I went into work and I felt that I just could not do it anymore. I didn't know why I felt that way but I had to get another job," she said. Ironically, my friend found a new job taking care of small children, but she remained very much in favor of abortion.

I was stunned by her shocking confession. The reality of my friend's past left me speechless for a moment. After a moment of silence, I asked her, "What made you change your mind? I know you are very pro-life now, what happened?"

She looked at me and in a very gentle whisper said, "Seth's funeral." She explained that when she attended the funeral for a baby that was just ten weeks in the womb, it dawned on her at that moment, that it was truly a human being, deserving of life from the very moment of conception. She was now teaching her daughters the same.

My heart filled with joy at the thought of what our little boy's life had meant to this woman. I had no idea the impact that He would have. God used the devastation of our child's death to bring life to a mother into the truth. In his little 10-week life, God had indeed used this baby to help bring abortion to an end.

Anita Usher

Anita Usher is the mother of eleven children. Three of those babies are now in heaven with Jesus. Anita has been homeschooling on and off for fourteen years and is now homeschooling eight children full-time. She has been married to her best friend, John Usher, for 17 years.

PEANUT BUTTER FROM HEAVEN

"Is this an emergency?" the receptionist asked as I paced the floor of my bedroom, nursing my baby. "It will be if I don't talk to the doctor or her nurse very soon." "Oh," she said, "one moment please." Believe it or not, she put me on hold. I glanced down at little Connor John in my arms, and I couldn't help but smile.

It had been a rather ordinary day in my rather ordinary life. As a homeschooling mother of ten, I would have to say that a day that goes as planned is quite out of the ordinary. Earlier in the day, a good friend from out of town, Jane, called. "How are you?" she asked.

"I'm doing great," I replied. I had just finished morning prayer with my children and had a great discussion with them about giving everything they do all day to the Lord as a gift. We had a long talk about smiling when things don't go our way because, when we give it all to God, He will use these things to build His Kingdom and help us become more beautiful for heaven.

Then Jane had to ask, "So how is everything else around there?" She knows me too well. By the time I was done with my litany she knew that our fourteen year old van was in the shop for the fifth time in a month, and it looked like it was the transmission this time; the dryer is broken, and there is no money for a repair man right now; Patrick's seizure's are out of control. He needs an MRI under general anesthesia, an EEG, and he has a very resistant staph ear infection that may require five to ten days in the hospital; (Patrick is severely autistic, and at 14, a hospital stay would not go over very well.) And last, but not least, I informed her that my husband Mark's back is out again. "Really, we're doing fine. God has a plan," I said. "Well, is that all?" she said. We both laughed.

After hanging up the phone with my friend I asked the Lord to help me truly see with eyes of faith that He is in charge and that He will use these trials to build his kingdom. In my heart I knew that Christ would show me how to handle all this, and at the same time He would strengthen my faith. Then I asked Him for one more thing. I asked Him to show me how to teach this to my children. In my heart I heard the same words I had spoken to my children earlier in the day, *Smile when things don't go your way because the trials of today will be the treasures of tomorrow.* It sounded so simple, and yet it made so much sense. If my children see me happy when faced with a difficult situation, they will learn to do the same.

Now I was on hold with the neurologist's office waiting to talk with the nurse about Patrick's seizure medication and his upcoming tests. He had recently suffered two grand mal seizures, and there was a problem with the dosage of his seizure medication. While I waited on hold I decided to peek out into the dining room to see how the kids were getting along with lunch. As usual, things were not quite the way I had left them.

"Kate, why are you and Bridget chasing Emily around the dining room?" I asked.

Just as Emily, my three year old, ran to me Kate said, "Because she was standing in the peanut butter."

Sure enough, Emily had gotten into the peanut butter. And I mean literally: both feet into the jar of peanut butter. She had peanut butter up to her knees. I had to ask myself why in the world I had thought I would actually save money by buying the huge mega tub of peanut butter. Thinking of my broken dryer, I said, "O.K., everyone grab something that is not made of cloth and start cleaning the peanut butter out of the carpet." God had blessed us with several days of rain, so I could not hang laundry out to dry. Fortunately, my kids, as great as they are at creating laundry, could not go outside and get dirty either.

While I was still nursing the baby and holding the phone I was able to maneuver Emily into a chair. I was instructing her not to move from the chair when finally the nurse on the phone said, "May I help you?"

Emily began to cry, "I'm sorry, Mommy." I knew she would not stop until I accepted her apology.

I whispered in her ear, "I forgive you." Then I rushed into the bedroom and closed the door so I could hear the nurse.

A few moments later I emerged from my room, assured that the medication problem would be taken care of. There before me was my resourceful crew, kneeling on the floor using my emergency supply of baby wipes to clean the carpet. They were discussing the fate of Romulus and Remus from the Roman history we had studied earlier in the day. Michael was having a hard time understanding how one brother could kill the other. Kate was at Emily's feet wiping the last traces of peanut butter from between her toes.

"You're doing a great job, guys," I said as I knelt down to help. Connor John toddled off with a baby wipe in his hand and then bent down to imitate his siblings.

As we all knelt on the carpet Megan glanced at the clock and said, "Mom, it's noon."

Everyone folded his or her hands and Brendan started with "The angel of the Lord declared unto Mary." We responded, "and she conceived of the Holy Spirit." God is so good. He got us all on our knees just in time for the Angelus. How could I not be smiling?

Elizabeth M. Matthews

Beth Matthews, mother of twelve, is the author of Precious Treasure, the Story of Patrick *and co-author with her husband, Mark, of* A Place for Me. *Beth is a frequent speaker on a variety of family topics. The Matthews live in Westfield, Indiana. You may find out more or contact Beth a www.chelseashire.com*

HOMESCHOOLING THROUGH SPECIAL CIRCUMSTANCES

As I walk through the hospital hallways behind my nine-year-old son's wheelchair, tears of relief stream down my face. The doctor has just told me that my son's sudden loss of vision is treatable. The nurse is taking him to his room, where he will receive intravenous steroids for three days.

As I walk through the hospital hallways again, several days later, with my son walking at my side, we don't know what the outcome will be. Will he regain the significant amount of vision that he has lost? He didn't respond to treatment, and now the doctor only hopes that some of his vision will return in the coming weeks or months.

"I probably won't be able to play baseball this year, but hopefully I can next year," Peter says to me.

As we step onto the elevator, I point out to him the Braille symbols for the floors. It's all Greek to me, but I have already decided this is something we will learn.

Soon we learn something else, something profoundly new and strange. Instead of optic neuritis, as originally diagnosed, Peter has a condition called Leber's Hereditary Optic Neuropathy. We learn that this is a gene, passed to the offspring only from the mother, which can cause legal blindness (or somewhat worse, as in Peter's case). Someone who inherits this gene may or may not experience vision loss. When they do, there is no cure or treatment. No, Peter won't be playing baseball next year.

Many people are praying for Peter and for all of us. We are touched by all the prayers. But when someone tells me to pray to this or that saint for a cure, I tell them, "Thank you. I appreciate your prayers! And you pray as you wish. But I feel this is God's will. The miracle He is granting, the answer to prayers, is Peter's good attitude and strong faith and all the people who help us along the way." I feel I need to just move forward toward helping my son to adapt.

But how?

I have homeschooled my six children for seventeen years, but now I begin to have doubts. Would it be better to put Peter into school where he can get specialized instruction from professionals?

One of my college-age students, running late to get to class, rushes through our schoolroom to the back door. Another young adult comes to the kitchen to get a snack, and starts up a conversation with the rest of us, some challenging the way I'm dealing with Peter. He can't read anything smaller than an inch in height. While we wait for a diagnosis and magnification, his reading and math abilities have plummeted. My husband works on the computer in the schoolroom, having been laid off from his job a few months before, and having begun a business of his own from home.

That same computer in the schoolroom connects me with Internet groups and websites where I meet people who generously offer various types of help. Sometimes it's an encouraging word, sometimes advice, sometimes materials they'll send us by regular mail. Finally we are getting special equipment from the Cincinnati Association for the Blind and the Kentucky School for the Blind. Later, a teacher of the visually impaired begins coming to the house, and also helps us to get more equipment.

Peter is learning to use enlargement software on the computer, learning to read Braille, learning touch typing.

My husband is ever supportive of our homeschooling, while working enthusiastically at his new business; but the economic time and region are not conducive to the thriving of a new business. I begin working part time in the evening, thinking about the possibility of working full time to help out; while he begins looking for a job.

For the first time in my children's lives, I ask if they would like to go to a regular school. For the first time, I consider alternatives, and give them a choice. Peter and his remaining homeschooling brothers give me the answer I had hoped in my heart to hear: an emphatic no.

On Holy Thursday of 2006, Jesus gives us an Easter gift: the saving telephone call to my husband, an interview for a good job in his original profession. He is offered the job, and we prepare to move to Baltimore, Maryland. Baltimore. This is the city where Catholicism first grew in America. And it's a city which has a school for the blind. We learn that Baltimore County is the best county in the region for getting visual impairment services at home. It's hard leaving the adult children behind, but by now they have moved out on their own.

We get settled into our new home, and once again a teacher of the visually impaired comes to our house for an hour a week. It's now been over four years since his vision loss. Had Peter been in school all this time, would his self-esteem be as good? Would he be a print reader or would he be a Braille reader? At home, we've been able to work on both each day. Finally I begin to realize how far we've really come.

Today, as Peter prepares to enter high school level work in the fall, he is now able to do research on the Internet and to type his essays and reports. His math is at grade level and he enjoys it. His auditory reading comprehension is above grade level. Although his print-reading is slow, he can make his way through a whole book with magnification and he can read Braille, too.

Homeschooling has been a very good choice. Indeed, it has given us the flexibility to help Peter adjust to his vision loss. But homeschooling has also given us unity and family joy in the midst of the trials and tragedies of life. Through it all, God has blessed our family and our schooling and his grace is always sufficient.

Margaret Mary Myers

Margaret Mary Myers and her husband Ed have homeschooled their six children for a quarter of a century. Margaret Mary enjoys writing about surviving and thriving through the challenges and joys of life. You can find her at http://margmary.blogspot.com.

WHY I HOMESCHOOL

Several years ago, my friend Tammy came to me distressed. Her husband was insisting that she put their two kids into regular school once they reached junior high. That meant the oldest would have been enrolled in school that next year. She asked my feelings about this, knowing that I schooled my kids past junior high. When I shared some of my own experiences and reasons, Tammy asked if I would put everything down in an email to her so that she could share it with her husband.

To my surprise, after reading my email and certainly guided by his wife's ardent prayers, he decided to keep them home a little longer. A little longer turned into all the way through high school. Their oldest recently graduated, so in the end, they surpassed what I was doing.

Going through my files to prepare for this book, I came across my email to Tammy. I decided to include in hopes that it will provide insight and thoughts for reflection...

Hi Tammy,

Since I homeschooled my oldest son, Aaron, only during the seventh, eighth and ninth grades, he can speak clearly of the differences. Although I can personally see the advantages of homeschooling, the ones that did it since they were little, don't see it as clearly. Aaron experienced a radical change in going from public school to homeschool then back again, so it's so obvious to him.

After three years of homeschooling, Aaron went to Bismarck High School for tenth grade. (Since that time, all our other kids have gone to the Catholic High School.)

Aaron's teachers raved about him. He did well in school and he was very, very social. He loved school so much that I was afraid to ask him how he felt about homeschooling. I had decided this was what was best for the kids spiritually. The younger ones were all at home, so I did not want to risk asking him, fearing he would tell me he felt like a prisoner and now was finally free. After all, he was clearly enjoying himself at school.

A couple years after he was in school, I was very surprised by a conversation between Aaron and his next younger brother Luke. Aaron was telling Luke he used to worry about what others thought, worked hard to fit in whatever the cost, and was hurt if others were cruel to him. (At this point in his life, Aaron was now a very self-confident leader among students. Other kids looked up to him and gravitated to him.) Luke then said to Aaron, "But if it wasn't for homeschooling, you'd still be that way."

Aaron responded: "Yeah, I know." This casual conversation between brothers was monumental to me. It totally blew me away that as teenagers they saw things so clearly.

Another time when I was speaking to Aaron about doing the right thing regardless of what others were doing, he said to me, "Mom, I never worry about what people think. I blame homeschooling for that."

My other two sons have gone from homeschool to St. Mary's High school as very confident, successful students. They've been on the high honor roll, active in many activities including student council and Tyler has been voted class president for the third year in a row. (He later became homecoming king.) Tyler received his first B this year; otherwise it's been straight A's. I never would have guessed this because he did not apply himself all the time at home. He did have the basics down, so once he was in a school setting, he had the skills to do well.

My kids are not angels by any stretch of the imagination--trust me. But I am confident that any and all bad choices they've made have been their own doing and not a result of peer pressure. I know it's a funny way to say that others do not influence my kids negatively around them.

Another point I'd like to make is that when I speak on homeschooling, I always point out that there are a wide variety of personalities and the fact that I have extremely outgoing kids cannot necessarily be credited to homeschooling. For instance, if someone is shy, people sometimes blame it on homeschooling. Yet, no one points to a shy public school student and blames it on the school. I simply believe that at home, our kids can learn and develop their personalities free from peer pressure.

Because of the fact that my five siblings and I were all shy and now all their kids, (my nieces and nephews) are shy, and the fact that all my own kids start out very shy, it seems to me that I can credit homeschooling with making a direct difference in how confident my kids are. My brothers and sisters and I all became very confident but not until we were adults. During a recent conversation, I listened to my siblings talk about how insecure and self-conscious their kids had become during the junior high years. That's when it hit me (in year seven of homeschooling) that those are the very years that I see my own kids absolutely blossoming--during junior high grades. This is a time when insecurity tends to be at its worst. Those are the years the other kids are intensely critical of one another and everyone worries about fitting in.

When that peer pressure was lifted from Aaron in the seventh grade—his first year of homeschooling—he enjoyed school days where he could be himself. He got into speech and ended up doing extremely well, even winning awards. He developed confidence easily because there was no one to criticize or make fun; instead, he received only encouragement.

Tammy, as you know, I am not always confident in my own ability as a teacher. I do great in the early years and then struggle more with the older years. I look for ways to supplement and complement their regular subjects (i.e. boy scouts, band, a science class being offered, etc.) My biggest strength comes from my faith in God and my trust in Him. If I believe He wants me to do this because it's what is ultimately best for my kids (remember, you can't take your test scores to heaven with you) then I can squash my insecurities and pray my way through the schooling. I trust that as long as I follow the path God sets out for me, things will turn out well. Not a year goes by that I don't ask: "God, are you sure you want me to do this?"

As you know, between writing a book and having a very, very busy two-year-old, I put the girls in public school for the past year. They will both be returning to homeschool this coming school year. I think it's important to note that they had a very successful time at school. They (and I) loved their teachers, they were "A" students, and they made a lot of friends. People are so surprised to learn I am bringing them home again. Some have actually been speechless, having thought that I had finally come to my senses. But I see the subtle things and I also see where such things can ultimately lead. Concern about styles, cool language, and what everyone else is doing and thinking, becomes a powerful source of control in a kid's life. It makes sense. It's the world they have to live in, so the controlling factor—peer pressure—is powerful in a kid's life. It's not the quiet, good students that make the biggest impact in a classroom. Too often it's the bad influences that are loud, bold and critical of others. Those are often the very kids that the others look to as examples. I've spoken to teacher's groups and when I say this, they all shake their heads in agreement.

By high school, kids have matured somewhat and the peer pressure begins to lessen. At that point, my kids enter full of self confidence and kids gravitate towards them. They have enough esteem not to feel pressured by negative people. Still, there are still elements of schooling that can be negative. The die-hard homeschoolers avoid this by going through high school. I've seen many wonderful examples of children homeschooled through high school, who are decent, high-achieving students.

I am convinced at this point, that I am not called to homeschool through the high school years. Given all the pros and cons of schooling, by high school, I believe my kids are better off at St. Mary's.

This has gotten very long, but I hope it gives a good perspective of why I continue to homeschool, even though it's not necessarily the easiest choice for me. You or your husband or your son, are welcome to call my son, Aaron, for his perspective. He is in college now at NDSU and supporting himself as a cook/manager at Perkins. Luke will be up there with him in the fall. I'll send up some prayers for you that whatever your family decides that everyone ends up in agreement.

God bless,
Patti Maguire Armstrong

HANG ONTO THE 'ROPE'

I had a vivid dream around the time I was reverting back to the Catholic faith. I dreamed I fell off of a huge ship and was being dashed about by large waves. A man in a tattered brown habit approached the rail and leaned over to call down to me. Alongside him, a woman in a flowing pale blue dress approached the railing too. I could only faintly make out the man's face. The woman's face was obscured by the haze. As I was tossed about in the sea, the man called down to me, "Hang on to the rope. Don't let go of the rope!" over and over. The dream was very realistic, and since I was crashing around wildly in the waves fearing for my life I looked for a rope to grab and saw none. At that moment I woke and was relieved to find myself safely in my room. A few days later at Eucharistic Adoration, I picked up a book on Padre Pio that was on the shelf in the chapel and immediately recognized the habit and the man from my dream. I opened the book and started skimming and my eye landed on a sentence that talked about the Rosary as "the rope". I've been hanging on to it ever since!

Mary Brown

'Mary Brown' is a former university professor who homeschools her children on the East Coast.

DOUBLE THE GRACE

John and I married when I was twenty-seven, and we were both anxious to start a family. I never had a number of kids in mind. I just thought we would see how things went. We both come from families with seven children, so a big family wasn't a foreign idea to us. Whenever I got pregnant it just seemed like the right thing, well, except maybe for the last pregnancy, which I'll tell you about now.

I had homeschooled various children over a span of six years. We chose home-schooling because it is such an efficient way to educate and we wanted our children to be strong in their faith. I loved the rhythm of the day when I was homeschooling. There seemed to be a more peaceful feeling, not usually something that comes to mind when you have five children under the age of eleven home at once. We had time for family prayer and frequent Mass, and I believe it strengthened my relationship with the kids. The children all returned to school at different times, most of them by the seventh grade. As with the decision to start homeschooling, it just seemed like that's where God was leading us.

It was after all of our five children were in school that I had big plans to find a part-time job (raising five kids is expensive) and do all those things that I had put off for years. I couldn't tell you what they were, but they would have been really big, something along the lines of world peace. We'll never know because at the age of forty-six, I found myself pregnant. This was a huge surprise and to say I was a bit upset is putting it mildly. First of all, I blamed my husband-- isn't that where we wives go first? Then, I blamed God. I thought I had proved myself when I had our fifth child at forty-two. What more could he want from me?

Then I turned on myself. What kind of person blames God and her husband? What kind of person looks on a child as a burden, not a gift? I decided to go to see Jesus in the Adoration chapel at my parish church to have a word with him on the matter. I asked him to please help me accept this gift with a loving heart, not the selfish one that I had. After a few minutes of tearful prayer, I felt this overwhelming sense of peace and acceptance pour over me and I heard in my mind, as clear as day, *I am giving you twins.* I thought, *Wow those crazy hormones are already kicking in.* I tucked that way back into the deep recesses of my mind. Denial works for me.

In the time that followed the discovery of my pregnancy, we were living (as we had been for thirteen years) in a nice, but smaller house in the city. There were three bedrooms and only one shower. The kitchen was small and as the kids got bigger, the house seemed to shrink. With five children, and the oldest being fifteen so we were definitely running out of space. We had tried several times in the preceding year to purchase a lot close to our home in the city (we loved the neighborhood and the fact it was close to John's work). We wanted to build, but the owner refused to sell. The neighbors said that the owner would never sell, and that others had persistently tried to buy this lot too. After a few tries we gave up, and decided to tough it out in our current home with the new baby.

Then I had an idea. My birthday is the same as the feast day of St. Joseph (March 19). I decided to invoke him with a novena and then ask John to ask the owner of the lot one more time if he would sell. At the end of the novena to St. Joseph, John called the owner of the desired lot, who, surprisingly, told him to make an offer. John made an offer, and the man accepted. None of our neighbors could believe that the guy actually sold us the lot. Soon after this I found out I was pregnant with.... twins! The voice I had heard in my heart in the Adoration chapel so many months ago was preparing me for this truth and responsibility and blessing! God gave us these babies, but also saw to it that we had the means to provide for them as well. He had blessed us in three ways—with two new lives and the wonderful provision of a home to take care of our rapidly expanding family.

Things just unfolded smoothly from there. We found and immediately started working with a Catholic architect who, understanding a large family's needs, designed a home that suited us perfectly. It had lots of closets, a big eating area, enough bedrooms, and a wonderful wrap-around front porch which I had always dreamed of where our family and neighbors could gather in the evenings. We were able to hire a builder who was more of a project manager than a general contractor so John could do a lot of the work and save our family money. I like to joke that I had plans for a part-time job in the fall, but God gave me a full- time one instead.

Megan and Grace were born on November 11, 2003. Six months later we brought them home to our beautiful new-old home. It is brand new but built to look old. The Catholic high school is within walking distance. We have finished a small apartment that is added to our home to rent out. It should provide some needed extra income so I might not need the part time job any more. I have my hands full with the girls, and running the older ones to their outside activities. God is so good!

Our oldest graduated from high school this past June, and at the graduation the speaker asked parents to stand who were graduating their last child. The twins are now two, so graduating the girls are in the distant future. When they ask us to stand then, I just hope we can, even with the help of a cane! Really, I just want to say that when God leads you somewhere it is always for a good reason. He led us into homeschooling early on, and then He led us out, both for very good reasons. As Mother Superior said in the Sound of Music, when God closes a door he opens a window. And for us the fresh air just rushed in! When you trust God and try to follow what you think He is leading you to, things are always better than you expect. And when times are difficult, as they often are with two year old twins and teenagers, there is always God's infinite mercy and grace to sustain you.

Erin Ryal

Erin, oldest of seven and mother of seven --"Sometimes eight, if you count my husband" --graduated from Saint Mary's College, Notre Dame, Indiana with a B.A. in history/secondary education certification, and worked in Chicago and Washington, D.C. She homeschooled several of her children over a span of six years and is active as a member of Corpus Christi Church in South Bend, Indiana.

SOMEWHERE OVER THE RAINBOW

Alice: I arrived home from the Dayton, Ohio Catholic Homeschool Conference around 7 p.m. on a summer Saturday, after having helped with take-down duties. I was happy, exhausted, and reminiscing about the day and all the wonderful speakers, including EWTN's own Father Robert Levis who had flown in from Erie, Pennsylvania on a small plane to be with us.

As I was winding down, I looked at the clock and it occurred to me that Fr. Levis was most likely still in the air at that moment, flying home. It also occurred to me that the pilot, Nino Vitale, had given me the link to a website that would allow me to track his flight via GPS technology. I hurried to the computer and logged on with interest. I found the tracking website and entered the plane's tail number.

Instantly, I saw real-time images of a radar screen with the flight being tracked right before my eyes. Amazing! The plane in the air was about two thirds of the way home. Earlier in the day I had heard thunderstorms over the area, and now I could see them clearly over Cleveland, parts of western Pennsylvania, and very heavy over Erie. Then, I noticed that the heaviest thunderstorms were hitting exactly where the little plane was flying.

Oh no! I immediately thought. Cessnas don't like thunderstorms--that was the one thing Nino didn't want to fly in.

I zoomed in for a closer look and noticed there was literally a ring or halo of clear sky in front of the plane. That's odd, I thought and I refreshed the image. It stayed the same. So, I refreshed again, and again. Each time I refreshed the image, the area directly in front of the plane remained clear, although fierce storms swirled around it. It was as if a big hand was swooshing the storms away ahead of the plane.

I was so puzzled and surprised that I just sat there, watching the radar image. This unlikely clearing of the storm in front of the plane occurred all the way into Erie. I could hardly pull my eyes away from the screen.

I received a call just a bit later --the plane had landed. All were safe and sound. I could hardly wait to tell the pilot what I saw. "Nino!" I said excitedly, "Do you know there were storms out there? Do you realize your plane seemed to just push them away? It was like there was a ring of clear sky around you. It was amazing to see this on the radar!"

He replied, "You will not believe what we just saw."

Nino: I've been flying for many moons and never have I had an incredible flight like this. First, at 4 p.m. Saturday, the storms actually seemed to connect Dayton to Erie. Storms were all over my flight path and even though this was short flight, the wind was blowing to beat the band. Normally, things calm down as the sun goes down, but not then. The storms were moving southeast so as the trip progressed, I had a chance the storms would have moved away by then. I also knew I had a safe and clear landing site at Cleveland Hopkins airport and Father said Cleveland is closer than Dayton so if we have to divert, that's fine.

As we took off from Dayton, my plane, which usually goes about 180 M.P.H., was clocking 220 M.P.H., indicating a huge tail wind. My equipment was showing that we'd be reaching Erie in one hour and ten minutes. Normally, this would be an hour and thirty-five minute trip. I am an experienced pilot but I admit I was a little edgy with the wind that was blowing and all the rain that was coming down ahead of me. As we moved along, with heavy rain all around us, the skies literally.... parted. I was watching radar closely inside the plane, and it was like watching the Red Sea part, only in this case it was storm clouds, and it was for us! It was absolutely unbelievable! I can't describe how it felt to see darkness and rain all around except right in front. I never fly within twenty miles of any storm cells and this corridor was at approximately sixty miles wide.

As we quickly approached Erie I commented to Fr. Levis, who was enjoying the rapid ride, that for every give there is a take and it would probably take me more than two hours to get home with that head wind. Although the rain was coming down in torrents near the Erie Airport, planes were still able to get in so the tower cleared me for the approach. The rain increased as we descended, and as expected visibility become difficult. I had to steady myself to concentrate. As we turned on to final descent, the heavy pouring rain suddenly... stopped. The sun showed as it was setting over Lake Erie, and it seemed to be dancing and shimmering all over the ground. The cloud deck was still above us, but the sun was low enough at our arrival time of 7:50 p.m. that the sun dropped 'beneath' the clouds in a break. It was sparkling and absolutely beautiful. What an amazing ride!

As we were retrieving our luggage, I heard, "Look outside." What we saw was a beautiful, bright, perfect rainbow. I have never seen both sides of a rainbow so tight or so clear. It was just at the airport. It was surrounding the airplane! And then I watched with surprise as gradually another rainbow formed, surrounding the first. It was so bright and absolutely incredible.

Well, of course, we told Father Levis it was him. He then spent an extensive amount of time blessing the plane, in Latin, with holy water for its future flights. When he was finished, I joked, "You're washing it with all that holy water you sprinkled on!"

Then I told Father, only half-jokingly, that he was going to have to fly with me more often. He replied jovially, "Any time." Then he said he thought there was a good sermon in this experience. I had to agree! He told me that this could not be considered a miracle as no laws of nature were actually broken. I told him that although that is true, I have never seen nature do that on any radar screen, flying or otherwise!

After that, I helped Father and Joe, the man that handles Father's publishing and distribution of books, into their cars, returned to the plane and took off. I ascended to 6,000 feet and it was smooth flying back home. There was absolutely no wind all the way back. I made great time with no problems whatsoever. I am convinced God's hand was the one pushing away the storm and reassuring us with His rainbow.

Alice: The weather that day was so unusual in Erie that it made the news that evening. The rainbow was so bright that it also made the news. My brother, who lives in Erie, was on his way home from a meeting at the time. He saw the rainbow from his car and pulled off the road just to photograph it. For us here in Dayton it was and remains a promise of God's loving protection for His children.

Alice Kompar is a '89 University of Dayton graduate. She is Mike's wife and mom to their six great kids. She enjoys hiking and gardening.

Nino Vitale is a husband and father of four boys with another child on the way living in a rural area outside of Urbana, Ohio. He has been a private-instrument rated pilot for over 10 years and flies a Cessna 210J.

.....Mrs. Jones invited Father Martin to dinner. She wanted Father to help her teach her young sons about God. Mrs. Jones wanted her boys to see that God was everywhere and in every person.

Dinner was wonderful and 7 year old Luke asked to be excused before dessert. Mr. Jones excused Luke from the table. With only Matthew staying for dessert, Father decided he had better attend to the task at hand and so he turned to Matthew and asked, "Son, where is God?"

*Matthew was only 5 years old and wasn't quite sure how to respond to Father's question so he just looked blankly at the priest which prompted Father to ask again, but in a louder, stronger voice, "Son, I ask you, **WHERE IS GOD?!**"*

Matthew became alarmed at Father's question and the tone of his voice and fled from the table. He ran into Luke's room and with terror in his eyes said, "Luke! Luke! God is missing and they think we've got Him!"

Chapter Five

LESSONS LEARNED

"Happy the man who finds wisdom, the man who gains understanding! For her profit is better than profit in silver, and better than gold is her revenue."
(Proverbs 3:13-14)

STUMBLING INTO SELF-DISCIPLINE

In the summer after my sixth grade year, my parents took our family on a vacation. My mother often said that her and Dad's big decisions were all made while away from home. That vacation's topic of discussion was whether to homeschool.

All of their reasons (better education, fostering of faith, etc.) didn't mean much to me. I begged to be homeschooled for the simple reason that I was terrified of the seventh grade teacher. Every night, I pleaded with God to let me be homeschooled. He answered my prayers, though not, I am certain, because of the teacher that made my palms sweat.

I was inclined to be lazy and take the easy way out of things whenever possible. I received impressive grades at school without having to try very hard, which suited my work ethic (or lack thereof) just fine.

The first year of homeschooling was (as anyone who has gone from the school system to home knows, be ye teacher or student), like walking into a glass door. Having escaped from the seventh grade teacher, Mr. Crack-the-Whip, I bounced my way into our kitchen on the first day of school, collected my pile of books and went off to learn.

This lasted ten minutes. My first assignment was reading comprehension, a subject I had excelled in the previous year. I read the chapter and prepared to answer the questions. Instead of the typical questions ('why was Sally very happy?'), there were questions like 'In your opinion, how could Sally have done a better job?' or 'What could be an alternate ending to this story?' In a panic, I re-read the story searching for my opinion and the hidden ending. My father patiently explained to me that the answer wasn't in the story.

"Well, how am I supposed to do this then?" I wailed. "This is impossible!"

I would love to say that I sorted myself out in a week, and turned into Little Miss Self-Discipline, the model homeschooling student. It took a year. A year of crying, yelling and slamming books around on my part, and stern talks and infinite patience on the part of my parents. By the time summer arrived, I had made friends in our homeschooling circle and adjusted to my new academic standards. I wouldn't have said I loved homeschooling, but I liked it enough to want to continue. My parents, however, weren't so sure. I had been a brat all year (not that they ever called me that), and had made it hard for them to teach not only me, but my brothers as well. I suppose Our Lord gave them a little nudge again, because they decided to keep going.

I graduated from high school and subsequently attended Christendom College, in Front Royal, VA. I now work as a writer and tutor, and my brothers and sisters, who range in age from three to eighteen, are still homeschooled.

My parents were never involved in the "un-schooling" method, in the sense that they had a set curriculum, but they also were very hands-off in the sense that their job was to organize field trips and provide a balanced set of courses. It was not their job to sit and hold our hands throughout each school day.

Teaching myself was exhilarating, yet frightening. The first year, (which I now refer to as the horror year), I didn't finish Math until late July. I hadn't followed the schedule they had set as a guideline for me, so I had to face the consequences. (When I asked Dad what would happen if I just didn't bother with this, he said that I would never pass to eighth grade without seventh grade math completed. He didn't care how long that took me.)

Self-discipline was not the highest goal on my parents list when they decided to homeschool my siblings and me. When I look at the advantages of homeschooling, and the profound impact it has had on my life, self-discipline is certainly very high on my list.

My homeschooling experiences have led me to a stronger faith, a more mature outlook and an increased depth of character. I am certain that in leading my parents to make this decision, Our Lord had all of this in mind for me, as well as for my siblings, but He also knew that I would be a writer, and that I would need to be self-disciplined.

And whatever happened to the seventh grade teacher who appeared in my childhood nightmares? The summer before I left for college, I worked on a pick-your-own berry farm. He came one day to pick blueberries, and to my surprise he recognized me. We shook hands and talked for about ten minutes. He wished me all the best in college and hoped to run into me sometime again. As I dropped him off in the berry fields, and drove the wagon back to the barn, I sat up taller. The realization that I was older and therefore less intimidated was immediately followed by the realization that I had never had anything to fear. Shaking hands with this perfectly amiable man, I knew that he could never be as stern a taskmaster as I am.

Maria van den Bosch

Maria lives and writes in Alberta, Canada. She also works as a tutor, currently teaching writing to homeschooled high school students. This article first appeared in Heart and Mind.

LEAF JUMPERS:
HOMESCHOOL TO SCHOOL AND BACK AGAIN

"Mom, there's just seven more days until the first day of fall!" My six year old son announced, giving me the usual morning 'fall countdown'. "How are we going to celebrate? Can we jump in the leaves?"

"You bet!" I responded. "How about jumping in the leaves and making caramel apples?"

"HURRAY!!!" He cheered, with his younger sisters jumping in on the excitement...

That was autumn, two years ago.

This was autumn last year...

"Look, Ben," I said. We just raked the first pile of leaves. Would you like to jump with us?"

"No. I don't want to jump in the leaves." My son responded flatly, barely looking up at the giant leaf pile or us. His sisters and I played while he "did his own thing." My heart broke to see a boy of such enthusiasm and spirit become a boy filled with disinterest.

I am His, and He is carrying out His work through me.
~ Oswald Chambers

What happened? Is the age jump from 6 years old to 7 so drastic that a boy who once got so excited about jumping in the leaves with his sisters, no longer cares? I doubt it. In my opinion, what happened was "school."

I was homeschooling my son until last year, but I started to question if I could continue to meet the needs of this growing boy. Does he need more? Can I give him enough? Does he need more social interaction? Then I started to answer. He loves structure. He loves activity. He is so social. The conclusion: He was made for school. It just seemed like we were supposed to put him there. We gave it to God, we started to pray, and the stones seemed to pave the way toward school. It seemed like it was the "right" thing to do and it seemed like God was leading us there.

Ben went from playing half of the day in the leaves with his sisters to playing half of an hour on a black top. He went from cuddling on the couch with his family doing math games, reading, and storytelling, to sitting in a classroom in a hard desk with thirty-one other kids, filling out worksheet after worksheet, raising his hand to talk, standing in line—a lot, and keeping his mouth shut. He went from lingering over lunch in his kitchen while talking about the latest topic of interest, to gulping down his food quickly in a loud lunchroom with concrete walls and little windows. It's no wonder that in just a short two month period this boy no longer wanted to play in the leaves... his spirit had forgotten how. It just didn't "fit" anymore. He went from actively experiencing God in his everyday life with his family, to mundanely learning about Him on paper...that was the difference.

I don't blame big schools for the approach that they take. With thirty-two kids in a room, it is impossible to cater education toward each child. Children DO have to "wait" a lot because there are a lot of other kids to "wait" for. It is necessary to provide tight order and structure or chaos would take over. It is important to start school at an early hour with a full seven-hour day in order to fulfill state requirements. This is the reality of most schools. And for some kids, "school" is the best place. For some families, "school" is the right choice. But for our family, it was not.

We went from sharing a peaceful breakfast with classical music in the background to the frenzied sound of my own voice shouting, "Hurry, Ben! We're going to be late!" Dishes were left piled in sink and baby was pulled out of her crib to get to school on time. We went from enjoying the presence of a delightful boy, helpful leader and friend to his sisters, to feeling a huge hole in his absence. We missed him, and he missed us, and what took the place was disconnect.

I took all of this in. I prayed about it—a lot. I listened. I journaled. I sought advice. The conclusion: I can choose something different for my child and for my family and I can choose to homeschool in a way that gives my child the freedom to be a child, and to actively celebrate and experience God within his family and within his world. I can choose to pray while snuggling on the couch, play games to learn phonics, bake cookies to learn fractions, and provide the space to play in God's creation. In doing so, my child will stay connected with himself, his family and his Creator in a deep and meaningful way. He will keep his "childhood" vigor and joy, the same joy that Christ refers to when he says, "For it is to such as these that the kingdom of Heaven belongs to...." God rejoices in seeing us play in leaves and delight in His earth...for in doing so, we are delighting in Him.

It seems that God called us to put Ben in school last year because it enabled us to clearly see the change in our son. We felt the "effects" of school on our family. As a result, we can now "get off the fence" and jump in the leaves with homeschooling once more.

It is now almost autumn again and the school year has begun. My son and I were just saying bedtime prayers after a day of learning games, reading, and a field trip to the zoo. "What do you want to thank God for today?" I asked.

"I want to thank God that it's getting colder," he said, as his eyes lit up. "Because that means that fall is coming soon, and we can jump in the leaves again!" I smiled a deep smile and gave him a big hug. "I thank God for that too, Ben...I thank God for that too."

Nikki Schaefer

Nikki is a former pro-life pregnancy counselor and art therapist. She is now a homeschooling mother to her four (almost five children) and a freelance writer and illustrator. Nikki's husband Bernie works at the Catholic radio station in Omaha, NE, which has become an important apostolate for her family.

LESSONS IN HOMESCHOOL VOCABULARY: MAGAZINE AND SISTERS

Magazine

When Maggie was little, she made clear distinctions between what reading material was hers and what belonged to Matt and me. Having received a subscription to "Highlights" from her grandmother, Maggie made sure that we knew that that was a "Maggie-zine." Of course, we agreed it was a magazine; we had several magazines that came to the house. "No,' she clarified, "only hers was a "Maggie-zine" emphasis on the 'Maggie'. My Reader's Digest was a 'Mommy-zine' and Matt's subscriptions were "Daddy-zines."

Sisters

Maggie and Amelia had gone to an overnight retreat. Matt went up the next day to pick them up. Meeting one of the mothers and her daughter who were greeting parents, he said that he was coming to get his daughters and the mother went off to collect them. The girl looked at Matt with surprise, "Maggie and Amelia are sisters?" "Yes," Matt replied. "Wow," the girl said, "I didn't think they were sisters. They didn't act like sisters." This comment made Matt concerned. "Oh, really? They didn't act like sisters?" The girl started walking away as Maggie and Amelia arrived. She turned back to Matt before leaving, "No, they acted like best friends."

Rachel Watkins

Rachel Watkins, wife to Matt, mom to 11 wonderful children. creator of the Little Flowers Girls' Club (www.eccehomopress.com) as well as the new series of stories on royal saints, "Princesses You Can Believe In". She is a regular contributor to Dr. Greg and Lisa Popcak's Ave Maria Radio Program, Heart, Mind and Strength as well as a freelance writer and blogger.

HEART MEDICINE

I have never let my schooling interfere with my education. -Mark Twain

Education is what remains after one has forgotten what one has learned in school. -Albert Einstein

Education is not preparation for life; education is life itself. -John Dewey

God will guide us on our way no matter how difficult it may be. -St. Francis de Sales

In bringing up children, spend on them half as much money and twice as much time. -Author Unknown

When you teach your son, you teach your son's son. -The Talmud

Family faces are magic mirrors. Looking at people who belong to us, we see the past, present, and future. -Gail Lumet Buckley

The only rock I know that stays steady, the only institution I know that works is the family. -Lee Iacocca

If you want your children to improve, let them overhear the nice things you say about them to others. -Haim Ginott

What a child doesn't receive he can seldom later give. -P.D. James, *Time to Be in Earnest*

He is the happiest, be he king or peasant, who finds peace in his home. -Johann Wolfgang von Goethe

Kids spell love T-I-M-E. -John Crudele

Before I got married I had six theories about bringing up children; now I have six children, and no theories. -John Wilmot

To bring up a child in the way he should go, travel that way yourself once in a while. -Josh Billings

Don't worry that children never listen to you; worry that they are always watching you. -Robert Fulghum

The quickest way for a parent to get a child's attention is to sit down and look comfortable. -Lane Olinghouse

It really doesn't matter how many kids you have. One child takes up 100% of your time, so more children can't possibly take up more than 100% of your time. -Unknown

A parent's love is whole no matter how many times divided. -Robert Brault

Conscience is less an inner voice than the memory of a mother's glance. -Robert Brault

Always end the name of your child with a vowel, so that when you yell, the name will carry. -Bill Cosby

What's done to children, they will do to society. -Karl Menninger

You have a lifetime to work, but children are only young once. -Polish Proverb

Motherhood—If it was going to be easy, it would not have started with something called labor. -Unknown

Teachers who inspire know that teaching is like cultivating a garden, and those who would have nothing to do with thorns must never attempt to gather flowers. -Unknown

The family is a community of persons and the smallest social unit. As such it is...fundamental to the life of every society. *Letter to Families* Pope John Paul II 1994 sec.17

Parents are the first and most important educators of their own children, and they also possess a fundamental competence in this area: they are educators because they are parents. They share their educational mission with other individuals or institutions, such as the Church and the state. But the mission of education must always be carried out in accordance with the proper application of the principle of subsidiary. *Letter to Families* Pope John Paul II 1994 sec. 16

THE CONSCIENCE
OF THE HOMESCHOOLED CHILD

The study of the Greek and Latin roots of English words was the subject under discussion with 10-year-old Cydney. "We are," I said, "going to learn about definitions and derivations."

First, though, we would have to know what derivations and definitions are. "We need to know the derivation and definition of 'derivation' and 'definition,'" I continued. When you are ten it is a lot of fun to wrap your mouth around such interesting polysyllabic alliterations. She was all ears and eyes, so with my trusty copy of English from the Roots Up at hand, I was ready to proceed.

We started with the derivation of 'derivation' from Latin de meaning 'down from' or 'away from' and rivus meaning 'stream'. I drew a picture of a river with irrigation canals coming from it to show how our words today are derived from the older stream of words. Then we tackled 'definition' from Latin de meaning 'down from' or 'away from' and finis meaning 'boundary' or 'limit'. I drew a yard with a fence around it to show how the meaning of the word is inside a boundary that separates it from what it does not mean.

The next day I asked Cydney to give me the derivation and definition of 'derivation' and 'definition'. She did great with 'derivation', but I could see that she just hadn't quite gotten the point of how the 'fence' (finis) was connected to 'definition'. So I put my hand on one of the chairs in our schoolroom. "I am calling this thing a 'chair'," I said, "Are you OK with that? Does that fit the definition of the word?"

"Yes," she said.

"Now I am also going to say that the stools around the kitchen table are also a kind of chair. Are you OK with that?"

She was.

I picked up a ruler. "May I call this thing a chair?"

"No," she answered firmly. And then with a sudden twinkle in her eyes she pointed her finger at me and said decidedly, "That is where I draw the line."

Bingo.

The 4th-grade class at PSR the following Monday was about the conscience. At dinner, my husband and I asked her what she had learned about the conscience. "It is a little voice inside of you that tells you what is right and wrong and you should always listen to it."

My husband pointed out that it was necessary for your conscience to be properly informed before it could be a good guide to right and wrong. "Is my conscience being informed?" she asked.

"Yes," I said. "Remember how were talking about definitions, and you said that it was like drawing a line?" She nodded.

"Well, you know what abortion is, right?"Her eyes clouded and she looked troubled.

"I think it is just like killing someone."

My husband said, "It isn't *just like* killing someone, it *is* killing someone."

"But what," I asked, "If you did not think that the unborn baby was a human being? What if you thought it was no different from an animal, or even a plant? Can you see how, if you draw your line in the wrong place, your conscience could be misinformed and you might do the wrong thing even though you were listening to it?"

She could.

"So, then, you see how learning what things really and truly are, is important for forming your conscience?"

She saw.

Mary Kochan

Mary is a senior editor for the Catholic Exchange website. She was raised a third-generation

Jehovah's Witness, worked her "way backwards through the Protestant Reformation," and entered the Roman Catholic Church on Trinity Sunday, 1996. She is a writer, speaker and counselor on religious cults. To arrange for Mary to speak at your event contact her at mkochan@catholicexchange.com.

PLANET EARTH

My kids have always been taught since they were very little that God made the stars, clouds and planets. They knew He is our Creator.

One day, I was reading out of a secular science book with my fourth grader. The article stated that the earth is just far enough away from the sun so that people do not burn up. This is crucial due to the enormous heat that the sun produces. The article proceeded to explain that the earth is also just close enough to the sun so that people do not freeze to death--an important and fragile balance. The book then went on to say that scientists are still trying to figure out how this could be.

My son stopped reading the book and looked up at me. "Don't they know that God made the universe and that's why it is in that position?" he said, sounding a little disgusted. He then asked how long it would take them to continue to study this situation while we as Christians could see it so plainly.

Virginia Dolajak has six children. She homeschooled for 13 years.

WHEN THE TEACHER HAT CHANGES

In a pride-filled moment, I mentally adjusted my homeschooling mom's teacher hat. After seven years in this game, I know how to play. My kids are the students, I'm the teacher, and my job is to teach them, correct their mistakes, and show them how to do things right the first time. If they balk or complain, my job is to crack down and let them know who the teacher is and who the student is. Or so I thought.

I'd learned that script years ago, when we studied phonics. The kids' phonics manual had a set daily script with flashcards, hands-on games, oral exercises, written practice, and spelling practice. All I had to do was pull out that day's materials and work our way through the lesson. If the lesson didn't click the first time, we just repeated it or relied upon the daily review to help the concept click. The weekly test helped me gauge what the kids knew and didn't know.

Suddenly, we entered middle school. The textbooks no longer have scripts. With preteens, the parenting no longer has a script, either. The mom who can change a diaper on the seat of any car, so discreetly nurse a baby in a sling while shopping that even her husband doesn't observe it, and manage 15 high-energy kids on a homeschool field trip, is suddenly at a loss. Sometimes it feels as though parenting older kids causes my I.Q. to drop five points per month. On bad days, it can feel like I'm losing 10 I.Q. points in a single hour.

Fashion emergencies emerge during this tumultuous time and can explode into family wars. If the adolescent's skirt is not too high, then the neckline is too low. And there are problems with the t-shirts, or rather the t-shirt sayings. One saying I didn't even understand until I did an Internet search of the phrase and discovered what it meant. My definition of dress-up clothes for a nice event does not include camouflage anything, which is not necessarily the same idea as my adolescent child's ideas. A mom can't ask to borrow someone's thongs because they are now called flip-flops, and thongs go places we don't discuss.

I go exhausted from the fashion war into the essay war. The kids' language books list the steps to writing a good essay. Math problems have steps, so I figured the kids would follow the steps, and the essay would magically appear like the sum at the end of an equation. The first step would be an outline and thesis, and so on.

But one thing was missing from the essay equation is my daughter's cooperation. I sat down with her, just as I sat with those phonics lessons years ago, put on my teacher's hat and was ready to begin, but my every attempt to work with her, to show her the "right" way to write, failed. It didn't just fail, but exploded into a clash of wills. She wanted to write her essay her way—not my way. The harder I pushed, the harder she pushed back. Finally, in frustration, I called a mentor mom, one whose daughters are older than mine and who has traveled this undiscovered country before me.

"What do I do?" I asked. I received a clear reply.

"Back off. Let her do it her way. See what she puts together and take it from there."

So I did. The next week, my daughter asked for my help: How could her essay be better organized? I had to think about this. Maybe we needed neutral ground on which to tackle this essay. I didn't want the tug of war again. I changed tactics because our kitchen table writing exercises had become a battle with ground gained and lost. The problem with that battleground is sometimes the child's work or the child's heart is the real loser. So I took her, just the two of us, to a bakery/coffee shop. I always enjoyed writing in restaurants, and maybe she would too. First we enjoyed scones and fancy coffee. So far so good. Next, we pulled out the instrument of torment: her essay.

For an hour, between bites of scones and sips of Earl Grey tea and mocha latte, I helped my daughter reorganize her essay. Some of her writing was thrown by the wayside, and we added more details here and there. We worked on that dreaded thesis statement and outline to make sure it made sense.

Amazingly, we didn't have a single fight. I suddenly discovered she had some good ideas to put in her essay and just needed to polish them a little. When we had argued at home, I had been so intent on winning the argument and putting her in her place that I didn't listen to any of her ideas, including her good ones.

We can't afford to go out to eat whenever my daughter has a writing assignment. However, I learned from our breakfast-out writing that I need a new teacher's hat. The old script needed changing. Now that the kids are older, I need to transition more into the role of a guide. Instead of sitting across from each other, we need to sit beside each other and work together. When we parent, the kids aren't the only ones who grow. And when we school them, we often learn far more than we teach.

Mary Biever

PIANO LESSON

My piano bench pad is wearing out. I suppose that is a good thing. Five of my children, ages 6 through 15, practice piano regularly—religiously, you might say. On Tuesdays, the piano teacher comes to our house for three hours. That's a really long time to keep the other kids quiet and out of the room, but that is not even the end of it. When she leaves the kids are so enthusiastic about their music they often want to practice all day. Sometimes all week. May I tell you a secret? It used to drive me crazy.

I know, I know. What an awful thing to say. Studying music helps improve test scores. It helps one think spatially. Being able to play the piano is a gift. It enriches the children's minds and lives. I should be happy they want to practice. But the plink, plink, plunk for nearly five hours on

Tuesdays, and other times during the week, is a long time. Even for a mother who likes classical melodies.

I really don't mind the mastered, sweet-sounding minuets or powerful concertos that my 13- and 15-year-olds practice over and over. Sometimes, in fact, I will slip into the living room where they are playing and lie down on the sofa, eyes closed, to enjoy the music that I never learned to play. As their fingers glide over the keys and bodies gently sway unintentionally to the rhythm of Bach's or Beethoven's or Mendelssohn's pieces, I am amazed at God's gift of harmony and song. I am amazed that my offspring can do this wonderful thing that I could never do. And I am equally amazed that God entrusted them (and their musical education) to me, who can barely find middle C on the keyboard.

But it takes so much effort to schedule the lessons, to keep the ones not playing quiet during them, to keep track of the younger ones' songs and practice times, to listen and encourage daily, and let's face it, to come up with the cash to pay our patient teacher. I have asked myself on days the children have struggled with notes and finger positions (neither of which I can help them much with), "Is it worth it?"

Last summer Caroline, who was 14, played in her first piano competition. It was held at a college in a real auditorium, with three somber judges scribbling notes from afar. Before the event she practiced for hours a day, for months at a time, honing her skills on the piece she had chosen—*L'Orage* ("The Storm") by Burgmuller—aptly named because of its intense, fast beat. The day of the competition Caroline looked beautiful as she approached the grand piano on stage. She wore a flowing black dress with ladylike but sensible shoes which allowed her comfortable access to the piano pedals. As she seated herself at the instrument with perfect posture—something not achieved without much effort if you know Caroline—I could sense both her nervousness and determination. At that moment I was ashamed that I had ever questioned if the music education was too much trouble, and that I had selfishly escaped to the upstairs bathroom for breaks from the sound of the piano in the early years. Right then I knew the effort was worth this one, single moment, when Caroline had the courage to walk alone on stage and play. That day she offered her talent bravely for the experts to judge, at an age when just walking into a room full of peers can sometimes be nerve-wracking enough.

Caroline started off beautifully, just like she practiced at home, but then stumbled over a few keys. I held my breath. Quickly she recovered and finished the piece rather well, but not quickly enough. I knew the judges would dock her for that error. She must have been disappointed, but I was immensely proud of her. She had worked hard. She had given it her best.

To anyone else but trained judges, her mother thought, the piece sounded spectacular.

It was then I thought that God must be like the parent and we are like the piano student. He applauds and encourages the sincere efforts of His children, but the incessant noise of the learning curve is surely no joy to hear, especially at the beginning. Without a doubt it seems we will never learn sometimes, as we plink, plink, plunk through the challenges God allows in our lives. But over time, with His immeasurable grace, we do learn. We may make mistakes at critical times, but God knows the intent of our hearts. Often we try again, and sometimes we may even gain some proficiency in doing His will.

Worthwhile objectives are always hard work. Good marriages, raising children, being good Catholics, and yes, even learning to play the piano are not goals quickly achieved, nor should they be. The effort itself is the chiseler, providing the very formation needed for the goal.

Caroline did not place at the piano competition, but the prize had already been won. I told her how proud I was of her persistence, determination and performance. Then I shared that she wasn't the only one benefiting from instruction in this instrument. Mom, too, I told her, had learned her own piano lesson.

Theresa A. Thomas

Chapter Six

FAITH

"If you had faith the size of a mustard seed, you would be able to say to this mountain, 'Move from here to there,' and it would move. Nothing would be impossible for you." (Matthew 17:20)

THE FAITH OF A CHILD

Foreli Kramarik was once strong in her faith—that there was no God—since she grew up in an atheist family in Lithuania. Religion in this communist country was commonly viewed as suspect, or at minimum unsophisticated. The widespread premise was that intelligent people simply did not fall for such delusion and wishful thinking as believing in a higher power.

Foreli's father, a talented theater director, had disdain for all things religious. Her mother must have been raised with some element of religion because Foreli has a vague memory of her grandmother teaching her prayers as a young child. Once Foreli's father realized his mother-in-law was trying to infuse religion in the grandchildren, however, he prevented visits between them. Since the state and Foreli's parents said there was no God, Foreli simply did not question it further.

One day, at the age of thirteen, Foreli woke up paralyzed in a hospital bed. Ironically, in a country where black and gray clothing was the norm, her prized red coat from Czechoslovakia should have been a red flag to the truck driver who hit her. But both Foreli and the driver were in too much of a hurry to see each other in time. She was hit hard.

The doctor delivered a grim prognosis. He announced, "You will not be going back to school and you will never be able to walk again or ever have children." Yet, the determined youth refused to accept such a dire scenario. "I kept telling myself to move," says Forelli. "I was determined to walk again. My brain was still working fine so I used it to keep learning and to convince myself that I would get better."

Since her handicap made attending regular school impossible, Foreli studied on her own. She also listened to the BBC radio and taught herself English. From the time Foreli was seven years old, she dreamed of going to the United States where she heard that conditions and opportunities were much better than in Lithuania. Her parents wanted to go too but could not get permission from their communist government. Learning English kept Foreli occupied and made her dream seem attainable. She studied a number of other subjects while continually pushing to move her unresponsive muscles. Gradually, her hard work and determination paid off. With no encouragement from her doctors or nurses—in fact they were usually indifferent and at times abusive—Foreli surprised everyone and healed within two years. During her time as an invalid, she had done enough independent studies that by the age of seventeen that she passed a government exam qualifying her to teach.

Foreli continued honing her English proficiency through books and conversing with foreigners, the latter of which was forbidden by the government. She even spent a couple days in jail after getting caught talking with foreigners. "I went by the hotels and special parks where the foreigners were allowed to go," she explained. "The KGB (part of the former Soviet Union's secret police) noticed I was doing this. People like my father—anyone in the arts, university professors or of high profiles—were watched carefully so I too was under surveillance."

When Foreli was nineteen, her father secretly paid a ransom to obtain a one-year visitor's visa for her. It was typical for such visitors to become runaways. The expectation was that she would send back money to help pay the ransom and also that she would likely never return. Her father made arrangements for Foreli to arrive in Chicago, and after she did, she worked at a number of jobs including babysitter, cashier and waitress.

Foreli's long-held dream of coming to the United States quickly turned sour. The people, customs and environment seemed so harsh and unwelcoming compared to her homeland. Even though she spoke four languages and learned quickly, Foreli did not feel like she fit in with the people around her. She was often sick with ulcers and missed her family terribly. Lonely and homesick, Foreli booked a return airline ticket to Lithuania for the following month. She continued on at her waitress job at a Lithuanian restaurant, planning to work up until the end.

One afternoon, a handsome young man caught her eye at work. Thinking she had nothing to lose, Foreli put on a big smile and brought a glass of water to his table. His name was Markus. He was teaching college cooking classes and had come to the restaurant looking for a translator to help with the Lithuanian dishes. The attraction was mutual and the two struck up a conversation. Unfortunately, all Foreli's attention to this one customer resulted in her getting fired. Markus was actually not even her customer since he was sitting in another waitress's section. On the bright side, they had made a date to visit the zoo together the next day where spontaneously Markus proposed marriage. Foreli and Markus's personalities had meshed immediately, and they felt they were always meant to be together.

"He was so charming," explains Foreli "My head was spinning. I had definitely fallen for him, but how could I make such an important decision on such short notice? ...I loved my country too. I was scared to say yes and scared to say no," she recalls. Foreli was 20 and Markus was 31 when Foreli decided to "take the risk and get married." That was in 1990.

Although the decision to marry was impulsive, Foreli never regretted marrying Markus.

"I was fortunate that he was the best man in the world for me," she stated. But they never could have imagined the incredible journey God had in store for them.

Now married, Foreli continued to hold fast to her atheism. Mark was agnostic, often wondering about a God, but never trying to influence his wife. Foreli continued to miss her family and homeland, but in 1991 with the birth of her first son, Delfini, she put down a little root. Two years later a second son, Jeanlu was born, and then Akiane, their first daughter arrived two years later. Unfortunately, health problems and job changes placed a heavy financial burden on the family. Still, Foreli accepted the poverty without complaint and raised her children with love and wonder for the world around them.

When Akiane was just three weeks old, Foreli received a call from relatives informing her that a woman named Victoria from the mountains of Armenia was telling people about a girl named Akiane who would have an incredible future that would impact many others. Later that day, Victoria called Foreli herself. With a thick Russian accent, she tried to explain the spectacular future that lay ahead for Akiane. Since Victoria was a Christian and Foreli and Markus were not, they considered the woman a fanatic and dismissed her predictions.

As Akiane grew, her easy affection and sunny disposition brought joy to the family's simple life. Recently moved from Chicago to a small town in Illinois, they could only afford a shack on the edge of a cornfield. The neighborhood was rough and the home decrepit, but their abundant love for each other richly made up for what they lacked materially.

Markus commuted a long distance to his job as a chef while Foreli lovingly mothered her three children. With little money and no friends, the natural world supplied their entertainment. Watching the setting sun, counting birds in the sky, raising monarch butterflies from cocoons, writing books, making swords out of branches and wreathes from flowers and pine needles, tents from blankets and forts from boxes or snow, filled their days.

Life continued to have its ups and downs. After taking a second job to ease the financial strain, Markus developed severe asthma and other health problems. Although Foreli cherished her time with their children, she took a job in sales with a national nutritional products company and experienced fast success. They moved into a ten thousand foot home in Missouri. But in time, Foreli found her demanding work interfered with the sacred bond she had with her children. Money did not compensate for such a loss. Foreli eventually felt directed to quit her job and devote herself full-time to motherhood. Markus found work, although his earnings were meager.

During this time, when Akiane was four years old, she came to her parents to share an amazing experience.

"Today I met God," Akiane whispered to her mother one morning.

"What is God?" Foreli questioned. Even the name "God" sounded primitive and ridiculous to her.

"God is light—warm and good. It knows everything and talks with me. It is my parent."

Foreli wanted to know about her dream but Akiane insisted it was no dream; she insisted that she had really been taken to heaven. Foreli wondered how her daughter even knew the word "God." The kids were homeschooled and her playmates were her two brothers. The family never prayed or talked about religion. Nor did the children watch television. Akiane's sudden and detailed descriptions of God and heaven were startling and unexplainable. And they did not stop.

With deep sincerity and wisdom surpassing her tender age, Akiane spoke often of the spiritual world and of God. At the same time, Akiane began drawing on whatever surfaces were available to her. One morning at 4:00 a.m., Akiane woke her mother by waving a drawing before her.

"Look! This is her—this is my angel," she said.

Akiane's sketches were those of an experienced and gifted artist not the scribbling of a young child with no formal lessons. Foreli and Markus were amazed but also confused. How could this be? What did this mean?

Watching the wonders unfolding before them, and hearing of Akiane's encounters with God brought Markus and Foreli face to face with the Divine. They had no idea why this was happening to their daughter, but it was clear that she was not making it up.

"Through Akiane's experiences, I knew there was something out there," says Foreli, "I began praying. It took a good year of little steps and another three years before we prayed together as a family. After awhile, I went into absolute immersion. I would often go to the fields or to the woods with the kids, bringing chairs and drinks to pray and try to commune with God for hours in all kinds of weather."

The family returned to a life of economic difficulty but because of Akiane, their newfound belief in God brought a harmony and joy they had never experienced before. At this time, in spite of the financial hardship, Foreli and Markus had a desire to have a fourth child. Another son, Ilia, was born in 2002. A difficult pregnancy for Foreli led them to put the children in regular school for a time.

Akiane's artistic abilities were advancing daily. By six she was painting. At this point, when her artwork was entered in local art shows, no one believed a child so young had actually created such pictures. Markus and Foreli moved their family to Colorado thinking the mountains would provide a wholesome atmosphere but instead it proved disastrous. Health problems pursued the whole family and attending public school left the children begging to come home again. Akiane had begun writing poetry and aphorisms at seven, her poems often coming to her fully conceived. Ironically, she had no prior interest in reading and writing. Akiane revealed that always she first prays and then sees words and images in her head. Sometimes, she is not even sure of the meaning herself. The compositions were astonishing for their level of sophistication, rhythm, imagery and beauty. Up until that time Akiane had read only nursery rhymes.

As Akiane's interest in poetry and art blossomed, her interest in school dwindled. She begged to be able to study at home so she would have the time and energy for art and poetry. Foreli was scared. Health and financial problems dogged at their heels and she feared the responsibility of schooling four children at home. For the first time, they began praying together as a family. Before long, the family packed up and moved to Northern Idaho close to a lake and amid nature.

Surrounded by family and nature, Akiane flourished. God and prayer comprised the core of her being. Foreli felt strongly that God wanted her to relax and not fret over subjects and grades.

"I came to understand that God is really there and He loves me," she explains. "God (also) revealed a simple thought to me: *Why are you having such a big burden? Are you going to please the world or please me?* Akiane's experience changed the way I homeschool because no longer am I fearful of the outside judging what I am doing... In a nutshell, I have learned that we should train our children to get a skill and with wisdom, find their interests and talents. Each one will develop on their own path." While Akiane is notably talented in art and poetry, her three brothers also have a number of interests and talents including architecture, real estate, cooking and producing plays, which they pursue at home.

Akiane's mystical experiences had brought the whole family together in faith, but now in Idaho, Akiane's talents would soon touch the world. At age eight, she was determined to paint Jesus' picture. After months of praying and looking for the right model, an acquaintance stopped by with a carpenter friend whom Akiane instantly knew was perfect for the portrait. It took her only forty hours of intense of focused work to complete "The Prince of Peace". Akiane had altered the model's expression and features to resemble the resurrected Jesus. People say that wherever you stand in the room, it appears that the eyes of Jesus are looking right at you. Akiane explained the finished painting by saying, "The light side of His face represents heaven. And the dark side represents suffering on earth. His light eye in the dark shows that He is with us in all our troubles, and that He is the Light when we need him."

Later a Russian television host, Jurij Sizenov Nikolaevich would say of this portrait: "We are all in total awe.... We compared Akiane's extraordinary painting "Prince of Peace" with the computerized image taken from the Shroud of Turin that was hanging in my office. To our complete shock and marvel, we found virtually an exact match! It is a miracle and it must come from God. There are no words to describe how a little eight-year-old girl could portray such wisdom, compassion and love in the eyes she painted."

Akiane's paintings were displayed in individual showings at art galleries. When she was nine, she appeared on the Oprah Winfrey show. As a result, the media and the world learned of this amazing child prodigy. Since then, Akiane has been featured on television and in newspapers and magazines around the world. Her art exhibits typically bring long lines that sometimes snake around the outside of the building. By the time she was ten, some of her artwork sold for upwards of $100,000. She uses proceeds from her two books and sold art to help needy children all over the world. Akiane has been internationally recognized as the only known binary child prodigy, accomplished in both realist paint and poetry. Her website, www.artakiane.com averages 150 million hits a year.

In spite of the fame, Akiane remains a humble and gentle soul. She explains, "I have been blessed by God. And if I am blessed, there is one reason and one reason only, and that is to help others." If she had but one wish it would be: "That everyone would love each other and love God." She says that her goal for each painting and poem is to be a gift to others and a gift to God.

In the book *akiane, her life, her art, her poetry*, Foreli summarizes Akiane and her family's incredible journey: "Akiane is convinced that the greatest gift we could give to God, who has everything and does not need anything, is for us to love one another and walk in faith, day by day, hour by hour. Now we as her parents believe that too. For by trusting Akiane and by listening to her messages, which were divinely inspired yet masked with childish laughter, we were rewarded with one of the greatest gifts of all—faith."

Today, at the age of 16, Akiane continues to homeschool and work alongside her brothers, Delfini, 20; Jean Lu, 18; Ilia, 9, and Aurelius, 3. She speaks four languages and her hobbies include playing piano, chess and helping people. Akiane rises in the morning around 4 a.m. to paint and write about four to five hours a day, five to six days a week. A single painting sometimes takes 100 to 200 hours, and she produces between 8 and 20 paintings a year.

A note from Patti and Theresa: As Catholics we approach mystical experiences with caution and make no final judgments on private revelations. We share Foreli's story here because we found it to be both amazing and inspiring. Akiane's artistic abilities are surely gifts from God and give testimony to His almighty power and love.

Readers may find it odd that Akiane refers to God as 'It.' Please note that pronoun usage can be unclear or even confusing in translation from one language to another. Also, please note that at the point in Akiane's young life when she made reference to God as 'It' she had no knowledge of God as a Person. We simply offer the retelling of Foreli's story for your own consideration and discernment.

BETRAYAL TO RENEWAL

Sitting in her grandmother's farmhouse in rural ND, Anissa Gartner often poured out her heart. Sometimes it was a problem at school or home and often it was just sharing some good news. Either way, talking with her grandmother was talking with her best friend. There was a cozy understanding between them. Her parents and three younger siblings lived on the same farm with her grandparents.

As the oldest, Anissa often helped with the younger kids during summer and pitched in with chores when her mother returned from working at the bank in town. Her mother had to go to work to help make ends meet when Anissa was nine. With her grandmother always around, however, Anissa never felt lonely. But then, during October of her twelfth year, her grandmother went to the doctors and discovered cancer had invaded her entire body. It was a shock to everyone.

Her grandmother immediately was taken to a hospital an hour away. Anissa didn't have many chances to visit her. Less than three months later, Anissa's parents took her to say good-bye to her grandmother. It was clear the end was near. Anissa had missed her grandmother so much. She could not bear the thought of her dying. Walking into the cold and scary hospital room, Anissa looked over at her beloved grandmother. She slowly approached the bed and reached out to hug her grandma, longing to be wrapped in the love and friendship that had been taken from her so abruptly. But as she put out her arms, her grandmother looked blankly at her as if she was a stranger. She was already gone.

Anissa gave her a hug but recoiled emotionally. Her dear grandmother, who had always been there for her, didn't even recognize her! *How could she not know who I am?* Anissa thought in horror. A couple days later she died. That was it. It seemed that one moment Anissa basked in the love of her grandmother as if it would never end and then suddenly, it was if she never existed.

Anissa went through the motions of the funeral and locked her anger and grief deep inside. *Grandma didn't even seem to care, she didn't even say goodbye,* Anissa thought. *She left me right when I needed her most.* With her beloved grandmother gone, Anissa began acting out, hanging with a bad crowd, lying to her parents and drinking at junior high parties.

"My mother could see what was happening, but I rejected her attempts to help me," Anissa explained. Yet, her mother understood that Anissa's teenage rebellion was mixed in with her grief and her mother's heart found a way to help her hurting daughter. She found a counselor that was able to get Anissa to open up and move past her grief. Soon, Anissa stopped sneaking around and no longer socialized with the wild group. Not into sports or feeling like she belonged with the smart kids, she began keeping to herself and spent most of her time at home.

Although her family went to Mass on Sundays, they had never been overtly religious though Anissa had recognized a deep but private spirituality in her grandmother. She began to see that her mother too had that quiet devotion to her faith. It was an example Anissa began to follow. She got involved with the church, singing in the choir and teaching religion classes.

Then, Fr. G. entered the picture. He had come to North Dakota from another state. This very large and jovial priest lit up a room and seemed to love everyone. At first, Anissa and her family enjoyed having him stop by the house for visits. But soon, his outgoing friendly nature crossed the line.

"We were hearing that he was getting too physically close with some of the ladies and girls in our parish," said Anissa. "The word was that sometimes in the confessional he would touch them inappropriately." Women and girls also began reporting that Father's hugs often included wandering hands. This made Anissa's family very uncomfortable to have him around so they often pretended not to be at home when they saw his car pull into the yard.

During the 70s, it was a different era. People were generally less inclined to speak out; then, it all came to a head. Anissa is foggy on the details, but she knows that Fr. G. was visiting at one of her friend's house. The parents were outside when Fr. G. began aggressively fondling their 6-year old little girl. Anissa's friend, the older sister, ran outside to tell the parents.

"After that, no one ever saw him again," Anissa said. "We heard later that he had a desk job at the diocese office and then shortly thereafter he died from a heart attack. I was an older teen when I heard he had died. I remember feeling some relief that I never had to worry about seeing him again."

Following this unfortunate episode, Anissa became resentful of the Church. The priest had been bad, so in her mind, the Church was bad. Going to Church and practicing her Catholic faith fell by the wayside before Anissa left for college to North Dakota State University.

If you have knowledge,

let others light their candles with it.

~Sir Winston Churchill

While in her junior year, Anissa met Lance, another lapsed Catholic. They fell in love and became engaged. Anissa looked forward to marrying the man she loved, but there was a slight concern about their future faith-life together. Anissa had started praying and reading her Bible. Even though she was still skipping Mass, she feared that if her faith continued to grow, would Lance grow with her? As a wedding gift on the day they married, January 5, 1990, Lance gave her a crucifix as a sign that in some way, Christ would be a part of their union.

Soon, children were born, starting with their first daughter Alyson in May 1991. As she grew and more kids came, Lance and Anissa felt it was important to attend Mass every Sunday rather than just when it was convenient. But still much of it was just on the surface. Then, one evening in 1997 Anissa was reading a book about the Blessed Mother and was suddenly overcome with the realization that she still harbored anger at the Church. "It hit me like a two-by-four and it came seemingly out of the blue. I was growing spiritually, praying and talking to God more, but my anger at the Church over the priest, was blocking me."

The anger welled up and exploded through a flood of tears. Relief and sorrow poured out between sobs. For so long, she had felt betrayed by the Church by a priest that had been sinful. Now, she understood that it was the priest that had betrayed the Church. The Church was still good, it always had been. The sin of one man had hurt both her and the Church.

It was at that point, in the quiet, peaceful aftermath of being drained of so much emotion, that Anissa felt God revealing to her that if she wanted to get closer to Him, she needed to go to the Sacrament of Confession. It had been twenty years since she had gone. During marriage preparation, Lance and Anissa were told they needed to go to Confession before they got married, but neither did. Once the tears had dried Anissa felt renewed in one way, but knew there was another renewal awaiting her, to confess her sins and receive absolution

Anissa felt scared but within a couple weeks she found the courage to go to Confession. "Bless me father for I have sinned," she began. She took a deep breath and continued. "It has been twenty years since my last Confession...." The priest was standing in for Jesus who had commissioned his apostles for this Sacrament after he rose from the dead by saying, "Whose sins you forgive are forgiven and whose sins you hold bound are held bound." (John 20:23)

A weight was lifted in Anissa, now replaced with the graces and love of God. "I felt like I was floating when I walked out," she said. After hearing of Anissa's experience, Lance soon took advantage of this gift also.

From that point on, Anissa said it seems that their family has been led by God to take big leaps of faith in their lives. The following year, they began to homeschool. Through homeschooling, Anissa says she and Lance have learned about the Catholic faith. "I have learned so much through the Catholic curriculum with our kids; things I never knew before."

After 12 years of homeschooling, Anissa says their family of six children is thriving. "My kids are happy we made this decision. We talk about Catholic issues all the time in our home. There's many times that we get talking late at night with the girls (two teens) so Jacob (age 11) hates going to bed early because he's afraid he might miss one of these late night powwows. Our children are on fire for their faith."

In recent years their family held a Sacred Heart Enthronement ceremony in their home to make Jesus their king and place themselves full under him and Lance is currently in the deaconate program.

"It's been a continual journey since that first confession," Anissa said. "We are so busy with housework, school and farm work, but my main desire is to be a good example and make our Catholic faith at the core of our family."

Anissa Gartner

Anissa and Lance live on a ranch in western North Dakota with their 6 children: Alyson 19 years, Elizabeth 16 years, Jacob 11 years, Michael 5 years, Joseph 4 years, and John 7 months. Anissa enjoys caring for her family, reading, gardening, and learning more about her Catholic faith. She also feels called to spread the message of Fatima and promote the Sacred Heart Enthronement.

But of Course...Inspiration

Jesus, help me to simplify my life by learning what you want me to be and becoming that person. -Saint Therese of Lisieux

How do you celebrate the everyday moment? Learn from children, puppies and other experts. -Harvey L. Rich, M.D.

You have to live a heroic Catholic life in America today. God will use you and provide you with the knowledge and the wisdom, providing you are living the authentically heroic Catholic life. -Fr. John Harden

The happiest moments in my life are those when I'm not thinking about myself. From the recovery website sober24.com

Patience is never more important than when you are at the edge of losing it. -O.A. Battista, chemist and inventor from Forth Worth, Texas

Live as if you were to die tomorrow. Learn as if you were to live forever. -Mahatma Gandhi

Do the math...count your blessings. -Unknown

Faith is the ability not to panic. -Unknown

He who dares to teach must never cease to learn. -Richard Henry Dann
If you worry, you didn't pray. If you pray, don't worry. -Unknown

Teaching should be such that what is offered is perceived as a valuable gift and not as a hard duty. -Albert Einstein

You can pay people to teach, but you can't pay them to care. -Marva Collins

Experience is the worst teacher; it gives the test before the lesson. -Vernon Law

The mediocre teacher tells. The good teacher explains. The superior teacher demonstrates. The great teacher inspires. -William Arthur Ward

OVERHEARD CONVERSATION

"Nothing can do ANYTHING!" Hank, age 6, said in a very heated fashion.

"God can!!" Jake, age 4, replied with confidence.

"Yeah, that's right", Spencer, age 6, jumped into the conversation.

Hank said, "God is not a person."

"God is a soul," replied Spencer.

Jake interjected, "He's right there next to you."

Spencer dramatically said, "Hank you just stepped on God."

"Yeah but I stepped on Him in a good way, I didn't hurt Him." replied Hank in a very solemn voice.

"But he doesn't make a sound" said Jake.

In a very quiet, knowledgeable whisper Spencer said, "The only way you can hear Him is in your thoughts."

"I am going to blow up a tank now" Hank said as the conversation jolted to an end.

Listening to my children and Hank, a child I baby-sit, have a conversation about God when they thought no one was listening was spellbinding to me. Frantically I was jotting down exactly what was said, I did not want to misquote anyone. Have you ever heard your child talk about God? Not when prompted to about homework, church or while praying? Well this was my first time and I was so proud I thought I was going to bust!

You can never be sure of exactly what is absorbed into those little sponge-like brains or if everything you try to teach them just bounces off into oblivion. Then you hear it, what you have been trying to teach them for years and it's as though you can sigh with relief, they get it, they really get it!

If our children actually listen, take in the information and then truly practice it... it's like it was all worth it, all 300 times I said that. There will be countless times we will never see the end result of what we have tried so hard to teach our children. So many times they will be put in situations when they will recall our voices and use that lesson from us to stay safe, and we will never know it. Seldom will be the times we will ever see it come to fruition but for the one time we do we should embrace the moment, savor the second and let it inspire us to continue on our path of loving, teaching and showing our children the right direction.

It works even if we never see it, it is so well worth the time and effort it takes to help our children to grow, mature and develop into responsible, generous, loving, faithful adults and it is in good part because of the parenting we administer, all the grunt work, the commitment and dedication for our children.

Never stop teaching, loving, guiding and nurturing your children even when you feel like they have not heard a word. Because one day you may be privy to a conversation I just overheard.

Lori Hadorn-Disselkamp

Lisa is a stay at home mom of four children and the volunteer coordinator of the children's learning service program at their grade school. She has always loved to write and derives pure pleasure from writing daily reflections on her blog http://faithfilledmom.com She is also a guest columnist at http://catholicmoms.com and http://gatherinspirit.com.

WHAT A DIFFERENCE A DAY MAKES

My father is very ill, in the hospital, on life support. Yesterday he said he wanted all the tubes removed and that he wanted to die. This was in the morning. As the day went on we talked to him again about the future and he wasn't so clear. He even said that, yes, he wanted to die, but then added "for now..." This assessing of a desire to live on the part of a person on life support is very difficult. Anyone who feels awful might say "I want to die" and really mean it at that moment, but only because their judgment is clouded by the suffering or depression of the moment. We finally decided that Dad was having mixed feelings, was certainly down, and that he wasn't thinking clearly enough to be making life and death decisions. It was a very scary time.

I told my father that his life was still very precious to me even on the ventilator. I told him that his life still had value, and that everybody who loves him still thinks so. I gave him some examples too of how he could still enjoy his grandchildren even in his condition—we could still watch football games together and he could still hear them play music. Then I added that "that being said, I don't know what it feels like to be in your condition and you are under no obligation to continue to fight and to stay on the ventilator. If you want to give up, we'll support you. Just know that your life is still valuable." I think when a person is suffering that much, if they are not reminded of the value with which others regard their life, it would be very easy to decide it would just be better for everybody for them to just die.

So today, he was much better. He smiled a lot and said (well, actually mouthed) some very funny things. For the last two days he has been on minimal assistance from the ventilator all day long and just on full assistance at night to give him a rest. When he heard that he mouthed, "Better than I thought."

I asked the nurse how she thought he was doing. She said that he's doing fine. I asked if she though he was improving and she said unequivocally "Yes, but he has a long way to go." She said, however, that he was making small steps toward getting better. I went in to my dad's room and told him exactly what she had said. He put a fist in the air (a gesture of triumph).

So for now, Dad is doing alright. This is not to say that there might not come a day when it is clear that my father will not recover and he might decide he wants the ventilator turned off. But I do believe that suffering is redemptive and that all human life is valuable and purposeful. I wonder how many times people have been pulled off "life support" because they were having a bad day or because no one told them that all life has meaning, even and maybe especially, life in a state of debilitation.

God's grace sometimes comes through the words and actions of others. We all have the power to pass on that blessing of hope to another human being. A word or a gesture of encouragement is often all it takes. The absence or presence of those simple things can make a difference on whether one decides to continue to fight on in this life, or give up and die. There may be a person thinking of committing suicide but for a kind word. There may be an ill person, like my father, who consciously or unconsciously depends on other's spoken words of encouragement to prod him on to fighting to live. In the morning my father wanted to die. By afternoon he was smiling about the future. What a difference a day (and God's grace) makes.

Rosemary Bogdan

Rosemary has been married for 29 years and is the mother of six children ages 13 to 25. She homeschooled some or all of her children for a total of about 13 years. She is interested in Catholic teaching, homeschooling, mothering, politics and, in particular, the life issues. She lives in Ann Arbor, Michigan.

LET THE LITTLE CHILDREN COME TO ME

What do you do with the 4-year-old who cries to go with you to Adoration (that is, your highly anticipated hour of peace and quiet) despite the late hour, her freshly shampooed hair, and the pajama-clad arms reaching up for you to embrace? You try bribery first. "Honey, wouldn't you prefer relaxing in bed? I'll put in a video tape for you to watch. Which tape would you like? Would you like Daddy to rub your back until you fall asleep?"

What do you do when she insists she wants to "go see Jesus?" You let her go, of course. After all, part of your children's *home* education includes *religious* training. It is through the parents that children are brought to Christ in these formative years.

While at Adoration, what do you do with the bag of books the 4-year-old insisted on bringing to Adoration "just like Mommy" and wants you to read aloud? You read them, of course. All five of them: *The Napping House* by Audrey and Don Wood, *If You Give a Mouse a Cookie* by Laura Joffe Numeroff, *A Child's Year* by Joan Walsh Anglund, *Ten Little Monkeys* illustrated by Danny Brooks Dalby, complete with something sticky and grimy on the cover, and *Cecily Parsley's Nursery Rhymes* by Beatrix Potter.

What do you do when the 4-year-old insists *loudly* "Mommy, why are we the only ones here? Where's Jesus?" even though she has come to Adoration before?

You explain to her (even if it's the one-hundredth time) that Jesus is here in the room "See! In that little white circle. Jesus is in that consecrated host. See? He's in that host inside that beautiful gold monstrance."

And you know from watching the expression in her eyes and the furrowed line across her brow that this 4-year-old mind isn't buying it. It doesn't look like Jesus. Where's his beard, for goodness sake?! And how can Jesus be in that white thing if he's everywhere in the world? This 4-year-old certainly had questions.

What do you do with the 4-year-old who wanders over to the crucified Lord hanging on the wall? You let her, of course. That's *her* moment of contemplation, *her* moment of meditation, *her* moment of Adoration.

What do you do with the 4-year-old who stretches out on the pew next to you, places her now-dry curly head in your lap, and requests you to "rub my back"? You rub her back, of course, while reading your own book.

What do you do with the 4-year-old who falls asleep before the hour is over after you warned her she would fall asleep if she came with you at this late hour? You knew you would have to lug her to the car but she *insisted* that she wouldn't fall asleep. You pick her up, of course. But, first, you calmly organize the book bags and slippers that have fallen off her feet, gently drape her over your lap until you can lift her onto your shoulder, rise without breaking your back and dropping everything, and navigate your way to the car where you unlock it, throw everything into the front seat—oops, that's a child in your arms, and gently place the four-year-old in her car seat. When did this 4-year-old go from small and compact to long-legged and spidery?

What do you do when you get home and the house is dark and everyone else is sound asleep...except you, of course? You do the same thing all over again, of course carrying her, this time upstairs, and place her in her bed.

And the next morning, when the 4-year-old awakes and asks if she *really* went to Adoration with you and did she *really* fall asleep and did you *really* have to carry her to the car and does Jesus *really* know she went to visit Him last night, what do you say when she asks in an excited whisper, "Can we do it again, Mommy?"? You smile and say "Of course! I'd *love* it!" I'll bet Jesus loves it too.

"'Let the little children come to me, and do not hinder them, for the kingdom of God belongs to such as these. I tell you the truth, anyone who will not receive the kingdom of God like a little child will never enter it.' And he took the children in his arms, put his hands on them and blessed them." - Mark 10:13-16*

Cay Gibson

Cay is the author of Literature Alive!, Catholic Mosaic, and A Picture Perfect Childhood. She lives with her husband, Mark, and their five children in Southwest Louisiana. Visit her blog (Cajun Cottage) at http://cajuncottage.blogspot.com/

ONE IN HEAVEN

Before I started homeschooling, I wondered how a parent could school more than one or two at a time. Yet, attend any homeschooling convention and it is full of parents of large families. Love does indeed does multiply and families open to homeschooling are often very open to new life.

My husband Mark and I became one of those families open to life and made a trip to the maternity year every couple of years. Given our track record, it seemed like a good idea to have an extra home pregnancy kit tucked away on a bathroom shelf. One month, I did not really think I was pregnant but I was not certain. I remembered the kit and thought, *I'll just check to be sure.* The pink line that emerged indicating a positive result, took my breath away. I would be 47 when the baby was due. We had recently added an orphan boy from Kenya so now we were a family of eleven.

"Hey Mark, we're going to have another baby," I announced to my husband, showing him the pink line. We looked at each other, wide-eyed. We shared a strong understanding that each little soul is a gift from God that will last an eternity. Still, I'd be forty-seven and Mark forty-eight. As we gradually adjusted to the news, I discovered that our willingness to accept new life led us closer to God. Instead of thinking of things like money, opinions of others and our advanced age we would trust God to provide for both the necessary material needs of this transitory world. New life had begun and would forever be a part of our family.

It had only been the previous week that my daughter Teresa, age eight, had expressed hope that I would have another baby. When I pointed out that older women did not usually have babies, she reminded me that Elizabeth was older when she had John the Baptist. I had just smiled and said: "You never know."

Well, now we knew. The younger kids were ecstatic. I thought the older kids would be taken aback (we had one in college, three in high school, one in junior high, and four younger ones) but they all said that given my history, they pretty much expected it. Friends and family registered surprise. After all, they had been secretly guessing that we were finally "done."

Then, at three months, I miscarried for the first time. I had some early warnings, so by the time it happened, it was not a surprise. The enormity of my loss did not really hit me until I was alone at morning Mass a couple days later. I had requested that my kids ask God to let us know the sex of the baby. My oldest, Aaron, suggested I give it a unisex name and leave it at that. "I would really like to know who it was," I explained, "so please ask God to somehow let us know."

It was just before Mass, two days after the miscarriage, that I suddenly felt a deep sense of knowing that the baby had been a boy—Matthew. We chose that name to go with our Mark, Luke and John, members of the family. Realizing I had a son suddenly filled me with a deep awareness that my very own child was with God now. I knew there was no greater place to be but still, a maternal sadness washed over me. My little son, Matthew, was our only baby I did not get to hold in my arms and have with me. He was the only one that his big brothers and sisters missed out on in this world.

I shed a few tears but was filled with peace that I knew who my baby was now. Then, after Mass, before leaving for home, the thought occurred to me that although I was convinced I had a son in heaven, other family members (especially the teens) might say: "Mom, you really don't know for sure."

For a stalk to grow or a flower to open there must be time that cannot be forced; nine months must go by for the birth of a human child; to write a book or compose music often years must be dedicated to patient research....

To find the mystery there must be patience, interior purification, silence, waiting....

~Pope John Paul II

I sent up a quick prayer. "Dear God, I accept that my son is with you now, but it would mean a lot to me if you would somehow let the others know the baby was a boy." I wanted my husband to know his son and the children to have a relationship with a little brother in heaven.

I kept the morning's experience to myself. Then, just a few hours later, Aaron called me from Fargo, where he attended college and was living for the summer. "Mom, I'm in a big hurry, but I just wanted to call to tell you I know the baby was a boy."

Aaron had dreamed two nights in a row of a baby. In the first dream, a baby had died but he was confused. The next night, he had the same dream but this time, when he looked at the baby, he knew it was his little brother. In the dream he looked at me and we nodded at one another in understanding.

"Oh, Aaron, I just asked God this morning to somehow let everyone else know it was a boy." I explained my own experience to him, marveling at my answered prayer. My oldest had connected with my youngest, from heaven to earth.

There was no time to talk, however, because Aaron was in a hurry to participate in a study, which paid very good money to college students. We said good-bye and I learned the rest of the story later.

Aaron arrived at the study site only minutes after our conversation. By all rights, he should have been disqualified during the screening because his heart started racing when his pulse was taken. Since the study had been overbooked, they were looking for any reason to start bumping students. Aaron knew from experience that an above-normal heart rate was a typical factor used to bump students.

It was Aaron's nervousness that caused his fast heart rate but he could not get himself to calm down. He began asking his little brother, Matthew, to help him. Aaron really needed the money for expenses. His pulse was taken two more times, each time measuring faster than the previous rate.

It seemed hopeless.

The study director looked at him and then at the nurse beside him who was recording the results. "Please Matthew," Aaron prayed, "Please help me get into this study." But Aaron braced himself, waiting to be told he was dismissed. *There's no way, now,* he thought.

Looking at Aaron in the eyes, the director paused and then stated quietly to the nurse at his side: "Let him in." The nurse registered surprise. She opened her mouth as if to protest but then quickly followed the doctor as they went onto the next participant.

A euphoric disbelief and awe filled Aaron's soul. It seemed impossible. He was in! And it was his little brother that got him in. It had to be.

It's been six years now since we lost Matthew. Although, spiritually speaking, we will never lose him. He will always love us, his family, and always hear our prayers. He knows more than we do, and his love is greater than ours. Even though it would have been great to hold him on this earth, it is a grace to have him holding us in his heart now in heaven.

Patti Maguire Armstrong

Chapter Seven

THE LIGHTER SIDE

"Gladness of heart is the very life of man, cheerfulness prolongs his days."
(Sirach 30:22)

GRACE FOR THE BAKING

My bundt pan is getting old and chipped. I bought it on sale at Sam's Club in the early years of our marriage—it was pretty, bright, blue and full of promise—and yet, at the time, I didn't think I would use it much. Oh, I had lofty ambitions, to be sure. Baking was something that every good wife did, right?

Nor was it a question of my not liking to bake. I *did* like to bake, and hoped to be good at it. The problem was that I already had a lot on my plate, so to speak, and dessert wasn't always a priority. I had several young children and a house to run. Who had time for cake?

Quite frankly, the thought of baking overwhelmed me on many levels. First, I hadn't had a lot of practice growing up. My mom and my sisters were excellent bakers; unfortunately, they didn't think to teach me and I never asked.

Second, I looked at baking as yet another kitchen mess to contend with. I was already spending too much time in that room as it was, filling sippy cups and making peanut butter and jelly sandwiches. Why add to my workload?

Finally, (and this is embarrassing for a homeschooling mom to admit), the thought of baking alongside my children stressed me out. I knew that there'd be an endless parade of messes—sticky fingers and spoon licking; sugar spilling and egg dropping—and I just sighed to think of the challenges to my patience and my sanity that all this represented.

Well, where was my courage? My mother's heart reprimanded me, gently at first and then with loud insistence. I thought of that Bundt pan and I dragged it out. I flipped through the little book of recipes that came with the pan and the words "Tunnel of Fudge" caught my eye.

I was sold. And my family could not have been happier! It was at that point that my life's lesson took off. I began to look at baking as a blessing and not a chore. Cooking and baking are such a necessary part of a large family, anyway; why not sweeten up my attitude and dig in?

All of my earlier fears were quickly dispelled as the kids and I baked one delicious cake after another. I stopped worrying about not knowing how to bake as well as not worrying about having my many budding chefs that wanted to assist me. My Bundt pan was very forgiving, and the more I baked with it, the more forgiving I became.

I quickly discovered that when I added a touch of love and let the children help me, the grueling was replaced by the grace-filled. As we cooked and cleaned together, the kitchen became a natural extension of our classroom. Many homeschoolers already know this, but I saw that the lesson plans fit right in with all the mixing. There is the reading of recipes, the math in the measuring, and the science of how the cake rises.

And how about the history? The Bundt pan was named for the German word bund, which loosely translated means "gathering." In 1966, a woman from Texas took second place in the Pillsbury Bake-Off using a Bundt pan for her now-famous "Tunnel of Fudge" cake and the sales and the fame of the Bundt pan skyrocketed.

Is it a coincidence that I was born that very year? I just don't think so.

Margaret Berns

Margaret is a Minnesota mom of seven (two of whom are in heaven). They are happy Catholics and happy homeschoolers, in that order. Please feel free to pay her a virtual visit at www.patentsgirl.blogspot.com.

THE HOMESCHOOL MOM

Oh, the life of a homeschool mom. Many gush with admiration at her skills to juggle home life and academics while others are skeptical wondering if she really can handle it all. But the homeschool mom knows full well, that she isn't so special or different at all. She's just a mom, making her way through each day, looking for direction from above and putting one foot in front of the other below. It's a lifestyle to be sure and every homeschool mom learns to lead a seamless life in which science, reading, math history, and all subjects meld into one with God at the center.

Her house is never as clean as it once was or as she wishes, but then when given the choice to create a learning environment at home or win a house beautiful contest, she knows which is of greater value. Sometimes she gets tired but then remembers that moms working full time and needing to do a second shift of homework, housework, lessons and sports, also get tired. She has less money and more mess, but more time and less guilt.

In the end, it's a matter of choice and not perfection. And the Moms that choose homeschooling don't ever take credit for the idea, just for following where they think God is leading.

How do you recognize the homeschool mom?

--Home economics class with is an integral part of her homeschool day—doing laundry, folding clothes, sorting socks, and cooking dinner.

--It's always okay to pray in school, even spontaneously like to ask for help finding Johnny's English book.

--Dead bugs on the windowsill are collected regularly and go straight to the microscope

--Time for a haircut? Right after class or maybe while baby is napping. Oh and might as well saves some hair for the microscope too!

--Mowing the lawn? Recess anyone?

--When her cat gives birth, that will do for the day's science class.

--No **snow days** for her kids but on the first day of snow, the kids can take a moment to run outside and play.

--Vacations are grand field trips to historic spots--but then, much of life becomes a field trip.

--The substitute teacher might be Grandma

--Lost teeth are returned by the Tooth Fairy, saved and examined; perhaps put in various glass containers with substances such as Coke and milk to watch deterioration

--A Saturday job for her kids: Dad might give the kids the yard length and width measurement and tell them to figure out the amount of fertilizer needed for the area of the yard.

--Who needs the *new* multi-age classroom offered by the schools? The multi-aged groups are sitting in the living room

--Teacher is sick? She teaches from her bed or uses educational programs they watch and discuss together.

--Sick children? They can rest in bed but can also just lie low and read a schoolbook under the covers if it's just the sniffles.

--The teacher's assistant for the kindergartener—the nine-year old who asks to help teach.

--Going to the zoo for a field trip? This mom just needs to wait for a nice day, not for permission slips to get returned and drivers to be arranged.

--It's hard to remember what grades the kids are in because they do school work at various different levels.

--Religion can be in every subject.

--When you walk into her dining room, instead of a centerpiece on the table, you will find science projects and other works-in-progress.

-- She is often one who fills up her cart when there's a sale on in-home pregnancy tests.

--In the doctor's waiting room, instead of reading the women's magazines, she has her red pen out and is checking papers or reading with a younger child.

--When she comes across mold in her refrigerator, she calls to her kids to get the Petri dishes.

--When school is out for the day, there's no homework--the rest of the afternoon and evening is free.

--Summer time doesn't mean learning stops but it's just time to catch up on some fun books they didn't get to during the school year.

--Her family's living room looks like the local library.

--She has more posters of parts of speech, maps, timelines etc than framed artwork in her house.

--She willingly stabs her finger so her children can look at blood cells under the microscope.

--Her kids know that dessert is "earned" by reciting multiplication tables She doesn't mind if her students recite the states and capitals while hanging upside down over the sofa.

--When asked how she does it, she thinks: "Well, how could I not?

THE FIRST TIME IS THE HARDEST

There's a slight difference between your first child and your fourth. The first child is your rookie season. By your fourth, you're getting ready to enter the parenting hall of fame.

With your first child, the conversation sounds like this:

"Honey, do you think its okay to take the baby outside? It's only 70 degrees and he might catch a cold."

After a lengthy debate, you dress the baby in a winter outfit that's as roomy as a straight jacket, check the weather channel for tornadoes within a 500-mile radius and arm yourself with a dozen cans of Lysol to disinfect the neighborhood as you go for a stroll.

With you fourth child, the conversation sounds like this:

"Honey, I know there's a blizzard outside but the kids are bored and I thought I'd take them bungee cord jumping."

"Okay dear, but you might want to take a sweater for the baby. The wind chill is minus 20."

Children are like martinis. The more you have, the looser you feel.

With your first child, you spend hours evaluating diaper brands and even perform a few of your own absorbency research studies in your kitchen. By your fourth child, you can construct a diaper out of nothing more than a trash bag, three coffee filters and a box of cotton balls.

With your first child, you think you need dozens of baby gadgets, such as an electronic baby wipe warmer. By your fourth, you realize the baby wipes will get warm if you leave them in the car on a hot day.

With your first child, you purchase an expensive diaper-changing table. By your fourth child, the diaper-changing table has been turned into a TV stand and you're willing to change your baby on top of the clothes dryer.

With your first child, you spend months researching baby names. With your fourth, you realize you'll end up calling your child by his or her siblings' names anyway. As you enter the hospital, you look at employee name badges for ideas. You settle on "Trainee."

With your first baby, you bring him or her to the doctor after every sneeze. After four kids, you make them show you signs of a compound fracture before you'll get in the car.

With your first child, you prepare special foods and cater meals to meet your child's whims. By your fourth, you realize that children can survive for years on nothing more than Cheerios and grilled-cheese sandwiches.

With your first child, you read dozens of books by parenting experts. By your fourth, you're simply glad when you can find a peaceful moment to read the newspaper.

There's a slight difference between your first child and your fourth. With your first child, you ask questions like:

"Are we really ready to be parents?"

With your fourth child, you find it difficult to remember life without kids.

That's just another way children are like martinis. The more you have, the worse your memory gets.

Tim Bete

Tim Bete is the former director of the Erma Bombeck Writers' Workshop and author of In the Beginning...There Were No Diapers and Guide to Pirate Parenting. You can read more of his writing at www.PirateParenting.com

Us Versus the Snake

As Mom was heading out the door to pick up my little brother, Noah, my 11-year-old brother Pavel spotted a four-foot long female rattlesnake near the doorstep. Mom freaked out, got the dog inside and instructed us to come in the house. She told us that she would get Dad to come home and kill the snake while she picked up Noah.

As soon as she disappeared down the driveway, I had an idea.

"Pavel, we need to do our duty," I said.

"What duty?" he hissed back.

"We need to make sure the snake doesn't escape and come back to hurt the little kids. Think how noble it would be to help the family out."

He hesitated so I said, "We'd have a good time with it afterwards."

Pavel at first looked at me as though I was crazy. Living in the Southwest, we both knew that the rattlesnake's venomous bite could inflict serious harm. Slowly though, Pavel's eyes lit up and he grabbed the hoe, rake and axe. Using these tools and thinking ourselves heroes, we pushed the snake out from under the bench by the door. Pavel, in a typical eleven-year-old fashion, threw a rock at the snake's head. It slithered into the grass. I got really annoyed at this and made Pavel climb the tree above the snake. From his perch, he took his Gandalf-type staff and pushed the snake toward the open driveway. I approached the snake cautiously and pressed my hoe behind its head to hold it down to the ground. Next, Pavel scrambled down and moved up behind it. Whack! He neatly chopped off the head with the axe. Success!

We discarded the head of the snake, but not before collecting some venom, (thanks to our many wild-life books we knew right where to find it) which looked a lot like soy sauce. Then I busied myself cleaning the dead snake, and dragging it to the outdoor table, where Pavel and I decided to skin it. Pavel handed me a razor, Mom's best steak knife, and a couple of plastic sandwich bags for gloves. I wore my reading glasses for protection in case blood or venom squirted. Next, we made an incision down on the under- side of the reptile.

Pavel pointed and said things like, "Is that the liver?" I guessed and nodded, or shook my head, trying to remember things from the science books I had read.

Mom returned, and eyeing us, she asked where the snake was. We glanced sheepishly at each other and I held up the partially skinned carcass.

"Right here," I said.

Mom was dumbstruck. She looked like she was trying to decide if she should give us a hug or wring our necks. I was definitely hoping for the hug. Instead, she called Dad on the phone, and thankfully he was on our side. He is, after all, an excellent science teacher.

With Mom's permission, we continued our work with the dead snake, and ended up with a beautiful skin, nice enough for a designer purse. Then I looked up online cookbooks and found all sorts of delicious-looking snake recipes: baked rattler with lemon, fried snake, rattler salad sandwiches. However, we ended up taking too long and eventually decided that the fleshy meat was left outside too long to be safe to consume.

Oh well...

Things went smoothly for Pavel and me that day. We cornered the snake without incident and were able to make our own home-made science project, even while we fell short of providing dinner for the family.

Zoe Federoff

Zoe Federoff, age 18, grew up with her parents and nine siblings in the beautiful Sonoran Desert. Her house was lovingly designed and built by her dad. Her mother did initially get angry but admits that the venom-collecting and skinning was very impressive. Her parents do not recommend killing rattlers as a homeschool science project.

TEMPORARY INSANITY

Maybe it was the big brown eyes that were to blame. Or perhaps it was the curly, non-shedding hair and turned up tail. Or it could have just been temporary insanity. Yes, temporary insanity was definitely the reason I brought the dog home.

After twenty-five years of marriage I knew better than to bring home another pet without consulting my husband. I also knew it was best to pray before embarking on life changing decisions. I usually prayed at the drop of a hat, but I had neglected to do so before putting the dog in our car.

My mistake began when I read an email on the homeschool message tree. "Due to allergies we must give away our beloved dog, Luis. He is a one-year-old labradoodle that loves children. He jumps through hoops, speaks, dances, plays dead, rolls over, and does other tricks."

Wow, I thought, *what a great dog.* Without stopping to think (never a good step) I picked up the phone. Like a dazed shopper racing for a limited supply of a much-desired item, adrenaline propelled me.

"Can I come out and see him?" I asked.

Within minutes my four youngest kids and I were petting Luis who was very excited to meet us. We watched with delight at his cute tricks. By now, I had become the victim of a multiple personality. The sensible mother and wife, who shopped wisely and avoided impulsive behavior, gave way to the crazy dog lady. "We'll take him," the crazy lady announced. Before the transaction could be completed, the family wanted time to say good-bye to their dog.

I was scheduled to meet at a playground with three other moms so our kids could play together, so I told the mom that I would return in a couple hours. I should have seized this "time-out" to regain my sanity. It was a missed opportunity for sure. Not until I was getting ready to leave the playground did I even admit to my friends that I was going to pick up a dog. My friends knew I already had two husband-approved dogs. So now you understand just how truly crazy the dog lady was.

I will forever be disappointed in my friends. Would they have let me reach for a third drink in the middle of the afternoon? I think not. Yet, they stood by and let me go for a third dog. Why didn't anyone slap me in the face and tell me to wake up? There were three of them. They could have formed a human shield and refused to let me leave the park. Instead, they did nothing but express surprise.

"You are going to have three dogs?" one of them said, her eyes bugging out.

Even though I tried to ignore it, there was a small thin voice within me, trying to make contact. "What about your husband?" the voice asked.

"Oh, that's right," I thought. I called Mark at work. "Hi Mark. We're going to be taking care of a dog for another homeschooling family." A bit of small talk ensued and then I said good-bye. "There, took care of that," I determined. It was actually the truth, sort of. Yeah, I know all about sins of omissions. Guilty as charged.

If there was no difference in the mom's and one child's allergies, with Luis gone, they wanted the dog back after two weeks. So I had convinced myself that we might not even keep him anyways. I'd let Mark in on the rest of the story after he realized how cute the dog was. Our own two dogs were getting old. They were happy to lie around all day, so one more dog would not really add much, I figured. But when I walked into the door and looked at the three furry animals in my living room, I suddenly felt like a zookeeper. Three was way more than two. "Let's pick up the clutter and move this toy box upstairs so there's more room around here," I ordered trying to stop the feeling that the walls were closing in.

One of the first things Luis began doing in his new home was barking loudly and often. Luis clearly had no affection for men and mine is a male dominated household. We have eight boys (six still at home) and two girls. The two little boys were fine, but the older ones were teens, so Luis found them manly enough not to like. (You probably have noted that the crazy dog lady also has four teenagers.) Our house not only felt smaller, but noisier.

We put Luis in his indoor kennel that evening. He barked and howled all night. As I lay awake listening to the mournful howls, which pierced through my bedroom door, earplugs and the hum of a fan, I had time to think. What had I done? I prayed about the situation-- finally.

But what was I praying for? For God to vaporize Luis? For a time machine to go back and conduct myself appropriately? I prayed for God's will to be done, whatever that was concerning Luis.

By the next morning, Saturday, I confessed everything to Mark. He did not like the dog. The kids cried. Luis would stop howling at night and barking so much once he settled in, I reasoned. Mark had errands and I had a meeting to go to. I stopped at church and prayed before the tabernacle: *"Your will be done, Lord."*

Back at home, Mark said we could keep the dog. The kids were ecstatic. I was not sure what I thought anymore. Day after day, the kids played with and loved the dog. Night after night he howled. He was not warming up to the boys. Things always seem worse at night, and that is when remorse overwhelmed me.

"Why had I been so stupid?" I asked myself listening to the howls. "I had been greedy to grab a dog I thought everyone else would want. I had been inconsiderate to my husband. I had neglected to pray first and now I was paying."

After several nights, I let Louis sleep with the girls. This made him happy and quiet at least at night. Then, the beginning of the end appeared under our dining room table. That's where he pooped. Years of diapers are one thing but loose poop in the house is another. My daughters' excused it stating he was probably whimpering to go out but they had not paid attention. Then, the next day, it happened again. It was then that I knew what I had to do--repent of my sin and return the dog.

I emailed the dog's owners late Saturday evening (minutes after finding poop Number Two) and explained the dog was not working out. Sunday morning, (we had gone to Mass Saturday evening) I took six of the kids fishing. Mark stayed home with two of the teenagers and slept in. I had to bring Luis with us so he would not howl and wake them up or poop in the house. It was this fishing trip that insured that the kids would not miss Luis. We tied him up very close to us, so he could see us fish.

But Luis howled and barked because he wanted to be with us among the poles, hooks and tackle. He made a nuisance of himself all morning. By the time we returned home, Luis's owner had called to say he would come by and take him back. My kids realized he would ruin our lives if he stayed. They were suddenly happy to see him go.

His original family had missed him and thought that maybe frequent baths could help alleviate any contribution he was making to their allergies. I apologized for the inconvenience I had caused. Then, when they drove away, I felt like doing cartwheels through the house. The mistake born of my temporary insanity was gone! The burden had lifted! Mark shared with me that he knew if he sent the dog away; the kids would think he was the bad guy. Yet, he did not want the dog. It seemed a no-win situation so he put it to prayer. Mark trusted that God would handle it.

Not working in union with God and my spouse had proved disastrous. God can use all things for good and I think this whole incident served as an example to my kids. They saw what happens when one acts alone without God's guidance and the difference when one puts a situation to prayer and trusts God to work it out. It's no fun serving as the bad example so I will try to avoid that role in the future. I am confident we have seen the last of the crazy dog lady.

Patti Maguire Armstrong

FROGS AND CIRCUITRY IN SCIENCE CLASS

I am listening from my office to the two ten-year-olds—Logan, my grandson, and Antonio, his friend, also homeschooled—as they are having a science class about electricity with my husband Dan. The boys are watching Dan fiddle with wires and switches and little light bulbs as he is setting up to show them the difference between a parallel circuit and a series circuit (don't ask me!) when I hear Antonio inquire of Logan as though it was the most ordinary thing in the world: "How many frogs can you carry in your underwear?"

Logan: "I don't know."

Antonio: "I can carry seven."

Me: (curiosity piqued): "When you carry the frogs in your underwear, are you wearing them or not?"

Antonio: "I'm not wearing them."

Me: "What does your mother think of this?"

Antonio: "She says I just have to get them out before my underwear goes in the wash..."

I understand. She has seven kids—fazed by nothing at this point.

Ya' know, ya' can't make this stuff up.

Mary Kochan

ABSOLUTION, DIAPERS AND CARRYING ON

Confession is the place I 'let it all hang out'. I just give it all to God during the sacrament of Penance. I figure He can handle it.

During one personal crisis in my life I went to confession for absolution of sins but also for some advice and guidance. Fortunately I was blessed to have a very compassionate confessor on this particular Sunday. When I had entered the confessional I felt chaos and confusion. Father was kind and listening. His understanding, compassion, advice and absolution really touched me deeply that day. The chaos and confusion melted as I felt peace and forgiveness flood my soul. It was so healing.

I am very emotional. When I feel something deeply I cry. And that day the tears came, and came. I was crying so hard I couldn't stop. I reached into my pockets looking for a Kleenex, piece of toilet paper...*anything* to blow my nose on and dry my eyes. And what did I find, rummaging through my purse, as I was baring my soul, crying my eyes out, wanting to clean up a bit? I found a disposable diaper, just a cute little red Elmo disposable diaper. I could almost hear his voice. The diaper was clean, yes, but still it was just a diaper in my greatest nasal need. Since I had no choice I wiped my eyes, and blew my nose with a honk. There I was in the confessional, bawling my eyes out, and.... blowing my nose and wiping my eyes in a Sesame Street diaper.

And as I sat there doing this, the irony hit me. I was receiving the greatest gift of God's forgiveness with a diaper meant for a baby's rear end smack in my face. It was humbling, and a little bit funny. We mothers eat a lot of humble pie, as they say. We make do. We improvise. We move on, despite moments of humility. And often, like experiencing the Sacrament of Confession, these doses of humility, making-do and improvisation make us stronger.

After confession and the burden of sin is lifted from my soul, I feel I have God's grace and strength to carry on and bear the crosses that I have been given. It's beautiful. One of the greatest things I have learned in my Catholic faith is to give it all to God in Confession. And a lesser thing I have learned, but still will never forget is that when I go to Confession it is always a good idea to keep a pack of Kleenex in my purse.

Karen Kuplack

Karen and her husband Chris are raising their large family in Texas. The family is involved extensively with Civil Air Patrol, Odyssey of the Mind, dance and horseback riding. Karen enjoys quilting and other crafts.

HUSBAND'S COMMENTS TO THEIR HOMESCHOOLING WIVES

Upon walking through the door after work and seeing an erupting volcano on the kitchen cupboard, a husband:

Might be tempted to say: "Well, *that* doesn't look like dinner."

Better choice: "Wow, volcanoes. Cool. Hey, can I *help* with dinner?"

> **Best choice of all:** "Awesome project, guys! Your mom really outdid herself on this one. Let's go to the library and get a video on volcanoes, then let's *go out* for dinner!"

Upon stepping over Legos in the shape of DNA a husband:

> **Might be tempted to say:** "Gee, the house is a mess."

> **Better choice:** "Wow. DNA. Can *I help you* put the Lego molecules back in the box and pick up?"

> **Best choice of all:** (Turning to wife) "You think of the *best* projects for these kids and I'm sure you could use some cleaning help. Let's get a weekly cleaning service so you can concentrate on the kids' education!"

A husband's and wife's eyes meet after a long day. A husband:

> **Might be tempted to say:** "You know you'd look so pretty with a little make-up."

> **Better choice:** (Handing his wife a tube of rose colored lipstick) "I saw this shade in the drugstore today and it reminded me of you."

> **Best choice of all:** "I love seeing your face in the candlelight. Let's go out for dinner."

A husband is quizzing their child on the state capitals. The husband:

> **Might be tempted to say:** "Honey, he missed one! He missed 'Delaware!'"

> **Better choice:** (Turning to child): "You got 49 out of 50! Good job. We won't tell Mom we missed Delaware."

> **Best choice of all:** "Delaware Schmelaware. Who cares? It's a small state...Let's take Mom out for dinner!"

On Saturday morning a husband:

> **Might be tempted to say:** (Rushing out the door) "My tee time's at 8. I'll see you this afternoon!"

Better choice: "Okay." (Sigh) "Where's the list?"

Best choice of all: "Honey, I'm going to clean out the garage, mow the lawn and take care of the miscellaneous fix-it projects you suggested, and I'll keep the little ones with me. Why don't you go work on your lesson plans...or better yet, just relax...."

Looking at a computer-generated library print-out left on the cupboard, a husband:

Might be tempted to say: "*32 books!?* How can you have fines on *32 books?* Who even reads *32 books?!*"

Better choice: "Well at least the kids are learning something."

Best choice of all: "You actually saved us money! Do you know how much it would cost to *BUY 32 books!?* I'm so glad the kids are reading so much. You're a great teacher. Let's go out for dinner!"

At 10 P.M. a husband:

Might be tempted to say: "Goodnight."

Better choice: "Wow, you're so diligent, staying up to go over the kid's worksheets. Atta girl! I'll make some popcorn."

Best choice of all: "Scoot over. I'll help you grade."

Sunday morning, before Mass, a husband:

Might be tempted to say: "I'll be in the car. Bring the kids when you are ready."

Better choice: "If you want me to dress them, just show me what to put on them."

Best choice of all: "I've got the church books, and the diaper bag, and the kids are buckled up in the car. Come out whenever you're ready. We'll be waiting."

At "that time of the month" a husband:

Might be tempted to say: "Didn't you already have chocolate this morning?"

Better choice: Nothing. Absolutely nothing.

Best choice of all: "I'll get you the candy Kisses stashed behind the cookie jar, and hey, you look great in those sweatpants."

At an ordinary meal a husband:

Might be tempted to say: "Meatloaf, vegetables and a fruit cup.....again?"

Better choice: "Hmmm. A balanced, nutritious meal."

Best choice of all: "Wow, you are amazingly creative with our meals considering the modest allowance you have for groceries and the fact you have little time because you full-time home educate our offspring."

On an important day a husband

Might be tempted to say: "What anniversary?"

Better choice: "You are the love of my life and to express that I brought you roses, some wine and chocolate."

Best choice of all: "You are the love of my life and to express that I brought you roses, some wine and chocolate AND a $100 gift certificate to the Teacher's Store. Now, let's go out for dinner!"

After receiving successful standardized test results of the kids, a husband:

Might be tempted to say: "Well, I should *hope* they'd do well."

Better choice: "Good job!"

Best choice of all: (turning to wife) "With a mother like you it is clear to see that the children are going to be both beautiful and brilliant!"

Theresa A. Thomas

AND THE WINNER IS...EVERYONE!

Last week I ran a 5K race. It was the first race I had run in 20 years. It wasn't my choice to run the race. My nine-year-old daughter needed someone to run with her.

I wouldn't say that I'm out of shape but my shape is closer to the Stay Puff Marshmallow Man than Mr. Universe. There was a single reason my daughter wanted to run the race: All kids nine and under would get an award. All they had to do was participate.

When I was a kid, there were no awards simply for participating. Woody Allen once said, "Eighty percent of success in life is just showing up." In today's youth sports, it seems 100 percent of success is just showing up.

We finished the race in an unimpressive time, and I was thankful I didn't cross the finish line in the back of an ambulance. Awards for the fastest runners were given out in dozens of categories: men age 40 to 45; men age 46 to 50; men age 51 to 55...born in May...on a Tuesday...before noon.

Many awards that should have been awarded were omitted. Hundreds of parents ran with their kids, which is a little like doing the high jump while carrying three bags of groceries. My brother-in-law's time would have been faster had he not had to escort his daughter to the Port-o-John during the race. His wife had to slow down because their son had a cramp. Once the finish line was in sight, however, he flew ahead, beat his mom and proceeded to taunt her for losing.

During the children's award ceremony, I had a brilliant idea. The kids had been motivated to run for miles in return for a small, inexpensive plastic trophy. Surely our kids would be thrilled to win similar awards. If I acquired a few cases of trophies, I might be able to get our kids to participate in the activities I'd like them to do...like cleaning their rooms and sweeping the kitchen floor.

Simplicity is the ultimate sophistication.
~ Leonardo da Vinci

"Hey kids!" I'd announce. "Tonight we'll be holding the First-annual Oscar Madison Memorial Room Cleaning Marathon. All children under the age of nine will receive a stunning three-inch plastic bowling trophy for just participating!"

The kids might wonder why I was offering a bowling trophy for room cleaning. I'd have to confess that I got them cheap at an estate auction. My daughter would think it was gross to get a trophy that belonged to a dead guy with the nickname Rocko, who had a 190 average. My son would think it was cool and brag about it to his friends. But they'd both be willing to work tirelessly to earn such a distinctive award.

Which proves it isn't whether you win or lose. It's whether you get a trophy.

Tim Bete

That's very creative dear, but NO, you can't use that for Phys Ed today!

Chapter 8

PRAYERS ANSWERED

"I love the Lord because he has heard my voice in supplication, because he has inclined his ear to me the day I called." (Psalms 116:1-2)

PRAYERS FOR A NEIGHBOR

A few years ago a neighbor related a story to me that I would like to retell. He was not a close friend, nor, for that matter a close neighbor. He would fall into the "Hi, how are you?" kind of neighbor. We had chatted a number of times and I liked him well enough but we had never shared a meal or were invited to each other's gatherings. I did, however, consider him a good neighbor. We looked out for each other and were neighborly.

He had had a heart by-pass surgery one spring and I had taken a meal over to the family during his recovery. I assured him that we were praying for him. At the time, he merely nodded his thanks. But later, when we had a moment to talk, he shared a story with me. During the surgery there came a time when the doctors had basically stopped his heart and he was only being kept alive by machines. It was during that time that he had the sensation of floating over the operating table.

But then he found himself in a room. In this room were people he knew. There was his wife, his children and others. He realized he was seeing all the people who were praying for him and that their prayers were what was sustaining him; keeping him alive, as it were. As he realized what he was privy to, he said he looked into the faces of those people who loved him. Of course there was his wife, and his children and then other friends and relatives and then to his great surprise there was his neighbor. I was taken aback when I realized he meant me!

"Me? You saw me?" I asked, astounded.

"Yes," he answered. "I saw you and your children. Were you praying for me?"

"Yes we were," I said.

What took him so long to tell me about it was that he had to heal and also digest this strange occurrence. You see, most of those in the "room" praying for him was expected. They were friends. They were family. Most important they were all Mormon, like him. Everyone that is, except us. We are Catholic. This took some digesting. He realized that all our prayers are heard.

"You know," I said, "I am going to have to hug you."

"It was a risk I was willing to take," He smiled.

It impresses upon me the priceless treasure of being able to spontaneously hit my knees with my children to pray—something we could not do if we were not schooling together. So many valuable lessons they have learned, not from a book, but by simply being there when life happens. There are many times that there have been simple joys and stunning moments and fabulous days that I think to myself, "I would do all the work of homeschool for this one moment." And yet, there have been many, many such moments!

Delma Atwell

Delma and her husband, David, have of six children and four grandchildren. She has been homeschooling for thirteen years and says she finds it more fun than should be legal. In her spare time she volunteers at her church, at the Idaho Historical Museum directing a marionette theater, and at the YMCA. In her spare time she stitches and quilts. In her other spare time she sleeps.

ON THE SIXTH DAY OF CHRISTMAS

It was a gorgeous fall day as my family ascended the hill in front of the Basilica of the National Shrine of the Immaculate Conception in Washington, D.C. The October air was so crisp and full of promise; the kind of day when everything seems just right. We were preparing to lead the congregation in the Holy Rosary before the Mass celebrating the 50th anniversary of the basilica's dedication.

As we walked along my eight-year-old son leaned over to me with a sense of urgency and said, "Mom, you know what, I only want one thing for Christmas." "What is it?" I asked him, expecting to hear about the latest Lego set on the market.

"A baby brother," he answered. I paused; surprised to learn this was what he wanted most. Since he is the only boy among his four sisters, it was not an unusual request, but it was the first time he had asked in this way.

I smiled understandingly. "That would be wonderful, but your baby sister is just one-and-a-half years old and we would like to keep her as the baby for a while longer," I told him.

He was not convinced that this was a good enough reason so I added, "But you never know what God has planned. You should pray about it."

After his surprise request, it also crossed my mind that we were still trying to sell our three-bedroom townhouse, which was already getting too small for our growing family. I was constantly struggling to maintain order within the limited space that we had! Throughout the eight years that we have been homeschooling, my son has heard me say that we are always open to life but I figured it was unlikely he'd be getting his wish that Christmas.

The great Feast of the Nativity of our Lord arrived and our family rejoiced in the joyful news of our Savior humbly coming among us as a sweet baby. At that point, my menstrual cycle was late but I chalked it up to being sick and to the stress of trying to complete our homeschooling lessons while preparing for Christmas. My husband and I were happy practitioners of natural family planning since our marriage nearly fourteen years ago. When I was several days late, I bought a pregnancy test just to rule out such a possibility but was sure it was only going to be negative. I was certain that there was no way I could be pregnant--I knew the signs of my fertility too well.

Well, that son of mine, who tends to be rather distracted during family prayer time to say the least, must have put in some great effort behind the scenes because he received a miraculous answer to his prayer. On the sixth day of Christmas, I found out that I was indeed pregnant with my sixth child! I kept checking the positively pregnant result window to make sure I was reading it correctly; it seemed so impossible. I could not help but to be thrilled and excited in spite of my complete surprise. I found myself thinking about the old adage that if you want to make God laugh, tell Him your plans. He knew that the best gift for our family was another child.

Later that evening, I grabbed an oversized silver bow from one of the Christmas presents and taped it to my tummy. I walked over to my husband and smiled. He glanced at the bow and asked, "What's that?" I continued to smile and then he asked if I was kidding when he realized what the bow signified. He was absolutely thrilled. I was so grateful for his enthusiasm and his great trust in God's providence.

The next morning we shared the good news with our five children and they were so elated and excited that Mommy had a baby in her tummy. Amidst tears and shouts of joy, they all agreed it was the best Christmas gift and unanimously said that they hoped it would be a baby boy.

I suspected that I was pregnant with a boy once my first trimester unfolded because I was so severely sick and nauseous, which was unusual for me. We all counted down the days until my sonogram, hoping that we would be able to find out the sex of the baby.

The big day finally arrived. After patiently waiting for all of the baby's measurements to be taken, my husband and children were invited into the ultrasound room. The technician asked each of the children what they thought Mommy was having and they each confidently answered in turn, "It's a boy!"

So when she slowly announced, "It's a (pause) boy!" the shouts of excitement arose into the air like a beautiful blast of fireworks. I think everyone in the waiting area must have heard the cheering.

The children responded with many sentiments.

"I can't believe it!"

"This is awesome!"

"Wow!"

While my husband exclaimed a drawn out "Yeeesss!"

What a blessing to have all found out together what we knew in our hearts: that God does hear and answer our prayers. We were so grateful to behold our beautiful baby boy on the ultrasound screen and the precious and priceless smiles of his siblings who were just beaming with pure love and joy.

Deborah Lynn (Corno) Porfiri

Deborah earned a B.S. degree in journalism and English from West Virginia University and studied on scholarship at the John Cabot University in Rome, Italy. She co-chairs the pro-life committee at Sacred Heart Church in Bowie, Md.. She tries daily to do small things with great love, as Blessed Mother Teresa so beautifully taught.

OUT OF A FOG

I was depressed and struggling. Even with medication I felt that I was seeing everything through a fog. Sometimes if that fog lifted for just a teeny tiny second, I still felt there was a huge brick wall around my brain that I couldn't see past. What was wrong with me? Why couldn't I simply snap out of it?

Simple things like preparing a meal or reading to my children as I homeschooled them exhausted me. I was only half-listening to conversations of others. My husband would talk to me and I reacted like a zombie. I felt more like an observer than a participant in life. I was so tired of the foggy feeling in my brain that I was almost claustrophobic of it. I could hardly remember what life had been like before this depression.

One night, I was lying in bed, so frustrated and depressed; at a real low point. I wanted to enjoy life, be optimistic, and have fun with my husband and children. I cried and then I thought, "Why not take this to Jesus?" Just like that I suddenly thought to beg Him for help. *Please, Lord, please, help me!* I begged with my whole heart and soul.

I closed my eyes and immediately I began to feel a peace run through my entire body. Every muscle just started to relax. Then I saw Jesus in my mind--kind of like the Divine Mercy picture, with the rays coming from His heart, but He had a white cloak or cape on too. As I watched, He opened the cape and the fog surrounding me just was taken up in to that cape and dissipated. And that was that. The foggy feeling was gone. I lay in my bed completely relaxed and at peace, and then I fell asleep. I slept longer than I had in a long time. The next morning I woke up refreshed and new.

This was a couple of years ago, and only once did I even begin to feel that foggy feeling start again. When I recalled that image of Jesus and how He took that fog from my head, the feeling went away faster than it started.

I have never had that feeling since. I am able to enjoy life like never before. My children make me laugh, I enjoy conversations with my husband and I even enjoy activities like scrapbooking and crocheting now. I still have moments of being down and I am still on the lowest dose of antidepressants, but I feel so much better and soon, I believe, I will be off them for good. I am again living life, and I am eternally grateful to Jesus for coming to me in my need the moment I asked.

Pam Milos

Pam lives in Saskatchewan Canada with her husband John and their five children, Eric, 21, Becky, 19, and Brett, 16, Evan 3 and Easton 1. When Pam is not homeschooling or chauffeuring children she enjoys scrapbooking, crocheting, making cards and quilting.

THE OTHER SIDE OF THE RAINBOW

When I first became a mother I also agreed to provide for the family while my husband finished college. My strategy included spending time with my needy infant when I arrived home and spending time with my husband when the baby slept.

I didn't take into account how tired I may feel after a long day or the added daily responsibilities of running a household. But most of all I never imagined the pain in my heart from walking out the door and leaving my little one behind morning after morning. One day I missed being "Mom" so much that I ventured for a sit-down lunch at a restaurant instead of grabbing a hamburger and fries, deciding to write my feelings in my journal. I imagined the sorrowful words filling the page to get them off my mind.

Unexpectedly when I began writing I addressed my thoughts to God. I spilled my emotions completely to Him asking for help. I wrote without stopping while trying to eat with my other hand. The time went so quickly. Soon I was walking back towards my car.

I knew nothing had changed. I still missed my son. "How am I going make it through this?" I said aloud. Then I looked up and saw a brilliant rainbow in front of a gray cloud backdrop. It was then I knew God would take care of me. It was as if He was saying, *I'll make sure you're okay. Remember my promise.*

Several years later, three more children huddled on the couch reading of a promise to Noah. God told him to build an Ark, put two of each animal on board, close the door, and trust Me. Noah patiently waited for God's will.

I stopped, tears of joy in my eyes, as I recalled my desire so many years before to be a stay-at-home mom. When my oldest turned five God fulfilled His promise to me, I quit my job and fulfilled my responsibilities of wife, mother, and teacher.

I turned back to the Bible excited to finish the story. The rains poured down for 40 days and 40 nights. Noah and his family remained safe inside the ark.

In God's time they walked safely onto dry land. *And God said, "This is the sign of the covenant which I make between me and you and every living creature that is with you, for all future generations: I set my bow in the cloud, and it shall be a sign of the covenant between me and the earth."* [RSV Gn 9:12-13]. There in the sky the promise appeared—the rainbow!

The children asked, "Why are there so many colors in the rainbow?" and "When do rainbows appear?" I decided we needed to delve into the specifics of a rainbow. I wanted to add some hands-on activities while explaining.

We started with the question of colors. A rainbow shows all the colors contained in white light—red, orange, yellow, green, blue, indigo, and violet. I taught them the acronym I learned in school to help remember the order, Roy G. Biv. Each letter represents the color.

Telling the children that all the colors together make white light sounded a bit confusing. We tackled this mystery by studying Isaac Newton's experiment in 1665.

One bright sunny day, Newton darkened his room and made a hole in his window shutter, allowing just one beam of sunlight to enter the room. He then took a glass prism and placed it in the sunbeam. The result was a spectacular multicolored band of light just like a rainbow.

Newton believed that all the colors he saw were in the sunlight shining into his room. He thought he then should be able to combine the colors of the spectrum and make the light white again. To test this, he placed another prism upside-down in front of the first prism. He was right. The band of colors combined again into white sunlight.

We took a paper circle, divided it into seven equal pieces and colored each piece one color of the rainbow. I attached the circle to a drill having the children stand a safe distance directly in front of it. When the circle spun the colors appeared white. My son, Michael's "Wow, cool!" told me it worked.

"Can we make our own rainbow?" my daughter, Nicole asked.

"Sure," I said. We filled a clear jar with water and set it on a windowsill with bright light shining through the window. The rainbow appeared on the floor below the window. We placed a large piece of white paper on the floor, traced and colored it. With delight the children matched the order of colors to the Roy G. Biv formula.

Now we came to the question of, when do rainbows appear? My son, Paul immediately responded with, "When it rains."

"Exactly," I said then gave them this information. When light and water meet in the sky on a summer's day, for a few moments, a rainbow will appear. What a spectacular display of colors! This happens during or immediately following a rain shower, when the sun is shining and the air contains raindrops.

We learned two people do not see the same rainbow because they cannot be in the same place. Since raindrops are constantly in motion the rainbow's appearance constantly changes.

After all the discussions about light, colors, wavelengths, and rainbows we sat down with colored pencils and paper. Everyone drew their version of the rainbow. Several colorful creations resulted including mountains, grasslands, and even a pot of gold. While looking at each other's works of art we remembered God's covenant to Noah using the rainbow as a sign.

A few months after our rainbow study, my fifth child, Heather Marie, was born on the Feast of the Immaculate Conception. At a month old she became seriously ill. I stayed at the hospital with her as oxygen sustained each breath. My other children remained home waiting for the few hours I would spend with them daily.

On the fourth day I was exhausted and tired. I felt alone and drained of any life within me. I didn't think I would make it through another day of watching health professionals poke and prod at my six-pound infant. I didn't know how I could give four tear streaked faces another kiss good-bye to drive back to the hospital.

It was time to go—again. I shut the car door, turned the ignition and allowed the tears to fall over my eyelids and down my cheeks. On the quiet, lonely two-lane road back to the hospital I lifted my head slightly to see in the distance ahead of me. I stared motionless into the sky. A beautiful rainbow beamed through my windshield leading me to my destination.

At that moment I knew I was going to be okay. Somehow I also knew my baby would be too. God not only sent His promise to Noah. He sent it to me too.

Lynanne Lasota

Lynanne Lasota, blessed since 1985 with her husband and five homeschooled children, writes from Queen Creek, AZ. She has contributed to local and national publications including Catechist, Religion Teacher's Journal, Scouting, Catholic Digest, Faith & Family, and National Catholic Register.

GOD REACHED THROUGH THE INTERNET AND FOUND ME

Last fall my son turned five, and I faced the time that I have been dreading since his birth--the time to send him to pre-school. He has always been home with me, and I loved the time we spent together. I loved reading to him, taking walks with him, baking with him, and answering all his questions about life and the universe. When he looked up at me with inquisitive eyes and wondered aloud about the spiders making its web on our windowsill or the birds which gathered near the pond in our yard I felt my life had meaning and purpose, and my vocation of motherhood was complete.

Then it was time for school. Right when he seemed to be the most fun, the most interesting, the most interested, I was going to have to send him away for the better part of the day to share these experiences with someone else. I felt miserable about the thought.

For various personal reasons I knew that I couldn't send him to a public preschool. I also knew that private preschool was simply not economically feasible. Besides, the one near us was not Catholic, and I wanted him to receive a solid Catholic education. I spent weeks agonizing over the decision.

Meanwhile, my son was having mixed feelings about going off to school. On the one hand he was getting very excited. He was imagining all the new friends he would make and all of the adventures he would be a part of. He was also apprehensive. The idea of leaving Mom and his little sister was really hard for him. All of this left me terribly conflicted.

One morning, I turned on my computer as I always did to check my email. I had been worrying about school more than usual that day, and suddenly I just felt compelled to search for Catholic websites. At the time, I did not know what was prompting me to do this, but I now know that it was the Holy Spirit showing me the way. In fact, it was almost as though I was not in control of the situation at all. One website lead to another, and with the click-click of the mouse, without really trying at all, I wound up finding all sorts of information about Catholic homeschooling. I was intrigued. The idea of Catholic homeschooling seemed to fill all of our needs--a relaxed learning environment, me being able to be with my son all day, going at my child's pace, the ability to put as much "Catholic-ness" into the curriculum as I wanted, *and* it was all within our budget. It was one of those moments in time where I felt the presence of God *right there*. He was holding my hand, guiding me to the exact information I needed and never could have found on my own since I didn't even know about the information. Click. Click. Click. Again and again I found page after page that addressed every concern and every need of mine about educating my child at home. It was uncanny how I'd think of a worry and that exact worry would be calmed by the very next page I clicked on.

Suddenly, intuitively, I *knew* I had to homeschool my son. It is difficult to convey how strongly I felt God's presence through the Internet. It was if He were standing there physically directing my computer. I still get a thrill each time I think about that morning. What's even more amazing is that never have I made a decision so impulsively before. I usually analyze everything (some say way too much), so for me to make this sudden decision was completely out of character for me. It was as though God reached right through my computer to what I needed most. I know it was Him because I was overcome with the most beautiful feeling of peace that I still cherish to this day.

While I immediately was very excited about homeschooling, I still needed to discuss this with my husband and son. Later that day, my husband agreed to my homeschooling plan. He knew that I was capable of teaching and managing my son's needs. He was confident in my ability to teach because I had an educational background. We agreed to take it one year at a time.

I knew the real test would come when I asked my son what he thought of the idea. Since he was so excited about going to school, I was truly surprised when he said that he would love to be taught at home. We discussed how this would be very different than going to a school building and that some of the things he was looking forward to wouldn't be the same at home. This did not sway his approval of the idea. His response was immediate and filled with joy. Then he said the words that not only made me cry, but set us solidly on the path to homeschooling: "Mom, you would be the *best* teacher." That was it. We started homeschooling preschool last fall.

That simple morning on the Internet changed my life completely. Since passing on the Faith to my son is now my full responsibility I take very seriously my job in that regard. I have grown tremendously in my faith since that day. I guess you could say it had a "bolt of lightning" effect on me.

I started out by designing my own curriculum and added children's bible stories and Catholic prayers to round out the basic subjects. Even my younger daughter joined in every day. When our schedule just didn't seem to be working, we changed it to better accommodate my children's needs. I was blessed to be able to watch an amazing change in my son in just one year. He went from a timid child who needed constant reassurance and attention to an independent young boy who wanted to do his work all on his own. I attribute this all to God's grace.

Very soon we'll start our second year of homeschooling. My son will be a kindergartener and my daughter will be at the nursery level. This year, we enrolled both of our little ones in a Catholic homeschooling program. My children beg me to begin their lessons. My confidence is growing, and knowing that I get to spend my days with my children is a gift from God. As a family, we have grown in our faith, and we have seen our children's love for the Lord and our Blessed Mother blossom.

We named our homeschool *Emmanuel Academy*. Emmanuel means 'God is with us', and He certainly is, just as He certainly was on the day He almost palpably reached through my computer and showed me directly and surely His will for us-- homeschooling. How perfect!

Kristen Trepanier-Henry

Kristin graduated from Smith College in Northampton, MA with a BA in Psychology and Education. She later received her Master's in Social Work from the Smith College School for Social Work. She is a full-time mom who lives with her husband Charles and two children, Noah, age 9 and Isabella, age 7 in Florida. They have homeschooled from the start.

HELP!
MY DAUGHTER WANTS TO GO TO SCHOOL!

For the past several months, my heart has been in turmoil: my daughter wants to go to school. Last year, she talked about going to school several times, but with school already in session, it wasn't even remotely possible. However, no sooner had we finished last year's schoolwork, than Sarah asked if she could go to school in fall.

"Why do you want to attend school?" I asked her.

"Because Alexa is there, and I want to go to school with her. I want to see what school is like. I'd like to have different teachers," Sarah said. "And I'd like to get some awards and trophies like Alexa." Sarah was envious of her friend's academic awards.

So, we talked about envy.

"But it's not just that, Mom," Sarah explained. "I want to study and learn and see if I can be as smart as Alexa. When I'm at home, it's just me."

So, my husband and I started talking about school. We had homeschooled Sarah since she was five and we vaguely planned to homeschool "as long as it worked."

Now, Sarah wanted to attend school. And we had to determine if her desire was one we should act on or not.

Part of me could completely understand Sarah's interest in school. She is a mature girl, ready to face the world, and what better place to start than the comfortable family of the small local Catholic School?

There was one problem, though. Sarah had just completed sixth grade work at home, but was the age to enter sixth in the fall. Should I put her in seventh grade? Her girlfriend was entering the seventh grade, and Sarah assumed she would go into seventh. I wondered how I could decide whether Sarah should go to school or not when I couldn't even figure out what grade she should go in.

Another thing was that Sarah was bright and quick. I didn't think she would enjoy all the waiting and explanations of things she already understood. I thought it would take her a year to adjust to school; my husband thought it would take two weeks.

"Maybe after two weeks she'll hate it and want to come home," I told my husband. "She doesn't know how slow it goes, and how you have to wait for the teacher to explain things to the students who don't get it. She learns fast. When she finds it boring, then what will we do? I'll want her home, but I don't feel two weeks will be giving it a fair shake. Besides there's the tuition factor, and what will the school think if we pull her out after only a short time?"

"Maybe we could find a gifted school for Sarah," my husband wondered.

"I checked into them. There are only two near us, one cost $12,000 and has a waiting list, and would take 45 minutes to drive to, the other cost $13,000 and would take an hour to drive to," I said.

"O.K. St. Peter is $2,500, which suddenly seems inexpensive. Let's send her to St. Peter, and make her stay till Christmas," Mike said. "That way she'll get a good idea of what school is like." But still I just wasn't sure.

We had another concern too. We would dearly miss her presence in our family each day if she were to go to school. Though her need seemed to be to broaden her horizons and move out into the world, our family needed her, as well.

As I began to see that this question about school was going to take some consideration and time, I began to pray. Was it best for Sarah to go to school this coming year? I prayed and asked God to guide me to the right answer. I asked the Holy Spirit to inspire me with the right questions to ask, the right books or websites to consult. Then, I called the school to make an appointment to meet with the principal. She sent me some papers and said to call her in a month.

This delay proved to be providential. We had time to think more, pray more and gain some additional information. I started a page of questions to ask other school parents and the principal. Then I called two school mothers I knew. I asked them their opinion of the school and how they felt it was run. This helped tremendously. The two mothers gave me both positive and negative things to think about. As the summer progressed, Sarah still asked about school, and continued to state she was looking forward to trying it. I told her that her dad and I were praying and thinking it over.

On the advice of a gifted program teacher, we decided to arrange privately for Sarah to be tested. The teacher explained that teachers deal with hard data. If Sarah entered school and I told them she was gifted, they would want some test results. I made an appointment with a professional. I thought I'd ask the psychologist her opinion about the sixth vs. seventh grade issue, and what advice she could give me about transitioning Sarah into the school environment.

Just before the testing, I was visiting with a friend who suggested praying to Saint Padre Pio, to whom she has a great devotion. I immediately began asking Padre Pio for help in knowing what to do for Sarah.

A most productive teacher in-service day

Life of a homeschooling mother....

At the psychologist's office, I found out Sarah is indeed gifted. The psychologist told me privately that she often saw gifted children who were bored with school. Her recommendation to those parents was to homeschool!

The psychologist's opinion about Sarah's grade level was that there was no doubt Sarah should not go into sixth grade. She already knew that information, and if she entered sixth simply for "social" and "adjustment" reasons, she would be very bored with the academics. The psychologist further told me that with Sarah's quick brain, she would need a gifted 7th grade program. Our local Catholic grade school has no gifted classroom or program, I told the psychologist. The two schools we knew of were out of our price and driving range. "Then I recommend you keep her home, you're doing a terrific job with her!" she said, to my amazement. "When she gets to high school, they'll have advanced classes she can take. Homeschool her until then."

On the way home, I kept smiling to myself. *"I'm doing a terrific job!"* I thought, over and over. Once home, I told my husband everything the psychologist had told me. At that moment, my husband relaxed. "We should keep homeschooling her, then. That's what's best for Sarah."

It was very difficult to meet the principal with our minds made up to homeschool. The principal gave us the tour and highlighted the positive aspects of the school. I knew that Sarah could survive there, and even do well there. It just was a matter of what was best.

When we returned home, Mike and I holed up in our bedroom for a long talk. We discussed school, the pros and the cons. We talked about the fact that we'd never really thought about the point where we would put Sarah in school. We discussed and reviewed the psychologists report. We talked about our daughter and what we thought was best for her. We prayed. Then we decided that the best thing would be to continue to homeschool Sarah.

I said a prayer of thanks to the Holy Spirit and to St. Padre Pio, and then I began to worry about Sarah's reaction to our decision. She had been operating all summer on the assumption that she would go to school in the fall.

After we let our decision rest for a day, and we allowed the Holy Spirit to fill us with a sense of calm and reassurance that we were making the best decision, we called Sarah to us, and told her our decision.

"Really?" she said, "and I was so sure you would say yes. Oh well, this way I can still go to chess club." (A homeschool group activity in which she regularly participates) And then, after we told her all the reasons why we decided, she skipped off to work on the computer.

"Well," Mike said in amazement. "Now I wonder how much she really wanted to go to school."

"Did I agonize all summer for nothing?" I asked.

"No, it was really good we went through this," Mike said. "Now we know just where she is academically and intellectually. And we know that our local Catholic school is not an option for us, now or in the future." (We had found out some things we didn't like about the school.)

"And perhaps," he said, "we'll send her to the local Catholic high school in three years, when she's at the right age to enter ninth grade."

"Or, we'll keep homeschooling her, if that's what's best," I added.

"Yes," he said. "We'll just keep trying to do what's best."

Nancy Carpentier Brown

Nancy is wife to Michael and mother of two daughters. Her homeschooling journey began with preschool, and she continues today with high school at home. Nancy writes for Gilbert Magazine and creates the podcast Uncommon Sense for the American Chesterton Society.
http://uncommonsense.libsyn.com/

MUSIC TO MY EARS

Ecclesiastes 11:5 Just as you know not how the breath of life fashions the human frame in the mother's womb, so you know not the work of God which he is accomplishing in the universe.

The Lord works intimately and continuously in our lives. I know this intellectually, but there are times when His nearness seems hidden. Times of sorrow or confusion can bring a feeling of being separated from God's sight.

I was experiencing one of these dark times in my life. A deep burden of sorrow had engulfed my spirit. I knew the Lord was with me. However, I was confused because he did not appear to be removing the cause of my burden. For several days I went about my daily chores in a distracted and hollow way. I was praying and asking to see God's power in my situation yet he remained (what seemed to me) silent.

My husband decided that a change of scenery would be beneficial to my mood. He suggested a late supper at a nearby restaurant. It was Sunday evening and the restaurant was nearly empty. Besides a few scattered diners, there was a party of eight to ten people. It was obvious that they had just come from church services as we overheard their conversation.

At their table, a man sat with three young boys. By the way they acted toward one another it was easy to guess that they were his sons. As we sat nearby, slowly eating and absentmindedly watching his happy group of people, I prayed within my spirit. "Dear Lord, please lift this cloud. Help me to see your work in this burden you have asked me to carry."

No sooner had this prayer left my heart, than several waitresses came near the church party's table. "Please sing it for all of us," they asked. Without hesitation, the young man and his three sons stood up and began singing a beautiful a cappella harmony. I cannot remember all the words because the first verse was so powerful, that it was all I heard: "*The God of the Mountain is also the God of the Valley.*" At that moment, I didn't just hear a song being sung. I heard Jesus directly speaking to me! I do not believe in coincidence, only 'God-incidence."

The Lord told me in that instant that he was with me in that valley. He remains all powerful, all knowing, and ever merciful. I was comforted by this sign of God's faithfulness. I am certain that praying always, especially when it seems to be unheard, brings grace beyond measure. With that grace fortifying our spirit we are able to see what we may have otherwise missed. Just like Elijah, we will hear God in the whisper of the breeze.

That night, the Lord did not remove the source of my sorrow but He helped me readjust my burden making it easier to carry. The Lord told me, miracles can happen in the valley because I am here. My spirit was refreshed and my hope renewed. Praise God!

Rita Munn

Ronald and Rita Munn were married in 1973. They have ten children and two grandchildren. The Munns began homeschooling in 1996. She is the author of A Family Journal, *published by Catholic Heritage Curricula.*

SURRENDER AND A KISS

I was a thirty-one-year-old single, and I felt the deepest longing to live out a vocation...as a wife and mother. Over the years my prayers had gradually moved from "Thy will be done" to a desperate, "Oh, please let *marriage* be Your will, Lord!" Finally, at thirty-one, Jesus gave me the grace to surrender all. Although I can't say I was particularly happy about it, I could, at last, truthfully say with resignation, "I accept Your will for my life, O God, even if it means being single for the rest of my life.

Ever since I was a very little girl, my desire, and my plan, was to be like my mother—to fall in love, marry young and be a mom to as many blessings as God would send. Being second oldest of a large, loving family with thirteen children gave me countless opportunities to care for and enjoy little ones. It fanned the flames of my desire to one day love and to nurture a family of my own. For many years I never considered that God might have a different plan for me.

Since I didn't date in high school, it was sometime in my late teens or early twenties when I decided I wanted to preserve even that smallest but most significant token of affection—my first kiss—for that person to whom I would eventually give all my kisses, indeed, my whole self. But when my college and graduate school years passed without meeting the right man, the thought started creeping in, "What if the answer is no? No spouse for you!" I tried to think of myself in a religious vocation, but it was always with a sense of despair.

Immediately after my conscious resignation to God's will, I immersed myself in my job as director of our local Catholic Charities Agency. I strove to make our little agency an image of Christ to others. I also volunteered at pregnancy help centers and my local parish, tutored and helped to care for siblings, babysat for nieces and nephews, and told myself that this must be my vocation. But that longing to love and be loved by someone special was left unfilled until I finally, at age 31, surrendered all to God.

It was not much more than a month after I finally completely submitted myself to God's will that I met Mike. He came into my life abruptly, encouraged by my future sister-in-law to call me. She knew my sister, and had seen me at church; from only that, she thought we should meet. I was totally out of my element accepting a blind date over the phone, but Mike's voice was warm and inviting. The connection through family made things more natural. Our first date was attending the local jazz festival which Mike was promoting as a graphic designer. The surroundings were musical and romantic. The date went easy and the night flew by quickly.

Before I knew it Mike was asking me out again.

Our relationship endured an early "bump" as we discovered that we had different ideas about approaches to dating. Mike dated quite a bit in high school and college and had a conventional view of going out. I viewed our relationship as more of what I would call a "courtship"—I wanted friendship first, then we'd see if it would blossom into romance. Mike understandably took my "friendship first" as "not interested" and it took us several months to figure out that we really both wanted the same thing.

Normally quite steady and calculated, I found myself happily in a whirlwind courtship, which was easy, and at the same time deep and profound. Mike and I talked about everything. Although we had attended the same high school, we ran around with different crowds. He went to Notre Dame and I graduated from Saint Mary's, a small Catholic women's college just across the street from the University. We should have run into each other a number of times, but we had not. Perhaps God was waiting for that perfect timing.

Through our late night talks, Mike and I discovered that we shared similar worldviews, were raised in families that had similar value systems including a strong Catholic faith. I was shocked to discover all our similarities and that he had literally been 'in my own backyard' all this time.

Within a very short time, Mike and I were engaged. And, the following fall, on an afternoon when the entire world around us was bathed in a beautiful white blanket of the season's first snow, Mike and I exchanged our vows and became one as husband and wife. Our promise was sealed with the traditional kiss. As I grasped Mike's hand during the recessional, I realized how special it was for me to have given and received my first kiss with the one with whom I'd spend the rest of my life. What a gift!

It isn't often that now, almost eleven years and many kisses later, as I am eight months pregnant with our sixth child, that I can find the time to stop and contemplate God's guiding hand and the lessons learned by following His path in meeting, courting and in marrying my husband. It is funny to me as I sit at the kitchen table, homeschooling our four oldest children while our two-year-old plays on the floor, that I once feared that my life would be incomplete. Truly, there is no greater joy in this world for me than to be the wife of my incredible, holy husband and to provide for the daily formation of my children's minds, hearts and souls in our little domestic Church. It is the gift tenfold that I never imagined back when I was hounding Heaven for a vocation. He took us down a beautiful path for our intimate involvement in shaping our children's spiritual, academic, character and social formation.

On our bathroom mirror, I have the following scripture passage scribbled on a post-it note. It was put there during a time when our family was carrying some heavy crosses, but it applies equally to the unforeseen graces, gifts and blessings God showers us with each day and very much applies to my life's path. My post-it reads:

O the depth of the riches and wisdom and knowledge of God! How unsearchable are His judgments and how inscrutable His ways! For who has known the mind of the Lord, or who has been His counselor? Or who has given a gift to Him that he might be repaid? For from Him and through Him and to Him are all things. To Him be glory forever. Amen.
Romans 11:33-36

Cheryl Murphy

Cheryl and her husband Mike are enjoying life to the full in raising and homeschooling their six children: Bonita, Jack, Jeff, Regina, Thomas, and Cecilia in the beautiful Midwest. They also thank God for their other two little ones, who are already with Him in heaven

THE START OF A FAMILY

When I was first married nearly ten years ago, I dreamed of nothing more for my life than motherhood. I wanted ten children. For a vibrant, youthful twenty-three year old who had only taken the first steps on her marital path, I recall how rare it was at that time for young women my age to desire a large family. I was not, however, surrounded by common modern women whose idea of fulfillment was a successful career and one or two children down-the-road.

I was blessed with friends and family who not only admired the bountiful home, but pursued it with every bit of grace given them. And their families were indeed beautiful. That beauty multiplied for each family as their fruits multiplied. This was where the combination of being Catholic and barren began to weigh more heavily on me. I celebrated the births of first babies and second babies and third babies, and though I was happy for each and every one of those miracles, I couldn't help but feel very alone, isolated from my closest friends and abandoned by Divine Providence. Why is she expecting her sixth child while I stand here with none? Couldn't I have one baby? Just one, Lord, that's all I'm asking! Even Holy Scripture shows the heart of the barren woman through Sarah, Hannah, and Rachel.

And Rachel, seeing herself without children, envied her sister, and said to her husband: Give me children, otherwise I shall die. (Gen. 30:1)

Two years into our marriage my husband Patrick and I began seeing infertility specialists. We then spent the following two years enduring much testing and a long list of treatments. I was willing to do anything within Church approval to attain that end.

As a young Catholic wife without children, the company of friends was often a heavy burden. It seemed to me that every friendly gathering involved the common young-mother discussions of breast-feeding, birth stories, and slings vs. baby carriers. Through those years I attended and hosted many baby showers for friends. These get-togethers were agonizing because I was stretched in opposed directions, the right hand towards happiness and rejoicing for a friend, the left towards pain and agony for myself.

Soon it had been six years that my husband and I had been trying to conceive. We began to walk the path of adoption. After the paperwork had been carefully filled out and the interviews and home studies had been completed, we waited. And waited. Suddenly, and not so suddenly, it happened. We were linked with a birth-mother.

This birth mother was a young girl who simply found herself in an unfortunate situation, but her openness to life gave her the courage to bring her baby—a boy—into this world. And she chose *us* to be parents to her baby. She chose *our home* to be his home. I was ecstatic! The birth mother had four months left in her pregnancy at the time we were chosen, and in that time we grew to love this little person as any parent loves his child. We gave him the name "Gabriel", and prepared for his arrival. I was given two baby showers. Two Grandmas knitted blankets for him. I thought about him every waking moment of every day, and in the last days before his birth, I restlessly "nested'—cleaning the house top to bottom, inside ovens and cabinets, and every place in between. Friends knew that I wanted Gabriel to have the nutrition of breast milk, and they gave us their own, carefully and cleanly collected, until our freezer was full. They scheduled dinners to be brought to us for weeks after his birth. We were so ready for him! And then, he was born.

Patrick and I received the phone call early on a Sunday morning and speedily packed our belongings—a take-home outfit, diapers, wipes, bottles, a car seat. Gabriel was born on the other side of the state, so we drove almost three hours to the hospital. When we arrived we were informed by the social worker that the mother seemed emotional. "It's ok," I thought, "We can handle this." We proceeded towards the room cautiously, but optimistically.

When we entered the hospital room, the birth mother placed baby Gabriel in my arms for the first time. My heart melted. Words cannot describe the love and joy that rushed through my veins as I held this precious infant in my arms. The feeling was something I had never experienced before. I waited six years for this beautiful boy. And at that first moment when I looked at him, his face only inches away from mine; I realized this present joy was worth every minute of aching and longing for him.

In the hospital room, Gabriel's extended family met us for the first time, and they asked us question after question. This started to make us nervous. I looked at my husband and he looked at me. We both were feeling that same anxiousness. We tried to push these thoughts aside, however, as we checked into a local hotel. Just after midnight, the phone startled us. It was the case worker who simply said, "(The birth mother) has changed her mind. She's decided to keep the baby. I'm so sorry." My husband and I both fell to our knees on the floor, holding each other, and uncontrollably wept. A fierce tornado of emotions whirled in my soul. How could this have happened? Didn't she know I already prepared for him? Waited for him? *Loved* him?

I didn't sleep all night. I vaguely remember thrashing in the hotel bed, devastated, and rocking back and forth while curled in the fetal position. I clutched my Rosary in my hand, "Hail Mary, full of grace.....Hail Mary, full of grace.....Remember, oh most gracious Virgin Mary......" and on and on.

I can't adequately describe how I felt as we drove that long road home with an empty car seat. But in the next few weeks I moved, with God's grace, from sorrow to acceptance to joy, even through the intense suffering. I came to realize that my Gabriel wasn't really mine at all. He belonged to the Father, who allowed me to love him. I only physically held him twice, but I decided to remain his "spiritual" mother for the rest of my life. I still pray for Gabriel, and his mother.

Perhaps God knew they needed me this way, and that this was God's way of connecting us. I learned, through this experience, that these little ones of ours are entrusted to us, but they are in fact God's babies, whether we are allowed to hold them for five minutes, for eighteen years, for many decades or not at all.

Following the loss of Gabriel, I knew I had to return to work. This was difficult for me since I had never felt called to the career life. From the beginning of my years as a married woman my desire was in motherhood. Just weeks earlier I had planned on coming home from this trip with my arms full of the rest of my life, immersed fully in my vocation as wife and at-home mother. That dream had been shattered. Before I could return to work I knew I needed a little time to grieve. I decided to take a week off and see my mother.

My mother flew in from out of town to be with me, as she was already scheduled to visit me and the new baby we were supposed to be bringing home. We made the best of her stay. We shopped, had lunch together, and relished heart-to-heart talks that only occur between a mother and her daughter. The most significant part of that week, however, was the day we visited the local Catholic bookstore. Here I found a book that would change my life—blessed Gianna Beretta Molla's biography.

I had never heard of the then-beatified woman before, but as I flipped through the pages, I was instantly drawn to the book and to her. The photographs of a stylishly dressed Italian woman with her beautiful children and of her and her husband in a tender embrace on their honeymoon first attracted me. As I perused the pages I saw that she was beatified. I figured that since she was beatified she must have led a holy, devout life. All this compelled me to make the purchase.

My mother and I read the book together, and when finished we resolved that we, mother and daughter, would pray to Blessed Gianna for a baby for my husband and me. We would pray for a girl, and should those prayers be fulfilled, we would name her "Gianna."

When I returned to work, the cards, flowers and prayers came flooding in. Sitting at my desk one afternoon, on a day that I just couldn't concentrate on office matters, I received a beautiful arrangement of roses, which was not only a floral bouquet, but also a spiritual bouquet. Each ribbon tied to a rose represented the prayers being said by friends and family on our behalf. It contained hundreds of prayers, rosaries, Masses and adorations offered up for us and our intentions in recognition of our loss. I have no doubt that those prayers were instrumental in the miracles that would soon follow.

On a dreary, gray afternoon after having returned to the office, I had just finished some work on the computer when my phone rang. A woman announced that she was a case worker from our adoption agency. I immediately sat down in my chair and took a deep breath. I listened while she told me the news: she had a baby for us. A little girl had been born six days before, and we were chosen to be her mother and father! The social worker filled me in on all the happy details, how many pounds she was at birth, her hair color, her sweet smell and how beautiful she was. I couldn't believe it! We arranged for Patrick and me to meet our little girl for the first time, and after the conversation ended I wept with joy. I knew this was the baby for us, and I also knew instantly who interceded on our behalf. I immediately told my husband the news, as well as everyone around me, that our Gianna was born!

We visited Gianna for the first time at her host family's home (A host family is similar to a foster family, but these families only take care of babies during the waiting period from birth until adoption finalization in court). The first moment I saw Gianna I was in love. Her sweet, beautiful heart-shaped face and rosy cheeks combined with her innocence and utter dependence seemed like a portion of Heaven itself. I felt deep and utter joy as I got to hold her for the first time, then feed her for the first time, and finally gaze on her new father cradling her for the first time. It was painful to leave that afternoon, but Patrick and I scheduled to see her again in two days, and having been very pleased with her host family, we were at peace.

After that, we visited Gianna as often as possible, spending afternoons with her for the next nine days at her host home until the day the birth mother was scheduled to go to court for finalization. Given our bad experience with Gabriel we were particularly nervous. The day that we could bring Gianna home couldn't come soon enough. The finalization date, upon which we would bring our child home for the first time, fell on March 19th, The Feast of Saint Joseph.

God could not have chosen a more perfect day for us, as Saint Joseph had been the patron saint of our family, securing jobs and homes for us and blessing us with countless material needs and spiritual gifts since the beginning of our marriage. And so it seemed perfectly fitting, Blessed Gianna whom Pope John Paul II had just named "Mother of the Family", and Saint Joseph, the foster-father of Jesus, the patron saint of fathers and our own spiritual father, worked together to bring us our first child, Gianna Marie Laurence.

Unlike our previous car ride back home bearing an empty car seat and enough tears to fill a well, this long drive was filled with love, joy, a tiny miracle beside me and the start of a family. The happiness Gianna has brought me since that glorious Feast of Saint Joseph is beyond comprehension, though perhaps not beyond the understanding of a mother who has longed for a child. Every moment of my mothering Gianna has been miraculous to me, and I have thanked God for her every day since that first meeting.

In the beginning of our marriage I wanted most of all to be a mother. And this has come to pass. Like other families, ours was born after much labor and love, and with, of course a few little miracles. Through the intercession of Blessed Gianna Molla and St. Joseph, and through the mercy and love of God, we now do indeed have the start of a family!

Kristen Laurence

Kristen Laurence is a Catholic, homeschooling mother of Gianna is 7, Madeleine 5 and Kilian 10 weeks. She is a graduate of Thomas Aquinas College and lives with her husband and children in California. She writes about the joys of the Faith, motherhood, and adoption at her blog, Small Treasures (http://smalltreasuresinorangecounty.blogspot.com).

Chapter: Nine

IT'S NOT ALWAYS EASY

"...when you come to serve the Lord, prepare yourself for trials. Be sincere of heart and steadfast, undisturbed in the time of adversity. Cling to Him, forsake Him not; thus will your future be great." (Sirach 2:1-2)

"...when the face is sad the heart grows wiser." (Ecclesiastes 7:3)

SPECIAL BLESSINGS, SPECIAL NEEDS

Many years ago, when I was fresh out of college, I took my first job teaching in a public school. The entire school was a "special needs school." I didn't apply for a special needs job. I wanted to teach kindergarten, preferably in the neighborhood school near my home.

Instead, I was in a special needs school, teaching first grade to 21 students. I had an aide for one hour a day. My principal had a strict policy against teachers talking with one another (I'm not kidding). I was on my own. Have I mentioned yet that I was 21? I got married the first week of school, was pregnant by the end of Christmas break, and didn't have a degree in special-education?

My friend Jan, who had been my study buddy all through college, reminded me that the special-ed majors had the same classes we did except for a very few. Perhaps I could do this...The children were, with few exceptions, from very needy and broken homes. There were days, almost every day actually, when I just wanted to take them home with me, feed them good food, give them baths, read them stories, and tuck them in bed. I definitely had classroom management problems. The school psychologist told me it was because I was too available. I didn't distance myself enough. She was probably right; how do you distance yourself from need? I could never get parent volunteers for anything from chaperoning field trips to classroom parties. My new husband bless his heart, was the de-facto room mother. It was there, in the utter chaos of that sad classroom that we decided to homeschool.

Our first child was born and eighteen months later, I was diagnosed with cancer. That experience cemented the decision. We were not sending this child out of our home for the better part of every day to let strangers shape his heart and mind. There is something about being reminded that you don't know how long you have to love your child that compels you to make certain that every day is lived according to its precious worth.

They warned us we'd probably never have another child. Our second son was born eighteen months after I finished treatment. Apparently, "they" didn't consult God. This child was wired differently. High need, certainly. "Special needs?" I had my suspicions, but I really didn't know. We bumped along with him until he was just four. Then, I was certain that there were special needs. We had him tested, eager to learn if the diagnosis was Attention Deficit or Sensory Integration Disorder.

No, the reply came, there's no problem here at all. Academically, he was right on track. And the experts all scratched their heads at that, given that he had had no formal preschool. We continued on, learning and living together and adding a new baby every two years. He struggled.

Things that made most kids smile--birthday parties, theme parks, big holiday gatherings, play groups--all made him cry. So we avoided those. We adapted and compensated and persevered. It just became integrated to our lifestyle. It took a very long time, but he learned to read. And all along, he had been listening. He heard all the stories read aloud, all the great language and literature, and he took it all to heart. He has the soul of a poet, but simple things evade him. And numbers are his nemesis.

With adolescence in full bloom and things like driver's-ed and SATs lurking in his not-too-distant future, we decided we needed to know more precisely what his challenges are. We began this summer with a battery of tests. The scores surprised us; his deficiencies were far beyond what we'd imagined. The tester puzzled over his "inconsistencies."

He didn't behave the way most kids, who were tested by her, did. He wasn't rude or poorly behaved or non-compliant. Despite substantial reading difficulties, he has a good grasp on stories and an amazing sense of literature. Though handwriting was literally painful and spelling evaded him, he can compose. He's been writing a novel late at night, when no one is looking. He's posted it to his personal blog and he is gathering a steady stream of faithful readers. "Still," the "expert" suggested with a knowing smile and a bit of a condescending air, "the test proves he can't write. You need a team to help you with your boy. He needs a special needs classroom or a special needs school." I shuddered. She kept referring to him as "your boy," as if she couldn't remember his name.

I kept nodding and blinking back tears. Oh, but I have a team, and it's growing every day. Within hours of returning home following the evaluation report meeting, I had heard from half a dozen women, scattered all over the country, who are experts at raising special needs children. They are mothers who have heard all the reports, read all the research, and endeavored to teach their children at home. To a woman, they all said the same thing: You know him best. God gave him to you. You can do this. We'll help you.

A team, indeed.

When I read the extensive report at home, I discovered that in some places, the evaluator did, indeed, get my son's name wrong. And, I think she got him wrong. There is no doubt we have serious needs here. But she missed the blessings entirely. She failed to see, from her institutionalized paradigm, how well home education has served him. She didn't understand that his strengths have been nurtured and his soul has been touched again and again. She missed his gifts entirely because they don't fit into her neat little boxes. She missed my boy. But I didn't. And I won't.

Elizabeth Foss

Elizabeth is a cancer survivor who lives every day grateful for the gift of life. She is happily married to Mike Foss and mother to nine children. She is the author of Real Learning: Education in the Heart of My Home *and* Small Steps for Catholic Moms, *with friend and colleague Danielle Bean. You can find Elizabeth online at www.elizabethfoss.com.*

FINDING OUT FOR MYSELF

There are good days and bad days in a homeschool. On good days, we sing the Lord's praises and thank Him for guiding us to educate our little blessings. On bad days, we ask God if perhaps there has not been a mistake. Did we hear Him wrong?

For nine years I had occasional bad days and asked, "God, am I really supposed to do this?" Inevitably, doubts faded with prayer and a touching homeschool moment. Or, my husband would remind me of why we homeschooled and peace would return. But in year nine, I could not shake off the bad days. I had already successfully launched three of my sons from homeschool to the Catholic high school. In all three cases, I knew I had made the right choice to keep them home through junior high. So, why was I struggling now?

Perhaps it was lack of sleep. I was working hard to meet a book deadline and getting very little sleep. Then, there was the two-year-old who enjoyed climbing to high places and removing child-safety plugs from electrical outlets. I had a junior high student, second and fourth graders, a pre-schooler and two-year old. Somehow, each day seemed more overwhelming than the previous.

I reacted in my usual fashion--asking God if I was really supposed to homeschool. The turmoil continued. I began thinking about the public school down the street. I knew a very nice mom with two exceptionally nice daughters who attended that school. I had met the principal and she was very nice too. I kept praying and not feeling very nice about myself as a teacher/mom.

After about month of feeling that learning was not taking place, I stopped thinking of enrolling my kids. I just did it. I did not want them to fall behind and God was not sending any perceivable signals to do otherwise. Still, I knew we were not done homeschooling. Jacob, my seventh grader would remain home. I preferred him not to have the middle school experience. Mary and Teresa would attend Roosevelt Elementary together at least for the remainder of the school year. John, who was four, was already reading, so this would give me more time to boost his skills. With two less students, I could also increase the odds that Isaac would live to see this third birthday.

It was November. I suspected that the teachers, who had never before encountered homeschooled kids, probably expected the worst: harried mother gives up and dumps uneducated barbarians off at school. They quickly learned otherwise. Both girls made fast friends and had no trouble with the schoolwork. Life at home began to run smoother. I had time for junior high subjects, John went from early readers to second-grade readers in just a couple months and Isaac had less opportunity to reach high shelves and remove the outlet plugs.

Roosevelt welcomed parents to come for lunch any time. I did so frequently and brought the younger boys with me. I could see the girls had friends and seemed to have adjusted. Teresa, however, wanted to come back home. The teacher said she was doing beautifully and I could see she had made friends. I told her that she would at least finish the school year. Mary loved school. There were a couple bouts of nasty-girl-encounters, but she overcame them very well.

As the year wore on, though, things emerged that I did not like. My girls were more than on par with their classes, but the classes were not up to par with their abilities. Subjects were lightweight and scant. I asked Teresa if she got bored when it came time for students to read out-loud. (We all remember being paragraphs ahead while some poor student struggled. Or perhaps we were the ones who struggled under the stress of impatient students.) No, she told me. She never got bored because kids never read out loud.

Years of traveling in homeschool circles had insulated me from the real world, so to speak. For instance, divorced moms having dates, a dad in prison and kids who did not know what religion they were because their family never went to church, was not part of the girls' world before. Then, there was the new vocabulary Mary brought home, like, you know, the kid-speak that says in so many words: I'm so way cool that like you wouldn't even believe it.

At Teresa's birthday party she had homeschool friends and public school friends. Big difference. Some of the public school girls were talking about boyfriends. Mind you, this was second grade. Then, a couple groups formed and there was stupid, secretive girl drama between a few. One could not play any of the outdoor games in her heels. Did I mention this was second grade?

By spring, I knew clearly why we were homeschooling and planned again to keep everyone home in the fall. Teresa wanted to return home. Mary wanted one more year at school so she could have the sixth grade teacher who was "so nice." I felt certain that the best place for my children was at home. Unfortunately, Mary thought otherwise. She begged, pleaded and cried when I brought up homeschooling her the following year.

My husband suggested we just not talk to her about it for the time being. I started a novena to St. Jude, the Patron of Hopeless Cases. After I had completed the nine days of prayer, Mary came home from school and had something to tell me. "Mom," she began. "I've been thinking. You always want what's best for me and you want me to homeschool, so that must be what's best for me." I gave her a hug and she laughed when I told her about the novena.

I'm in year sixteen of homeschooling this year. This is not to say that our way is the only way it is simply "our" way as we feel God is calling us. God directs people onto different paths. For instance, a friend of mine who once thought of homeschooling was frustrated by her husband who felt strongly that their two girls should be in school. The mom now works with homeless families and does incredible work. Her girls are exceptionally good kids, providing very positive examples in the public school.

As for our year of public school for the girls, maybe God got tired of hearing the same question from me over and over. Perhaps he was telling me, "If you don't believe me, find out for yourself."

Patti Maguire Armstrong

FACING MORNING

No! I don't want to get up! I pulled the covers over my head and scrunched down under them deeper. *Please, no, please! It can't be morning!*

The sun streamed through the sides of the shades in my husband David's and my bedroom, making a narrow line of light on the wall. Birds chirped outside, and I heard a car drive down our subdivision street. Next to me, in a white cradle, our new baby girl, Angela, just a few weeks old, slept peacefully. She was curled on her side. Up and down, up and down went her little chest as she breathed in and out.

Just hours earlier, a sharp telephone ring had pierced the softness of the night. David had been first to grab the phone. When I looked at the digital clock radio next to him and saw it was after 2 a.m., I felt a pit in my stomach. Who calls at this time unless tragedy has struck?

"Hello?" I heard him say. He cleared his throat. "Yes. No, it's fine. What? What?"

I got up instinctively, restlessly, knowingly. *What is it? What has happened?* Infused with nervous energy, I walked to our bathroom, which was within earshot of David. I opened the window and looked at the dark houses in our neighborhood where everyone was undoubtedly asleep. A streetlight flickered. I put my face close to the screen and breathed in the night air. It was cool and damp, typical for rainy April in northern Indiana. *Something terrible has happened. God, I don't know who or what but help them and us, please. Oh God, help us.* I cringed, wondering who it was, and braced myself for the punch.

"Are you sure? Oh my gosh," I heard my husband say. His voice dropped. "Oh my gosh…"

I took a deep breath and turned from the window.

"What can I do?" David said into the phone, "What do you need?" He was silent for a few minutes, listening. "You don't want us to come now?" He continued listening. "Are you sure? OK, goodbye…"

I was pacing now. Our lives had just forever changed. I knew it. I wanted to know how, but I also didn't.

"Who is it?" I whispered. *Which person in my family of 12 brothers and sisters or his four, had met with tragedy?* "Who is it?"

"It's your mom," he answered. At first I thought he meant my mom had died, but then I realized he meant it was my mom on the phone.

"Who is gone?" I pressed, "What happened? Did someone die?"

"It's Johnny," he said quietly.

I slumped down against the wall. Johnny.

Johnny was my youngest brother, aged 20, adopted in our family when he was two years old. My mother told David that he had been coming home just before midnight from Taco Bell with a friend, a young lady who had been driving. It was raining. Somehow they went off the slippery road. Their car hit a tree and both were killed, almost immediately.

The whole thing seemed surreal. Earlier that day I had attended my high school son's track meet with my new baby, our first outing in public. We ate dinner. I put the children to bed. I nursed the baby. Things were just starting to get back to normal after Angela's birth. Everything was fine. Now, everything was not fine. It was wrong, tangled, a mess. A searing pain and sick feeling ripped through my gut. I crossed my arms against my stomach and bent over. I felt like throwing up. Johnny was gone.

David told me that my mother said that there was no reason to go there at that time. Only some of my siblings were at my parent's house. The police had already left. We couldn't do anything. We'd meet at Mom and Dad's house in the morning.

David and I were in shock. We were silent for a long time. At 42 and with nine children, I was old enough to be Johnny's mother. In fact, many days when Johnny was little I took care of him. Mom would drop him off at our house so she could run errands. I'd read to or do crafts with him and my two little boys, who were just a few years younger than him. We'd take walks. We played with Play Doh on a plastic child's picnic table on the back patio. I'd felt protective of him, like a mother. I was frustrated with him sometimes too, like a mother, as he liked to live on the edge and as he grew older pushed all limits.

David had a special relationship with Johnny, too. When he was little and before David and I were married, David would come over to our house and head right for Johnny. He'd toss him in the air and wrestle with him on the floor. He was David's little buddy.

After receiving the phone call alerting us of John's death, David and I were simply stunned, not saying anything. Slowly and quietly we started talking about him, his life and his death. Finally, we cried, then, embraced. In each other's arms and with nothing left to say, we dozed off in the early morning, exhausted.

Now, the sunlight was streaming in through the windows. It was time to get up. Our high school-aged children would be waking up to get ready for school. I homeschooled the younger ones so they would be sleeping a little while longer. Thank goodness. As I lay in bed thinking about the day ahead of us I felt sick, sad, and angry.

No! I don't want to get up! I pulled the covers over my head and scrunched down under them deeper. *Please, no, please! It can't be morning!*

The next time I felt that way, wanting to stay under the covers and go back to the make-believe world of dreamless sleep, was Friday, three days later. David's brother Scott, a surgeon, had stopped by the house to offer condolences the night before. Uncharacteristically, I asked him about a lump I had on my collar bone. I was stressed. I was tired, up all night from the grief of Johnny's sudden death and taking care of a newborn baby. I had so much on my plate. I had found this lump and simply wanted him to assure me nothing was wrong during this tumultuous time. He didn't.

Scott examined the lump and palpated it with his hand. His alarmed look was frightening to me because as a trauma center chief he was used to seeing everything and dealing with emergencies calmly. Why this demeanor with me? What was the alarm?

"I want you to see my partner in the morning," he said, "I want that biopsied right away."

The next morning was the morning of my brother's wake and Rosary at the funeral home. I'd be spending it in the hospital instead. What would the day bring? This was too much.

No! I don't want to get up! I pulled the covers over my head and scrunched down under them deeper. *Please, no, please! It can't be morning!*

Two days later it was Sunday. Scott would bring over the results of the biopsy. I was lying in bed with David, resting on his chest with his arm around me. It would be time to go to Mass soon. John's funeral had been the day before. I could hardly remember it. Things had been happening so fast and I was so weary from a lack of sleep, that I simply couldn't process everything. Sometimes I was in a daze and the world seemed to moving in slow motion. Other times, it sped by and I totally missed a comment directed right at me. I couldn't help it. My brain was numb. That morning in bed David agreed to say a Rosary with me. *Whatever happens, God is here, even though we don't feel Him.* I inhaled the fresh scent of the cool, fluffy pillow beneath my head and tried to forget the recent happenings. The pillows smelled so clean, and felt so normal, so comfortable. The covers which enveloped me were soothing.

No! I don't want to get up! I pulled the covers over my head and scrunched down under them deeper. *Please, no, please! It can't be morning!*

It was cancer—Hodgkin's Lymphoma. Scott had brought over bagels on Sunday and broke the news. I wanted to scream and hit something. Instead I stared blankly, a tide of emotion welling inside, not matching my vacant stare. I said, "Ok... thanks for the bagels." I felt gut-punched, with no breath left in me. *Take your stupid bagels and go home!* I was screaming inside, *I don't want your stupid bagels and I don't want this! What else could you do to me, Lord?!*

There would be more tests to 'stage' me. Scott got me in with the best oncologist in the area. "You can't believe the luck I had this morning," he shared, "(Dr.) Ansari *just happened* to be in the hospital today—Sunday morning—can you imagine? I haven't seen him in three weeks and there he is, walking down the hall as I'm holding your results. He never goes in on Sundays!" Scott continued, "He said he'll see you tomorrow morning. Isn't that great? He'll get you started right away." Scott bent down and looked me in the eye, "Theresa, he'll speed these tests along. He's the best. This will be a blip on the screen of life before you know it. You're going to beat this." After that, either Scott or my husband—I can't remember who—hugged me.

Immediately, I felt claustrophobic in my own body. I wanted to get it out of it. *Take it back and fix it and give it back!* Something was growing inside me. It was dirty, toxic, and ugly. *Take it away.* What about my baby? What about my other children? What about my husband? Was I going to die?

In anticipation of the radioactive tests I needed, I had to quit breastfeeding. This was devastating to me. Nursing was a way I bonded with my babies as well as gave them nourishment. What's more, my children had allergies and the few times I tried formula with one or two of them they developed rashes. I thought Angela would probably be no different.

My sister-in-law Margy had some breast milk in the freezer as she was nursing a child, and she offered it to me for Angela. Angela took to it so well that Margy agreed to try to pump for her, although she wasn't able to produce enough for her to be fed fully on that alone. My sister Lisa, also nursing, had some breast milk and gave it to me, as did my sister Karen. This milk Angela gobbled down ravenously, but it was not enough to feed her entirely. I started her on formula, and as I expected she started developing a rash.

Spurred on by this knowledge and a deep generosity, my sister Cheryl, who was expecting a new baby in a few short weeks, offered to provide as much milk as Angela might need.

"I'll just get an electric pump in the hospital and pretend I'm nursing twins," she offered. I couldn't' believe this kindness and was hesitant, knowing how worn-out she would surely be after the birth of her fifth child.

"Hey, between all of us, we ought to have her (Angela) covered," she said.

Cheryl offered this in such a light-hearted, natural way that I felt it was OK to accept. And so began what I playfully nicknamed 'The Great Milk Run', thinking of old stories of the Pony Express. Once she had her baby, Cheryl would pump after every feeding of her own infant then fill bottles for Angela. David would pick them up every night after work. And this is the way Angela would be nourished the first year of her life.

As promised, Dr. Ansari saw me at the beginning of the week. I had blood work, pulmonary and lung tests taken. An MRI and CT scan were also done. He was a Speedy Gonzales in ordering these tests, not taking 'no' when various labs claimed they couldn't fit me in. I was grateful. He also ordered a bone marrow biopsy. This last test would tell doctors if the cancer had spread to my bone marrow, indicating later staging.

The room where the bone marrow extraction procedure was to take place was small and clean. The dominating feature was a low, flat bed where patients lay during extraction. I was given a relaxant and a pillow to squeeze. I was nervous and made small talk with the nurse assigned to me, as David chatted with the doctor. The nurse was impressed when another nurse told her we had nine children.

"You're so lucky!" she told me. I smiled and nodded.

"Do you have children?" I asked, trying to turn the conversation away from me. She deeply sighed.

"No, my husband and I have been trying to get pregnant but we're not having much luck."

"I'm sorry," I answered.

"We've been trying for years, and when I did get pregnant once, we lost the baby early on through miscarriage. I haven't gotten pregnant since," the nurse continued. She turned to a cabinet and started taking out gauze and some sort of medicine in a container.

I didn't feel it was my place to inquire whether she had seen any doctors about this problem, but I urgently felt inspired to say, "Well, I'll offer up this procedure for you!" She stopped what she was doing, turned and looked at me. As soon as I said it I felt silly. I didn't even know if she was Catholic or understood what it meant to offer up pain for an intention. It was a completely impetuous, out-of-character act for me to blurt that out to a stranger, but she smiled.

"You might not want to waste that on me," she said. "This procedure can be very painful."

Her expression indicated she was touched by the words but that I might not fully understand what was about to come. It was a mix between tenderness and pity. Her comment and expression only moved me to reassure her.

"That's OK, I'll offer it up for you—that you and your husband have a baby!"

Although I had only known this woman a few minutes, I felt a sincere empathy for her. I thought of the tremendous blessing my children have been in my life and how empty my life would be without them. I wanted this blessing for her, too! *Please, Lord! Help her conceive and carry a baby to term!*

The doctor returned with a needle aspirator and syringe. I lie down on the bed, face-down, and grabbed onto my husband's arm and the pillow simultaneously as the doctor prepped the area to be poked.

"At the count of three I will insert the needle," he warned me. "One...two...three..."

As the doctor thrust the needle inside my buttock and began rotating it, I could hear crunching and I nearly screamed at the intense pain and pressure. I bit into the pillow as hard as I could and dug into my husband's arm with my fingers. It seemed like an eternity before the doctor said, "There, we're all done. Good job." In reality this procedure only took five minutes. When I found out that my doctor was known as an expert at quick, efficient and as painless as possible, bone marrow extraction. I felt sorry for the patients of other doctors.

Preliminary tests aside, I was staged. IIA. The "II" represented the fact that both sides of my body were affected by the cancer. The "A" represented the fact that the cancer was in the early stages. I was asymptomatic. More advanced stages of lymphoma would have included symptoms such as intense itching and night sweats, neither of which I had. Thanks be to God for that.

The morning of my first chemotherapy treatment arrived. I had a familiar, desperate thought.

I don't want to get up. It can't be morning.

This thought was short-lived, however, as I had to get going or I was bound to be late. My mother was going to watch the kids, and David was already up, dressed and gathering our paperwork. I showered, put on some clothes, kissed my children goodbye, and went out to the car.

My brother Bobby, interestingly, had been diagnosed with the same type of lymphoma three years prior to my diagnosis. (He was eventually to battle cancer two more times.) He met David and me in the parking garage the first day I was scheduled for chemo. It was a surprise. As David and I rounded the corner of the first turn in the parking garage, Bobby came bursting out from nowhere with fists of triumph, beating the air and with cheers.

"All right! We're going to beat this cancer out of you!! This is the day you start your cure! Let's go!!! Woo Hoo!!"

This was a little over the top, but to tell you the truth I liked it. I was sorely lacking confidence, and like a child literally putting her feet into the huge footprints of an adult in the deep snow so she wouldn't sink in uncharted spots, I grabbed onto whatever positive feelings Bobby could provide. I wanted to believe him. I had to believe him. I clung to this positive attitude like a drowning person clutches onto a life raft in a storm. I gave him the 'thumbs up'.

The chemo room itself was both depressing and pleasant. It reminded me of a nursing home in a way—nobody really wanted to be there but it was the best available under the circumstances. Fresh flowers were displayed on tables, and a water fountain—for a calming effect, no doubt—bubbled nearby. But those pleasantries were in stark contrast with the sick people sprawled out on the chairs, some coughing, others simply staring out into space. It was an ocean I definitely didn't want to swim in. Unfortunately, I had no choice.

Collections of recliners in various cozy arrangements were the staff's attempt to make the chemo room homier. Some recliners were facing the windows, which almost completely covered the walls around the room. To find an empty chair there, by the window, but not directly in the sun, was like finding a shiny coin on a crowded beach. I found out quickly that those window seats were the most coveted spots. Sitting in those chairs by the window, I was to find out, meant being able to watch the busy people on the street below as they drove to work, to the park, to the Burger King just down the block. As those people below turned left into the side road or ordered a Whopper for their lunch, they were oblivious to our pain and suffering, as we watched them from our perches up above. As they briefly flitted past our gazes they never knew how we longed to be in their shoes, to be living a boring dull day in a healthy body. In those window seats we could remember what our normal lives were before cancer, and we could imagine what we hoped they would be like again.

Scattered among the chairs, on small tables, were cheerful colored glass bowls of hard and chewy, bite-sized candy-peppermints, toffee, and strawberry crèmes. At first I thought the nurses were merely attempting hospitality. Later I found out the candies had a practical purpose. Chemotherapy leaves an awful taste in your mouth. The candies temporarily relieved us of this minor suffering.

I was shocked that the room was, for the most part, always full. Did that many people really have cancer? What was wrong with our society that so many suffered from this affliction? Was our American lifestyle predisposing us to this disease? I had to remind myself that God wasn't punishing us, although it felt like it at times. I tried to draw upon thoughts of God's love, provision and care. I was reminded of Matthew 10:28-31:

> *And do not be afraid of those who kill the body but cannot kill the soul; rather be afraid of the one who can destroy both the soul and body in Gehenna. Are not two sparrows sold for a small coin? Yet not one of them falls to the ground without your Father's knowledge. Even all the hairs of your head are counted. So do not be afraid; you are worth more than many sparrows.*

I often brought my Bible to the chemo room to read, and try to absorb. I figured God allowed this to happen to me so I would learn something. God was asking me to trust Him. Job had a lot of troubles too, and things worked out for him. I had to go on. What else could I do?

Each evening before my chemotherapy treatment, I continued to think, *I don't want to get up! It can't be morning!* I just got used to putting one foot in front of the other and taking one step at a time. I was walking blindly, but I was learning to walk with the Lord.

The day after each chemotherapy treatment, David gave me a shot of Neulasta, a white blood cell builder, directly into my stomach fat. It made me nauseous and my stomach tender, but it kept my white blood cell counts where they needed to be, and for that I was grateful.

One night, I snuggled under a homemade quilt that my homeschooling friends had made me, block by block, piece by piece. There was Mary Ann's signature. Kathy's quote. "Jesus I trust in You," which Kelly wrote on one of the squares. Karen had quilted it all together. Burrowing under these covers, enveloped literally in a blanket made of love, I felt for the first time in months that maybe I was going to be alright. Just then, my seventeen-year old son walked in the door with a surprise—my favorite chocolate ice cream sundae.

"I just thought it would taste good after a day of chemo," he said.

It did.

Three months later I was well into my chemotherapy regimen when I saw the nurse who had assisted at my bone marrow extraction at the oncologist's office. She stopped me in the hall.

"I'm pregnant! I'm pregnant!" she told me excitedly. But that wasn't the only news. The date of her conception, she couldn't wait to tell me, corresponded with the week of my bone marrow biopsy. God is so good!

I underwent a total of six months of chemotherapy. My hair fell out. I gained weight. I reached my lowest of the low points in all of my life. I continued to grieve Johnny's death, and desperately hold onto life.

And then, one October morning, I woke to the sound of chirping birds. I had been declared in remission the day before by my oncologist. Life was hard, but I was going to be OK. As I lay in bed I knew instinctively, too, that it was time to get up. And so, I pulled the covers back off my body and my feet touched the ground. I opened the shades and took a deep breath. It was a beautiful morning.

Theresa A. Thomas

SURVIVING THE HOMESCHOOL PANIC

It hits every year right around now. Getting cranked up in January after Christmas is hard enough, and once you do get going again, suddenly, the end of the school year, which way back in the fall seemed a mere speck on a distant horizon, rushes toward you, filling your field of vision with catastrophe.

"We are so far behind. We will never get caught up. Why did I ever decide to do this? I am such a failure. And what is worse, I am failing these children."

The messages start bouncing around in the mind of the homeschooling mother like super balls on a tile floor. It is homeschooling panic time.

OK, take it from someone who has been through this so many years that it isn't funny. You will be OK. You have accomplished more than you think you have.

Go back and look at your children's work at the beginning of this year. Now compare it with what they are currently doing. Do you see the progress? See, they are learning. They really are.

I know what it is. This year was going to be different. *This year* you were going to be perfectly organized. This year every form was going to be turned in on time. This year you were going to plan well ahead for all kinds of wonderful, enriching field trips. This year you *would* do lesson planning weeks in advance and you *would* have all your supplies on time. This year you were going have a schedule that ran like a well-oiled machine and you *would not* spend entire quarters of hours searching for lost sneakers.

And it wasn't just the external things that were all going to go right. This year you were going to be perfectly patient and never raise your voice. This year you were going to *calmly* ferry the children from place to place while you played classical music CDs in the car. This year you were going to go to bed each night knowing that you had spent the day in the most productive manner possible—and your husband was going to find you in a good mood. Not like last year when he asked you if you were going to bed soon and, surrounded by stacks of paper, you gritted out through clenched teeth holding a pencil, "Do I *look like* I am anywhere near being ready for bed?"

So, what happened really? Kids got sick and things got broken—cars, washing machines, and computers. And what did the kids see on those days when "we didn't accomplish a thing?" They saw you figure out how to solve problems, how to find alternatives, how to cooperate when you are under stress. How to put a fever above fractions and put helping above history.

It is so easy to forget why we are homeschooling. Sometimes the "home" part seems to get in the way and especially all these *people* in the home. We could homeschool the children so much better if they weren't so messy and energetic to the point of bouncing off the walls. If they weren't children, you see, it would all be so much easier to homeschool them.

January is when we really have to get a grip. Might as well, you know. It is too late to turn back now. In for a semester, in for a year.

So don't panic. You still have nearly half the year to go. You will adjust and reassess. You really are doing a great job. And as for the perfection that eluded you—hey, there's always next year.

Mary Kochan

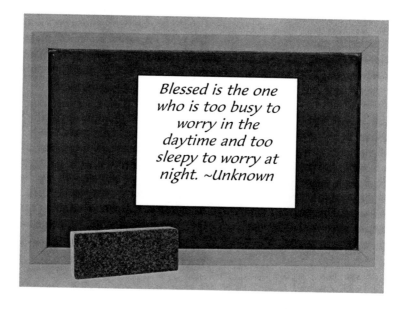

FR. JOHN HARDON ON HOMESCHOOLING

Excerpted from a speech originally given by Fr. John Hardon, S.J. (June 18, 1914 – December 30, 2000) at a homeschool seminar in October 1991 in St. Paul, MN.

There is no single aspect of religious instruction that, over the centuries, the Church has not more frequently, or more consistently, taught the faithful, than of the parents on how to provide for the religious and, therefore, also human education and upbringing of their offspring. So true is this that it is the second and coequal purpose for Christ instituting the Sacrament of Matrimony—for the procreation and the education of children.

Where has the Church survived? Only and wherever—and this is historically provable—homeschooling over the centuries by the Catholic parents has been taken so seriously that they considered it their most sacred duty, after having brought the children into the world physically, to parent them spiritually.

The necessity for homeschooling is not only a natural necessity; it is a supernatural necessity. Have parents over the centuries, in all nations, from the dawn of human history, in every culture, had the obligation to teach and train their children? Yes, the same ones who brought the children physically into the word have a natural obligation binding in the natural law, to provide for the mental, moral, and social upbringing of their offspring. Yet since God became man, the necessity, and therefore the corresponding obligation, becomes supernatural.

What do we mean when we say that Catholic homeschooling is a supernatural necessity? We mean that in God's mysterious but infallible providence, He channels His grace from human beings who already possess that grace. It is a platitude to say that we cannot give what we do not have. Nobody would ever learn the alphabet. We would not know how to read or write...or even how to eat.

The main reason for homeschooling is that He only uses those who have God's grace as channels of grace to others. Over the centuries, our principal Jesuit apostolate has been teaching. And we are told, in the most uncompromising language: *"You will be able to teach others—you will share with them only what you are yourselves."*

No one else can teach the faith—except the person who has it. But possessing divine grace, beginning with the value of faith, is not only a condition; it is also the measure for the communication of grace. Weak-believing parents will be weak conduits of the grace of faith to their children. Strong-believing parents will be strong conduits of the grace of faith. This is not good psychology and it is not good example. This is Divine Revelation.

In the mysterious providence of God, this is the law: Only those who possess the supernatural life and the measure of the possession of faith, hope and charity will God use as the channels of His grace to their children.

How are parents to provide for the Catholic homeschooling for their children? First, the principal and most fundamental way is by living strong Catholic lives. All the academic verbiage and planned pedagogy are useless. Only persons who have God's grace will He use as the channels of His grace to others, and no one, but no one, cheats here.

For Catholic parents to live good Catholic lives in our day requires heroic virtue. Only heroic parents will survive the massive, demonic secularization of materially super-developed countries like America.

And consequently, far from being surprised, parents should expect that homeschooling will not be easy. Any homeschooling in the U.S., which is easy today, is not authentic Catholic homeschooling. If it is easy, something is wrong.

Today, Catholic parents must not only endure the cross, resign themselves to living the cross, but they are to choose the cross. In case no one has told you, when you choose homeschooling, you chose a cross-ridden form of education. You have to live a heroic Catholic life in America today. God will use you and provide you with knowledge and the wisdom, providing you are living the authentically heroic Catholic life.

If you want to teach and train your children, you must know your faith. You must grasp and understand the faith. Read the 14th Chapter of Matthew where Our Lord tells the parable of the sower sowing seeds. Seeds fell on four kinds of ground. The first three kinds were unfruitful. As Jesus said, birds came along and picked up the seed, and nothing grew. The disciples asked Jesus for the meaning. The Lord explained that the seeds falling on the wayside are those persons who have received the Word of God into their hearts and fail to understand it, and therefore the evil one comes along and steals it from their hearts. That is why America now has millions of ex-Catholics. They have never understood their faith.

I have strong encouragement from the Holy See to train parents. You are all welcome to learn your faith so that you grasp and understand your faith. Then God will use you to teach your children as a channel of faith. Teach, not only by rote memory, to grasp the faith.

Next, Catholic homeschooling must be schooling. There must be organization, administration, a pattern, a schedule, and a program. Somebody has to be in charge. Mother and father must cooperate in the homeschooling.

Homeschooling must be sacramental. In other words, the Church that Christ founded is the Church of the Seven Sacraments, especially the Sacraments of Eucharist and Confession. You, yourselves, should receive the Sacraments of Holy Communion and Confession. Train your children to live a sacramental life.

Finally, to be authentically Catholic, homeschooling must be prayerful. The single most fundamental thing you can teach your children, bar none, is to know the necessity and method of prayer.

You must pray yourselves. Without prayer, all the schooling in the world will not produce the effect which God wants homeschooling to give because homeschooling is a communication of divine grace, from Christ to the parents to the children. And the principle way parents communicate grace from Christ to their children, the grace upon which those children will be saved, is prayer.

THE GOOD GIRL'S SIN

I would never ever consider committing adultery. I feel guilty killing insects. I return extra change accidentally given to me at the grocery store. I would not physically bow down to any brazen image and yet until recently I regularly bowed down in my heart to an extra serving of just about anything on my plate, and my body was visual proof of that.

Carrying and giving birth to seven children had been a big excuse for me in explaining the way my body looked. It is not easy gaining and losing weight just about every two years with each pregnancy. Making it even more difficult is the fact that I turned to food instead of our loving Father every time I was weary and needed rest, when I was hungry for companionship, when I was nervous, aggravated, angry or frustrated.

For more than twenty years I tried many diet and weight loss programs. I am ashamed of the diet food and special diet products I purchased, but also of the clothes I've had to buy to accommodate my growing body. I also felt guilty about all of the time I have spent, (time that should have been

God's and my family's) going to weight-loss meetings, making special food, focusing on myself.

Many times I confessed my sin of gluttony, but was at a loss as to how to rid myself of this unhealthy love of food. Spending my days in the kitchen preparing meals for my family, I felt like an alcoholic who was required to work as a bartender in a saloon. I turned to food for a large variety of reasons, very few of which were God's intended purpose of fueling the body. How could God expect me to overcome this problem when I had to face food continually (and with six sons I mean continually!); and, did God really want me to be concerned with my body shape? Wasn't that vanity?

I was struggling with those questions when our loving and merciful Father showed me a way out through the simple and amazing grace of a friend. Amy told me about a program called "Weigh Down Workshop" and the corresponding book called "The Weigh Down Diet". I was very surprised when she shared with me that she had struggled with her weight and relationship with food because she is not heavy at all. I am sure that her sharing was God's moment of grace for me as I had been crying out to Him almost daily to save me from my obsession with food. (I have since seen the Catholic alternative Light Weigh which I believe would have accomplished the same goal in me). I was tired of trying to lose weight and was a little leery about trying something new, but something nudged me to explore the program, read the book and be open.

As I was reading the book and during time of prayer, I felt God was trying to tell me something about my relationship with Him. I began to feel that my unrealistic relationship with food was connected in some way with my relationship with God--something I had not read about, heard about or thought about before. I began to realize that dieting is following man-made rules. Just "fix" the food by manipulating the calorie content, fat and sugar and one can eat more, the man-made rules seem to say. I began to see that overeating may actually be a spiritual problem, when one is out of balance with a relationship with God. I began to realize that God did not put wonderful things like pecan pie, ice cream, pizza and butter on this earth to torture anyone. I started to recognize that He has given us all of these wonderful things to enjoy in moderation. I started to wonder if most people's problems do not stem from eating these foods, but from eating them greedily. It only made sense that God made our bodies perfectly. He gave us a hunger and fullness mechanism to let us know when our bodies need fuel and when they are full. I began to understand in a way I hadn't before that we have to learn to listen to those mechanisms.

As I learned to recognize true hunger, I slowly cut my food intake in half and ate unhurriedly, savoring the food and thanking God for his wonderful creativity. I learned to pay careful attention to my body and stop eating when the stomach hunger was gone. I began to choose healthy, nutrient dense, body-supporting food instead of junk and empty calories. I saw that I needed to choose to eat food the way it was intended, to nourish the body God gave me, not stuff it to ease pain or substitute for something else. In time, I came to realize that I need God to fill all of those desires that I was previously using food to fill.

Reading the book my friend gave me was just the beginning. God guided me and sustained me through prayer. Now, instead of running to food for solace, I run towards God in His word, spiritual reading, or Mass. I have lost and kept off fifteen pounds, slowly getting closer to my goal of fitness, not a particular dress size, and am happier now than I have been before. My mental attitude has changed about food, and that has made all the difference. God's amazing grace came to me in the form of a friend, a book and a little nudge. And these simple things, along with being open to God's will in my little daily struggles, have made my life so much more manageable, much sweeter, more fulfilling and lighter than I could have ever imagined.

Lori Massa

Lori is a Catholic homeschooling mother of six sons and one daughter. She lives in Indiana and once again enjoys cooking for her family.

I CHOSE YOU FOR THIS

I knelt in Adoration, my mind a deep black pit where no prayer could form; offering Him my whole troubled heart, full of pain and confusion. Was He punishing me? How could He make me come back to this town? It was like a jail sentence, or Hell. Why? How could any good come of it?

We had lived here six years ago. Just prior to moving, my active duty military husband of eleven years confessed to an affair with a friend of mine; one whose children were friends with my son...and she was pregnant. We had a 5-year-old, and I was eight months pregnant myself. We'd experienced plenty of pain already, having lost our previous three pregnancies, one of those, a child at full term. Suddenly, my world was a nasty soap opera drama: betrayal, shattered trust, broken dreams, and hard choices.

I leaned on the Lord as never before. Although not a professing Christian at the time, I had learned to listen to His quiet voice during the deaths of our babies. During those difficult times, I had the comfort of my husband as well. Now I could not even lean on him. God was all I had, and Jesus became my best friend. I began longing for a church home.

Fast forward. Despite the excruciating pain, I was determined to forgive. My husband was penitent. And so, with a counselor's help, and time, our marriage healed and thrived. We loved our new military base. So did our two children. I was grateful to homeschool them after thinking at one time the demise of our marriage would prevent it. My husband paid child support faithfully after DNA confirmed parentage of the child of my former friend, but we never expected to be a normal part of that child's life; we simply lived too far.

Through study and the friendship of a fellow homeschool mom, I came to see beauty in the Catholic faith. Although my husband did not convert, my experience of the Church's truths, of RCIA, of the Sacraments: Baptisms, Communion, Confirmation, and particularly the Church's blessing of our marriage, gave me joy and new life. Through prayer and little miracles, my husband and I were even able to adopt a baby! We had a wonderful support network. Life was good.

Then, our request to extend my husband's service at the base we were living at was denied. Suddenly, my husband got orders to return to the previous base, where the former "other woman" and her children lived; where we had so many bad memories of lies told, babies lost, and hearts shattered. There was no escape. The move was rushed and hard.

My husband and I were both miserable and full of dread. Privately, I wondered what had I done to deserve God's wrath. Had I not endured enough? Did we not deserve the new joys we had? The questions were endless, the memories and reminders, unnerving.

In the stillness of Adoration one evening, as I poured my heart out to Jesus, I heard a short, sacred reply, *I chose you for this.*

Huh?! That's it?! He chose me for this? What did that mean? Feelings and thoughts flew through me... and then I "got it"!

This was *not* punishment! He did not choose this for me, but chose me for something which would exist with or without me. God had confidence in me, that this was a job I could handle through His grace and the gifts He gave me. I need not take the faults, problems or issues of others personally. For this was not, per se, about me at all. I knew many people would take their cues from how I handled this situation. My new job was as a role model and guide, not victim. I scheduled counseling, set appropriate boundaries, and supported my husband and children. We came to gradually know and love my husband's other child, and share her with others.

Today, I can say I am lucky to know this child, and this path. It has been rocky and very painful but God has healed some of my hurts and the experience certainly stretched my growth. I pray the outcome will be positive for those reading this or who must experience the same type of sorrow in their own life.

God does not abandon us, and the Bible tells us we see imperfectly. Let us trust in Him to guide our paths slowly, not as we project they should be, but let His Will be done. He will console. Always ask yourself: what would Love do? I rest in the grace of knowing I can endure and even thrive with God's help. I have peace in knowing "He chose me for this."

Jenny James

Jenny's husband suddenly left the family after 20 years. Jenny now teaches in school and cherishes her homeschooling years. Her children's sister sometimes visits and the family has a great time together. She offers a Bible quote for those in similar circumstances: "At present we see indistinctly, as in a mirror, but then face to face. At present I know partially; then I shall know fully, as I am fully known. So faith, hope, love remain, these three; but the greatest of these is love." 1 Corinthians 13:12-13

THE TWO BECOME ONE: FINDING GOD'S GRACE IN A MIXED MARRIAGE

When Steve and I got married, he was in the process of becoming Catholic. Six months into our marriage and one month before things were final he backed out. There were still many doubts in his mind about the Catholic faith and he just couldn't go through with it. As devastated as I was, I did not want him to convert just for me. I wanted him to truly believe everything that the Church teaches.

Steve had agreed to practice Natural Family Planning (NFP) but was not completely sold on it and did not fully understand why the Church was against contraception. Looking back I see that we both practiced NFP with a contraceptive mentality. For this reason, our first year of marriage was the hardest. We were like the "ledger people" keeping track of what the other had or hadn't done.

Our first daughter, Mary Rose, was born seven weeks premature, just two weeks after our first anniversary. The stress and anxiety we experienced and the work that was demanded of us during the first year of her life brought out the best in my husband. He was positive, upbeat, and cheerful. I have to say that I, on the other hand, saw the worst in myself and was not too pleasant to be around. I blamed myself for our daughter being premature, and for months I could not get over the anxiety and worry about her health. We did not have very many visitors for the first two months of her life and then, when we did, I practically made people boil their hands before they were allowed to touch her. I struggled to produce enough breast milk and considered that a huge failure as well. I was stressed out and strung out and was trying to do it all on my own strength.

During this time, I was also desperate to help Steve "see the light" of the Catholic faith. I read apologetic books and tried to get him to read them too. I admit that I was a bit vigorous. Wanting to share my faith with him probably felt and looked like me trying to control him and he backed away.

As Mary Rose started heading towards school age, I thought about homeschooling. Our NFP instructor homeschooled, and a woman at church called me out of the blue because she heard that I practiced NFP and she didn't know anyone else who did. She wanted to meet one other person from our huge suburban parish who practiced NFP. She also homeschooled. These coincidences were gentle taps, nudging me even more towards this choice.

Homeschooling sounded so great on paper and there were many reasons why it looked like the best option. First and foremost, I wanted my children to know, understand and embrace their Catholic faith. Sending them to school seemed like it would limit our time together as a family and thus limit the time that I could share the faith with them. I remember how hectic it was being the last of eight children and how as much as my parents wanted to pass on the faith, extra-curricular activities got in the way of what was most important. I saw homeschooling as a way to simplify our lives, and a way to not get caught up in the agenda that a school set, but instead have the family and the Church be the center of our lives. I wanted

> *Each person finds his good by adherence to God's plan for him, in order to realize it fully: in this plan, he finds his truth, and through adherence to this truth he becomes free.*
> *~Pope Benedict XVI*
> *Caritas In Veritate*

to create a truly "Catholic culture" within our home with sacred pictures, music, educational toys, maps and books on hand. I wanted my children to experience "total immersion" in the faith. I did have some hesitations, however. I wasn't sure if I had what it takes to make it work. I thought, "I am not organized enough, I am not patient enough."

I mentioned the idea of homeschooling to my husband and surprisingly he was interested. He became completely sold after reading numerous books on the educational system in our country and how it has deteriorated over the years. His reasons for homeschooling were more defensive (i.e. keep the bad out) and my reasons were more on the offense (i.e. let the good in). But we agreed that it was the right decision for our family.

As my children and I studied the lives of the saints, I read in horror about the nasty parents of some of the saints. I wondered if someday I would go down in history as the "horrible mother" that created a saint. In the first years of homeschooling I remember literally breaking down in tears thinking, "*The kids are going to say 'Daddy was Protestant and he was nice and Mommy was Catholic and she was mean.'*" I imagined them rejecting their Catholic faith based on my bad example. This was a very humbling thought.

One night, my daughter Mary Rose and I were at Adoration and there was a statue of our Blessed Mother in the corner. Mary Rose knelt down in front of the statue for a minute. When she got up and came towards me I felt inspired, pointing at the Virgin Mary, I said, "*That* is your perfect mother." And then pointing to myself I said, "*This* is your imperfect mother." Mary Rose got a knowing smirk on her face that let me know she understood perfectly.

Homeschooling has forced me to take a good look at myself. With the birth of each additional child, I have mellowed ever so slightly. It has been a long, painful process of conversion for me. I have been "measured and found wanting." I know that on my own strength I cannot do what needs to be done. It demands growing in virtue and relying on God's grace and strength day to day and moment to moment.

Even though Steve is not Catholic, he goes to Mass with us each week and never openly contradicts what the Church teaches. He reads the Bible to the kids, prays spontaneous prayers with them, and does devotionals as well. I pray the Rosary with them, take them to Adoration, and daily Mass during the week. We are finding ways to work together to bring God's love and truth to our children.

In the past five years, various family tragedies, mixed with fervent prayer and abundant spiritual reading has helped me to grow more mature in my faith. God has been and will continue to work on me through my husband and children. Frequent reception of the Sacraments keeps me going. Reading the lives of the saints has given me strength and hope as well. God is amazingly good. I told the priest the other day in confession, "I have learned humility now. Do you think God would let me move on to another virtue one of these days?"

Through Steve's questions and doubts coupled with my desire to teach our children the faith, I have studied a variety of Catholic issues. I wanted to be able to explain the Catholic faith to Steve and have him understand the church's teaching on sexuality, specifically contraception. A friend introduced me to Pope John Paul II's *Theology of the Body* and it has revolutionized the way I look at life. It has opened my eyes to so many truths: In marriage we are meant to mirror the life of the Trinity. What we do with our bodies affects our souls. We were made to give ourselves away in sacrificial love as Jesus did. I never had seen it that way before, but through God's grace I am learning to see now and can share that with Steve.

Discussing and exploring different aspects of the Catholic Faith together has brought us closer than ever and made us both better people. I have learned that a mixed marriage can be an opportunity for God to show His amazing grace.

Ruth Beier

Ruth graduated from the University of Notre Dame with a BA in English and Theology in 1990, did a year of volunteer work with the Jesuit Volunteer Corps in the Pacific Northwest, and then returned to the Midwest to teach religion at Bishop Luers High School before marrying Steve and starting a family. She is a stay-at-home homeschooling mother of five blessings.

BE STILL AND KNOW THAT I AM GOD

Two pink lines. That is how it all started. I didn't need the box to tell me what they meant. This was the eighth time in eighteen years I had hovered over the bathroom sink anxiously waiting for confirmation. Once again the answer was yes, we were having a baby. It was the perfect way to celebrate at that point in our lives. For eighteen years we had been Air Force gypsies, moving thirteen times total before my husband Allen's twenty years were completed. He had just submitted his retirement paperwork and we had bought a home in rural Colorado to settle down and raise our children. All was well with the world. Or so we thought.

As it turned out, it was 'well' for approximately forty-eight hours. That was when the phone rang. Allen was very quiet through the call. Then he hung up and told me the news. He was going to Iraq. Not right then, but in four months, which would put me halfway through this pregnancy. I could be having this baby by myself. My worst fear.

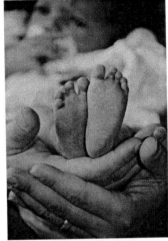

At that moment my world, which had just seemed to settle into a comfortable orbit, suddenly began spinning out of control. I didn't cry, not much anyway but my peripheral vision began to go, the telltale sign a migraine was hitting. It had been twenty years of sacrifice, twenty years of upheaval, twenty years of "we can do this." We were so close to the end, yet I was going to be alone and pregnant.

The next few months passed in a flurry of activity with me in a sort of dazed state. We tried not to think too much about the deployment and to just relish the time we had together. The children seemed to deal with the upcoming separation very calmly. We plugged away at the pre-deployment to do list: getting the power of attorney, locating the essential paperwork in the event of a disaster, getting our nearly sixteen-year-old ready for the driver's test, transitioning the bills over to me, etc. By summer's end we learned the baby I was carrying was our sixth baby boy, a strapping fellow who looked to be in excellent health. Before we knew it the time came for Allen to leave.

I didn't cry on the way to the drop-off point. We listened to the radio and made small talk. Allen stopped at the convenience store and got some snacks for the flight. He had a few cell phone calls about last minute supply issues for his troops. It was like any other drive to base and only the snippets of discussions I overheard about packing the weapons hinted at what was coming.

When we got to the drop point Allen pulled off across the street. It wouldn't do to have the commander's wife fall apart in front of all those people, and right then I didn't feel up to putting on my show face. We said goodbye in that parking lot and he went on to meet his company. I slowly pulled out onto the road and all the tears I had held in for four months escaped in a torrent I could not hope to stop. I shook. I drove. I ached. I turned the car towards home and prayed that this was not the last time I would see my husband. I wondered how I would carry on if it was.

The sight of the house growing larger on the horizon signaled me to put aside the anguish and to put on my mom hat. I dove back into housekeeping and home education with the surreal normalcy you

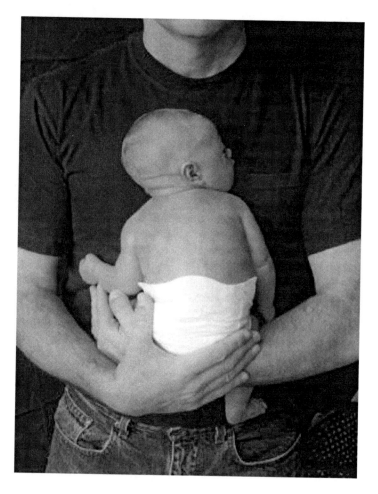

experience while your husband is in a war zone but your kids are still hungry and need clean laundry.

Our kids were also military deployment veterans of a sort and responded the way so many military kids do. They pressed on, essentially. We reworked our schedules and errands and got the sixteen-year-old his license. I was pregnant and we live thirty minutes from the edge of the nearest city. Someone had to be able to drive me to the hospital in the event of an emergency. He was it.

Those first few weeks went pretty smoothly. We did learn the baby was measuring larger than my dates suggested. I tried not to think about that. I tried to not think about an awful lot of things. Denial can be a good thing. I set the Internet home page to a scrapbooking site and we went without the evening news. I started to toss the main sections of the newspaper without reading them, leaving us the comic page and the food section. In short, I did my darnedest to create a little news-free haven for us. The last thing either I or the children needed was to soak ourselves in images of the battlefield.

Our honeymoon period of self-sufficiency was not to last however. Before long I began contracting. This was nothing new for me. I have a history of irritable uterus and was apparently not going to escape it this time. There was no way around it; I was done with doing my own shopping and errands. In fact, before long I was done with an awful lot of things. Life as we knew it officially came to a screeching halt. The whole thing seemed beyond unfair. Not only was Allen gone but so were all the opportunities we had to distract ourselves. Even worse, I couldn't take care of our basic needs.

What was God thinking anyway???

Amazingly, despite the long distance from town, people rallied round. Other moms volunteered to implement my homeschool party plans for All Saints Day. Our piano teacher and her family brought us a complete Thanksgiving dinner that year since I couldn't travel to them. A good friend, whose husband had been unexpectedly laid off from work, decided they would jump in with the newfound time they had to make weekly trips to our ranch to bring us groceries and do the guy jobs. Not only did they bring us essentials like food, they brought us things to do. My friend taught the girls and me to crochet and left us, each week, with more yarn and further instructions.

Along with the physical changes the climate of the house was changing. The days that were previously filled with moving here and there were now filled with things that could be done with an incapacitated mom—reading aloud, handcrafts, piano duets, baking, painting, and hours and hours of playing with each other.

We accomplished an awful lot academically. We did all those things people always say they never have time to do.

Because of our unique circumstances, I learned a great deal about the children's fears and worries about their dad. In our rush to get things done before he left those concerns had been buried. It became clear that God wasn't punishing me, but He was giving us exactly what we needed to work things out together. For us, love and healing was definitely spelled T-I-M-E.

Christmas gifts were made or mail ordered that year. I finally passed the danger point and was given the go ahead to labor if that was what happened. We had a quiet holiday together and did get to visit our friends and watch a tear jerking computer presentation Allen had sent to us. We saved a set of presents to open when Daddy was home. Shortly thereafter we found ourselves just two weeks shy of Allen's return. Suddenly this baby who had threatened to appear weeks before was now laying low.

New Year's came and went. Contractions effectively stopped. The end was in sight now and I allowed myself to hope that maybe Allen would be back in time for baby's birth. The day came when Allen left Iraq and began the commute home. It was several days of hopping from one plane to another, out of touch with us. I breathed deeply for the first time in months when he called and was in friendly territory once again. I went to bed the last night of his trip after speaking to him in Maryland on his layover. At eleven a.m. he would be here. Unbelievable. It was finally over. I went to bed and let that reality wash over me.

That whole reality-washing-over-me part lasted about thirty minutes, which was when my water broke. All I could think was, "No stinkin' way! This is happening **now**?" Oh yes, though, it definitely was. I called my midwife, who was scheduled to attend my home birth. I called my faithful friend, who had just settled in for the night, thinking her standby labor partner job was no longer needed. And I called Allen at the hotel in Maryland. He joined us by phone as labor began.

This eighth birth turned out to be one of the most challenging. The baby was in an unusual position and just was not descending as well as we hoped. The pain and the effort involved notwithstanding, there was a quiet there too. That same unexpected serenity that had carried us through all those months was seeing us through this final struggle. There was to be no panic, just hushed determination and Allen's voice on the other end of that phone.

The baby was born at nearly 2 a.m., just as his Daddy was leaving for the airport to fly home. The last thing he heard before boarding the plane was his new son Brendan's first cries. The timing was perfect. The calling card he was using had held out and the whole birth, fit between his landing and taking off again so at least he could be virtually present for the entire event.

While I would never wish to do that alone I can see now that God used the fullness of the experience to help me trust more and to show me what I was capable of when I let go of my white-knuckled grip of control. It also helped Allen to discern what place his military career needed to take in our lives. It had been a marvelous ride, but that time in the desert had turned his heart towards home and family. Another unexpected blessing was that, after months of their own "desert experience," our dear friends were offered a spectacular new job the very week Allen returned.

Most importantly, it helped all of us reorder our lifestyle and priorities. Instead of seeing myself as having been sideswiped by life, I realized God showed me the abundance that was overflowing right there in front of me. That was perhaps the greatest grace of all, to see what was right in our hands all the time. Life is good. Sometimes it is even better when it seems like it is at its worst.

Kim Fry

After 20 years of traveling around the country with the USAF, followed by eight years on a ranch in rural Colorado, the Fry family (now boasting ten wonderful children) has recently relocated to Germany. They believe the very best place to be is within the will of God.

HEALED BY GRACE

I was sexually abused by an uncle when I was six years old. I told no one because he told me I was a bad girl and that no one would believe me. It was a one-time thing; however, I constantly lived with fear. At age thirteen, I was brutally raped by someone I knew and trusted. I think at this point I might have told someone that if the earlier incident hadn't happened this might not have either...but it did. At my young age, I felt I had no one to turn to. To ease the pain, I found a way to get alcohol and I started drinking daily.

In high school I was a good student and an accomplished athlete. On the outside, I am sure it looked like I was a successful teenager, but on the inside I felt used, dirty, worthless. After the early abuse it was easy to give into sex. After awhile, however, I felt like I had become a prostitute. I used alcohol and sex to deaden my pain, but the alcohol and sex caused my pain. I fell deeper and deeper into a destructive circle. I didn't see any way out.

One of my boyfriends was several years older than me. We dated for over a year and planned on marrying. My parents found out we were sexually active and they put me on birth control pills. We broke up a few months later. A few nights after our break up, I wanted to talk to him so went to his house. He wasn't home and his father molested me. The next boyfriend I dated for two years in high school and then on and off during four years of college. He beat me up on occasion. It was with him that I became pregnant. We never even thought of having a child together or getting married. I don't remember ever considering keeping the baby. In fact, I don't remember ever thinking about "it" being a child. I went to Planned Parenthood where I was given a pregnancy test. I was left in a room the size of a closet to wait for the results, and then was silently ushered into a large office with a huge cherry wooden desk. There, the clinic worker gave me a business card with the name of a doctor who would perform an abortion.

A few days later I made an appointment with this doctor. I don't remember if there was any kind of consultation. I don't remember clinicians at Planned Parenthood or the doctor himself ever talking to me about any options. No one mentioned to me that this was a *child* and I might consider adoption or keeping him or her. No one said they'd help me tell my parents, or find resources to keep my baby. No one offered me any choices, just an abortion. I was pregnant and no one but my boyfriend knew, so I guessed I would have to have an abortion. I went to the doctor's office one afternoon and they put a reed into my cervix that would slowly dilate me over a twenty-four hour period. It was very uncomfortable and caused lots of cramping. The next day I was to return for the procedure.

The day of the abortion was a bright, southwestern summer day. It was in direct contrast to the gloom I felt in my heart. I was all alone in the waiting room. Everyone had someone there for support but me. Even though it was twenty-eight years ago, I remember it vividly. I was very afraid but I never thought about the fact that I was carrying a child within me. Now I realize that God was crying out to me. My soul knew what I was about to do. I was just too numbed by the world to hear my own heart.

After sitting in the waiting room for what seemed like an eternity, the clinician called my name. I was taken to a private room. They gave me anesthesia and performed a suction abortion. The only problem was that the anesthesia didn't last long enough for the clinic workers to clean the room after the abortion. I woke up and saw on the counter a glass gallon jar filled with blood and tissue. I immediately became hysterical and started crying; now realizing what had just happened. The workers shushed me and brought me milk and cookies to calm me down, as if milk and cookies could make up for what we had just done. My boyfriend arrived shortly after that since I wasn't supposed to drive home. I am certain that otherwise he would not have come at all. A clinic worker brought him back to the room where I was sitting and sobbing. I don't remember him giving me any comfort. He did, however, eat the cookies.

On the drive home, my boyfriend was still hungry so we stopped for a pizza. I didn't eat. I just stared out into space and felt numb. I felt no grieving, no awareness of what I had just done. I just felt ...nothing. I know now that shame and guilt were beginning their dance within me, but I pushed them away. I didn't know God then but He knew me. He was calling me, but in my pain I refused to hear.

I was a rodeo queen that summer and was supposed to be training a new horse for a national contest. I lived at home with my parents for the summer and even though I wasn't supposed to do any physical labor for at least two weeks, after a few days I couldn't keep putting off my parent's questions about why I wasn't riding and training like I was supposed to be doing. I decided I had to ride in order to avert questions, so I saddled up and just did some slow work. The next day, I was hit with excruciating cramps and started hemorrhaging. I left work and went home, but was met at the door by my mother who had called me at work and was told I went home sick. She looked at me bent over in pain and all I could blurt out was, "Mom, I had an abortion." I am sure this news hit her like a ton of bricks, but the one I was really worried about was my Catholic father. We weren't raised with any faith. But he had remained true to his Catholic heritage. Mom said I had to tell him.

When Dad came home from work that night I went out to the living room. He was sitting in a big recliner. I got tears in my eyes and told him what I had done. His eyes welled up. His arms opened. I ran to his lap, and we sat there crying together. Looking back, I believe that was one of my first encounters with Christ through another human being.

No one ever spoke of my abortion again. My boyfriend and I broke up and I started dating my boss. He was quite a bit older than me. We dated for a few weeks and then one night he raped me. I now realized that I was obviously attracting the wrong kind of man. By the time I was 20, I had been sexually violated by an uncle, molested by my boyfriend's father, violently raped twice, beaten by boyfriends and violated in many other ways.

I graduated from college that year with a degree in science but continued to live a life of sin. I went from one relationship to the next, never really thinking about what I was doing to myself. I never once thought about having a soul. I never once thought about there being a God who might care about me. How could anyone ever really love or care about me? It was too painful to even think about.

A few years later I moved in with a family to help them with their kids and horses. I talked with them about God and His hand in the world. Since my degree had been in science, I argued with them about things like how the mountains were made. It was eye-opening to me that some people thought God created the earth purposely rather than it happening randomly through up thrusts and earth movements. I debated them with vigor but it started me thinking. A short time later, I met my husband. He had been born Catholic and still occasionally went to Church. I had been baptized Catholic, so we were married in the Church. I remember saying I would marry in the Church as long as it didn't mean that I had to say I believed in something that I didn't believe in. I am sure the Lord was laughing!

I had been drinking regularly since the first rape at age 13, and after seven years of marriage my drinking was out of control. I knew this was bigger than me and started being curious about the possibility that there really was a God and Creator. I asked questions, went to different churches for Bible studies and mostly put this "God" to the test. I frequently challenged Him with things like..."Okay God, if you are real then do such and such for me."

During this time, I had become friends with the local Catholic priest. He loved horses and we would ride together. We developed a close friendship over the course of a year or two, but I never thought of becoming a Catholic. He was moved from our area by the Bishop, but I kept in touch with him. Over the next year or so, my drinking became worse. By that time we had a son and he was paying the price of having an alcoholic mom. Every night I drank either a six-pack or more of beer or a fifth of hard liquor. I wasn't violent and could hold my liquor well. Most wouldn't know I had had that much to drink, but I was irritable and short-tempered with my son.

I couldn't continue to live this way. I had hit rock-bottom. I tried a support group for alcoholics, but it didn't seem to work for me. Then, I found out this priest was returning to the area for a wedding. I sought him out and fell to my knees before him. Through my tears I begged him to help me. We made arrangements to get together where he heard my first Confession and gave me my first Holy Communion. Remember, I had been baptized into the Church as a baby. At my Confession, this priest asked me to offer up my alcohol—not as a penance, but just for an intention of his. I walked out of that Church and never took another drink. That was seventeen years ago. Since that day, May 20th, the Lord has taken me on an incredible journey of healing and forgiveness.

I was so filled with zeal when I returned from meeting with the priest. My husband and I had been at odds for some time. In fact I had almost left him on several occasions, but after my conversion I felt able to endure anything! My life changed drastically. I went from spending time drinking at home or in bars to going to prayer groups and studying the faith. In fact, when I went to my local priest to ask what I needed to do to prepare to be confirmed, he told me I knew more about the faith than most people sitting in the pew. I continued to study, pray and grow in faith and trust. The only difficult part for me was that the stronger my faith became, the unhappier my husband became. He was angry with the Church and didn't want to have to follow any of its rules, like Natural Family Planning. Many times I felt that he liked me better as an alcoholic than a Catholic...and that hurt.

About that time, a friend told me that she was going to homeschool her children. I remember thinking and saying to her that she was absolutely NUTS! It sounded ridiculous and radical to me. Then one day my sister-in-law and I were on a trip together and I found out that *she* had embraced this homeschooling thing! I was trapped in the car with her for eight hours so I had to listen. By the time we got home, God had worked a miracle once again in my heart and I was open to the possibility that this *might* be something the Lord wanted even me to do. I embarked on a summer of reading and research. I told no one, but took my thoughts to the Lord and asked for His guidance and His will to be done. By August, with our oldest son just weeks away from entering the public school kindergarten, I presented my case to my husband. I had asked the Lord to use my husband as my answer. If he was in favor of it I would proceed; if he was against it, our son would attend public school. When I was finished presenting the pros and the cons, my husband simply turned to me and said, "I think you would do a great job." God had given me His answer.

So we began the homeschool adventure. Not much Catholic curriculum was available back then, but I chose what I felt was best. My son had difficulty keeping up with the reading and the math. It took me most of that year to realize that something was amiss. It took several more years to fully understand that our son was severely dyslexic and had auditory processing difficulties to boot. I decided to educate myself on dyslexia, and it is a good thing because all of our children have some form of it, ranging from mild to severe. But still, I pressed on and God was faithful to me.

I don't think I had doubts about homeschooling that were strictly tied to the abortion. Actually, I didn't think at that time that my abortion was having any affect whatsoever on my adult life. I had confessed it when I joined the Church and that was that. Or so I thought. It wasn't until a few years after I had begun homeschooling that I came face to face with it. I was encountering problems in my marriage and in dealing with the demons of the past. I started seeking healing in many ways.

Your sins are forgiven.
Mark 2:5

One evening my best friend and I attended a talk on conversion and forgiveness. The speaker focused on forgiving ourselves and what a loving God we have. The pilgrim image of Our Lady of Guadalupe was there, and the speaker's talk touched on abortion. After the talk as we were all visiting, my friend came running over to me saying she was going to buy us each a t-shirt. I went to look at it and turned inside out. On the back was an image of Our Lady of Guadalupe with a pro-life message on it. I was very agitated and told my friend "NO! I don't want one!"

On way home that night, I decided I had to tell her about my abortion and why I had reacted the way I had. At that time, it seemed completely hypocritical to defend life when I had taken a life myself. Our Lady was working on me though because this was the first time that I realized I was still carrying around the weight of my abortion.

Several months later, I attended a healing service that was being offered with hopes that I could find healing for my marriage. You see, I was still in denial that I needed healing for the abortion. The priest laid his hands on me and began to pray. Within minutes, I was sobbing uncontrollably. This was a new experience for me but somewhere deep inside of me I knew it was about the abortion. My best friend was there with me.

Later I told her that my tears were about the abortion. She looked me in the eye and said, "I already knew because during the prayer time I looked up and you were sitting under a full-size image of Our Lady of Guadalupe!" I knew then that God had not forsaken me, that God does love me, and that Our Lady of Guadalupe was watching over me. After that, I became involved with Rachel's Vineyard, a ministry for healing after abortion.

The Lord blessed us with four more children, and we continue to homeschool. My life is not perfect, and our marriage has its ups and downs, but I am confident that with God's help I can overcome any obstacle and remain in His peace and healing. I want to give hope to other Catholic homeschooling moms who may have experienced the pain of abortion. It can be overcome with God's help. He makes all things new with His amazing grace. ·

"Rachel" lives out West with her husband and five children. She has homeschooled since 1992.

A WORD FROM YOUR FATHER

You say:

> I can't do this. I'm too tired, and I'm not smart enough. I'll lose all my good friends and feel all alone. I don't think I can figure this out or manage house and schoolwork at the same time.

God says:

> With men this is impossible; but with God all things are possible. Matthew 19:26
>
> Cast all your cares on me. I Peter 5:7
>
> I will give you rest. Matthew 11:28-30
>
> I give you wisdom. I Corinthians 1:30
>
> I will never leave you or forsake you. Hebrews 13:5
>
> My grace is sufficient for you, for my power is made perfect in weakness. 2 Corinthians 12:9
>
> I will direct your steps Trust in the Lord with all your heart and lean not on your own understanding. Proverbs 3:5-6
>
> I will supply all your needs. Philippians 4:19
>
> You can do everything through me, who gives you strength. Philippians 4:13
>
> I am able to make all grace abound to you, so that in all things at all times, having all that you need, you will abound in every good work. II Corinthians 9:8
>
> For I did not give you a spirit of timidity, but a spirit of power, of love and of self-discipline. 2 Timothy 1:7

And Further More...

> Behold, children are a heritage from the Lord, the fruit of the womb a reward. Like arrows in the hand of a warrior are the children of

one's youth. Blessed is the man who fills his quiver with them! He shall not be put to shame when he speaks with his enemies in the gate. Psalms 127:3-5

And when Esau lifted up his eyes and saw the women and children, he said, "Who are these with you?" Jacob said, "The children *whom God has graciously given* your servant. Genesis 33:5

You shall teach them diligently to your children, and shall talk of them when you sit in your house, and when you walk by the way, and when you lie down, and when you rise. Deuteronomy 6:7

Fathers, do not provoke your children to anger, but bring them up in the discipline and instruction of the Lord." Ephesians 6:4

"Train up a child in the way he should go; even when he is old he will not depart from it. Proverbs 22:6

A kind mouth multiplies friends and gracious lips prompt friendly greetings. Sirach 6:5

Do not give into sadness,
Torment not yourself with brooding;
Gladness of heart is the very life of man,
Cheerfulness prolongs his days.
Distract yourself, renew your courage,
Drive resentment far away from you;
For worry has brought death to many,
Nor is there aught to be gained from resentment.
Envy and anger shorten one's life,
Worry brings on premature old age.
One who is cheerful and gay while at the table
Benefits from his food. Sirach 30:21-25

Chapter Ten

FAMILY FIRST

"(Children) are a gift from the Lord." (Psalm 127:3)

A Promise Kept

Two bright-eyed girls whirled round the dance floor at the Knights of Columbus St. Patrick's Day Party—one a slim and lively eleven year old, the other a dimpled baby. The baby squealed delightedly with each bounce and bump, the deep burbling sounds of a well-entertained nine-month-old. The older girl twirled as if she would never stop, spurred by that irresistible laughter—more musical than music itself.

Watching these two girls—my own daughters Theresa and Eileen—it struck me how unusual a thing it is these days to see sisters a decade apart. My mind wandered back to a time in the almost-forgotten past:

> My fiancé and I are leaning over black and white composition books, comparing the answers to questions asked of us at the Cana Conference Retreat. We are completing an exercise meant to ensure we each know the other's plans for married life. The first question reads:
>
> "How many children do you hope to have?"
>
> An optimistic "At least eight" appears in my feminine slant, and in my fiancé's masculine scrawl, "About half a dozen."
>
> We both want a large family. So far, so good.
>
> The next question continues:
>
> "How soon do you want to start a family?"
>
> A confident "Right away" appears plainly in the feminine slant, but this time the masculine scrawl is nowhere to be seen.
>
> What is the meaning of this, I wonder. Aren't we both ready to start a family?
>
> My fiancé looks at me seriously and explains, "I would love to begin a family right away, but my fear is that, years from now, you will remember the career you left behind and feel sorry. I don't ever want you to have any regrets."
>
> "I will never feel that way," I assure him with confidence.
>
> "How do you know?"

"Because I know myself. It would not be possible for me to feel that way."

And that was that.

I woke from my reverie to find my husband motioning something to me, his eyes twinkling meaningfully—our little boy was on the dance floor attempting the "Cotton Eye Joe" in awkward, oversized red snow boots (none of us had noticed his unconventional footwear until we arrived at the party). We laughed as only two parents, united through the Sacrament of Matrimony, but also in infinite love for a child, can laugh. Sitting there at that table, with our children dotting the dance floor like violets in a May meadow, we shared another moment among millions to remember the undeniable Truth of the Catechism: "Children are the supreme gift of marriage and contribute greatly to the good of the parents themselves." (CCC 1652)

And I secretly gloated, thinking upon my own prescient words of self-awareness, "It would not be possible for me to feel that way." Indeed, I never have and never will.

Years ago, I remember telling a dear friend and former classmate of mine we were expecting our first child. She responded as our culture has taught her, and, as she heartily believed even without any real life experience, "What a waste!"

Please understand, as I repeat these words, they held no sting for me then or now. I know, in fact, she meant them as a backhanded compliment, a tribute to my "worth." Her sensibilities were steeped in society's pervasive notion that children should be, particularly for the educated woman, an afterthought, best left until prominence, profit and partnership are all checked off the to do list. (Here I am not talking about the many mothers who sacrifice for the good of their families by working outside the home, but those trapped in a spiral of unnecessary ambition, postponing the deepest joys in life.) My heart went out to her in honest sympathy, as I imagined her wearing her youth away, perhaps never tasting the joy I was already feeling just knowing a precious heart was even then beating beneath my own.

And what of that to do list? What price would have been exacted for prominence, profit and partnership?

Prominence would have required my twenties. The children of my twenties were Agnes, Theresa, and Margaret.

Profit would have sought my early thirties. The children of my early thirties were Marie and Patrick.

Partnership's capital investment would have been paid during my late thirties. The children of my late thirties were Catherine and Eileen.

Somehow, I think I would have been working off the wrong list.

Is it any wonder I reaffirm today, but with even greater fervor and emphasis, that promise, spoken all those years ago: "I will never feel that way. It would be impossible for me to feel that way."

But this time, I am uttering a heartfelt Deo Gratias to go along with it.

Alice Gunther

Alice is a wife and mother of eight children. (One more was added since the story was originally written.) She writes The Catholic Home column for The Long Island Catholic. Alice is also the author of "Haystack Full of Needles: A Catholic Home Educator's Guide to Socialization," published by Hillside Education. Find her online at www.alicegunther.com .

MOTHER AS A HUMAN BEING

We mothers can be so efficient. We can do laundry, clean a dirty kitchen, and calm sibling spats in between spooning Gerber's best into our babies' mouths. Once, just for fun, I wrote down everything I did during a one-hour period one morning. The list took up two pages.

I often get wrapped up in juggling tasks, in accomplishing, in doing. I know I am efficient. Most mothers are. But I am here today to admit that maybe that's not always the best thing to be.

Once, one of my sons, in the fifth grade at the time, invented a new game. He spent hours devising rules, cutting out game pieces, and gluing the pieces to toothpicks. (It was a very involved game.) The object, if I remember, was conquering the world, which wasn't a bad goal considering he was just ten. At any rate, I was busy the morning he finished the game. I was doing laundry, cleaning up baby spit-up, changing diapers, sweeping the carpet and tending to a dirty kitchen. You know, I was being efficient. I was "doing."

When my son finished creating the game he immediately wanted to play. I admired the game from the stairway, my arms full of miscellaneous objects I was putting away, and I promised to play "in a bit." I had, in my mind, a list of things I needed to do, and I was on a roll. I would play later. He could show his sister now. When the clothes were put away and my other chores were done, I asked my son to show me his creation. He simply gave me the short version of his game. No one told me his initial enthusiasm and willingness to explain every detail would wane. It simply dissipated and didn't come back. Even a little motherly prodding didn't elicit more than, "Well, you just roll the dice and follow the instructions on the card. It was fun when I played it awhile ago. What's for dinner?" Now, eight years later, I still think of that moment lost. It's a little thing, but I wish I hadn't been quite so efficient that afternoon.

Another time my efficiency cost me something really special. It was early spring. I had been trying to teach the children to come to me when they wanted something instead of yelling out "Mom!" from wherever they were. That morning I was in the basement, switching a load of laundry, with the baby in the swing.

"Mom! Come here!" I heard. Again, "Mom! Come here!"

There was no alarm in the voices, just a sense of urgency.

"I'm in the basement," I answered cheerily, giving them notice but not budging.

"Mom!" Now more than one child was calling my name. What did those kids want? Why wouldn't they come to me? What was so important? I finished pouring liquid detergent into the machine, folded a couple more towels, grabbed some garbage bags which I needed in the kitchen, took the baby from the swing and climbed the stairs. In the family room five children were standing, staring at the sliding glass door.

"You missed it!" said Michael, visibly disappointed.

"Missed what?" I asked, peering out the window.

"Two deer," he continued, "A buck and a doe...in our backyard."

Now, if we had lived on a farm or other rural area, that might not be such a big deal, but we live in a subdivision with a smaller yard that is fenced in on two sides.

"Really? Deer?" I exclaimed, coming closer to look.

"It's too late, Mom," Michael said, "They're gone."

The kids turned away from the window, leaving me there, standing alone.

That was the second moment that I lost because I was being efficient.

It's true. My kids won't be scarred forever on account of these two incidents. But you can bet that both events taught me something. I learned that no work I am doing is so vital that it can't be put aside for just a moment, if something important comes along. My children should not expect me to come running at the drop of a hat, but nor should I be so busy that I can't take advantage of a precious moment that spontaneously arises. The Martha-Mary dilemma presents itself every day, and moms need to discern quickly to make the right choice. There is a good reason God calls us human "beings" and not human "doings." From now on I strive to "be" just a little bit more.

Theresa A. Thomas

THE CHOICE I MADE

There was a cherry tree in the backyard of my childhood — a fragrant, bulging cherry tree whose branches sprawled out in three different directions. On summer afternoons, my sister and I would climb and dream in that cherry tree, oblivious to the world below.

In its branches we were riding dinosaurs, soaring into space, or just hiding from our little brother. In that tree we made plans for the rest of our lives and for the rest of the afternoon. The possibilities were endless.

Flash forward twelve years. I am a sophomore in college declaring a major. I choose English because I love the written word and a good story, and I choose a minor in American history because I finally figure out that history consists of good stories that happen to be true. Ignoring well meaning advisors who suggest a practical major, I study what I love and worry about a job later.

It is a hot day in May when I turn my tassel and join the ranks of alumni. *"Magna Cum Laude"* reads my diploma. I am so proud. I have a practical job at an advertising agency waiting for me, but my secret desire is "just" to be the best wife I can be to David, the man I will soon marry, and to be an extraordinary mother to the brood of children we hope we will have.

I have kept all my Shakespeare notes so I can introduce him to my not yet existing children. I have saved all my history papers so one day these children can know the magnificent stories that have created the fabric of modern life. I am yearning, not for advancement through the agency I have just joined, but to excel as a helpmate to my ambitious, smart, soon-to-be husband. I am feeling stronger that this desire of mine is a vocation to which God has called me. I am feeling that God wants me to be His missionary at home, to some little people who don't even exist yet. After graduation I ask my father if he would regret his financial assistance to me in college if I did no more than stay home and raise children. He smiles and replies that in educating me he has educated an entire family.

Today I sit on the green painted, peeling rocker on the front porch of my home. The street is lined with cottonwood trees. They are messy, and aren't good for climbing, but they are sturdy, prolific, and provide nice shade on hot summer days. In my arms I hold my baby daughter. She and I sit rocking, watching her seven brothers and sisters play in the yard. It will be fall soon, and we will start school again, in the schoolroom in our home, as we have done for years.

My vocation has become my passion, which has become my full-time job. Day after day I explain addition, sew on buttons, read and interpret stories, read and interpret hearts. Through home schooling and performing my duties as wife and mother I come to believe that service is at the heart of authentic womanhood. We love those whom we serve, and by serving we learn how to love. Serving my family has given me great joy. Many days I feel I fall short in my mission, but I move on, go forward, reminding myself of Mother Teresa's gentle command: "Do ordinary things with extraordinary love."

In the years we have homeschooled, I have been able to introduce my children to Shakespeare ("Mommy, Puck is so funny!" exclaimed my little daughter referring to a character in *A Midsummer Night's Dream*), and to the events leading up to the American Civil War. (These true stories rival any present day adventure book!) My children and I have endured monotonous memorization of state capitols, and have reveled in the discovery of history come alive by traveling to Gettysburg, Pennsylvania and Washington, D.C. We have had family poetry nights, where we share original poems, and have played our own version of Jeopardy with science topics.

My oldest children have made the transition to the diocesan high school. One has gone on to college. My service to them, now, has shifted to letting go, little by little, so they can eventually learn to stand on their own. I must work myself out of a job, free them to make their own choices, and then repeat this process again and again with my other children.

When chaotic days unfold, as they inevitably do, I remind myself that I am living a vocation which, in its best moments, allows me to pass the richness of my education on to another generation, and in its worst moments, allows me to practice virtues, such as patience, that I will probably never master. During the day, like so many other mothers, I teach and learn, cook and clean, and drive kids to soccer practice and violin lessons, all while trying to help my children know, love and serve God. At night, I do what I love best — tell stories and snuggle with my children. They invigorate me. They exhaust me. They form me just as I form them.

After I close their doors at night, sometimes I think about their futures. I do not regret not pursuing a full-time paying job. I do not worry what might have been. My education has not been wasted. On the contrary, it has been well-used. My choice isn't the only one, but it is a valid one. I have made a good decision, and with God's help my children will make good decisions too. I realize, almost twenty years later, that the possibilities are still endless.

Theresa A. Thomas

NOT WHAT WE PLANNED

"Daddy, I'm pregnant."

My unmarried daughter's announcement last February forever changed our family. No longer could "unplanned pregnancies" or "single mothers" be spoken of in abstract terms, as things that only happen in other families.

This was a flesh-and-blood reality that challenged us to renew our commitment to Christ and to our beloved firstborn daughter.

The early weeks of 2006 had some remarkable twists. On New Year's Day, hours before heading to Boston for my annual Ignatian retreat, my wife Maureen gave me the surprising yet wonderful news that she was pregnant. In February we learned that she was carrying twins, but the joy tuned to sadness as one died in utero, then the other. While Maureen was still recovering from her seventh and eighth miscarriages, we learned that we were to become grandparents for the first time. Over the course of the next several months, we had our ups and downs, but we've come to see in a more profound way God's providential love for our family.

Like all Catholic parents, we strive to provide all our children with a solid formation in the Christian faith. While parents might disagree on the exact amount of "sheltering" that needs to take place, clearly during our children's formative years it's crucial to maintain some control over their environment and activities. Yet when our children become adults in their own right, we can't exercise the same type of control. We desire good things for our adult children, but we can't make decisions for them.

Maureen jokingly says, "I hate free will" when our children make bad decisions. If it were only up to us, our children would always choose Christ and His Church, and they would always choose that which is morally good. Yet they are all on their own journey home to God, and we have to trust that the Lord in His time will lead them to repentance and conversion.

In this particular situation, we obviously could not undo the sins and bad choices our daughter had already made as an emancipated adult. Even more importantly, going forward we could not "control" the outcome, despite my conviction that "Father knows best" how to handle the situation. Maureen and I had to learn that what was needed was not control and coercion, but love, support, and wise guidance. Our daughter had to make her own difficult decisions, and that was scary.

In the weeks following this "bombshell," my daughter was inclined to choose to place her child in an adoptive home. There is substantial irony in this, as Maureen and I have had several experiences of adoption as the adoptive parents. I affirmed my daughter's inclination to go the adoption route. The totality of her circumstances, not to mention the absence of a father, seemed to point clearly in that direction. At her request, I began looking for a couple that might be open to an independent adoption.

As a matter of principle, I knew that adoption would be a good, loving decision. At the same time, what grandparent does not want to be part of their grandchild's life? I have frequently called upon grandparents in that situation to be generous in supporting adoption and not to lay undue pressure on the mother to keep their grandchild. The shoe was now on the other foot, and so now I had to walk the talk. I'm glad I did, but I learned to have more compassion and understanding for grandparents who don't want to "lose" their grandchildren.

As it turned out, however, our daughter really wanted to keep the child and be a full-time mother. She just couldn't see how it could all play out given her difficult circumstances. I continued to encourage adoption and lovingly set forth the harsh realities of single motherhood. Even more, we encouraged her in her spiritual and personal life to grow in faith and responsibility. Over time, it became increasingly clear that her heart was set on keeping the child. We did our best to change gears and support this decision once it was firmly made. We invited her to move home rent-free so that she could be full-time, nursing Mom. She accepted.

Our daughter's moving home required quite an adjustment for everybody. After being on her own for several years, our 26-year-old had to deal not only with meddling parents, but also five younger siblings ranging in age from 14 to less than two, as well as her elderly grandmother. For our part, we had to get used to having an adult child in our midst, learning to balance parental concern with the desire to give her appropriate freedom and space.

Slowly but surely, our daughter blended back into our household. She grew accustomed to the rhythm of our daily life, from our more conventional hours to prayer time, family meals, and our busy homeschool day. I have commented in recent months that she has become, in some sense, more a part of our family than ever before. I'm very proud of her.

I realize that our society in general is too accepting of many evils that touch upon human sexuality and marriage and family life. All the same, as the pregnancy became more obvious to the entire world, I was so grateful for the love and compassion showed us by the families in our parish and community. I don't recall hearing any judgmental or condemning remarks.

For myself, I remember a priest once saying that God's love, when focused on us sinners, shows itself as mercy. I want my daughter and all my family to come to a profound experience of God the Father's love for us. As a human father, I thought it was absolutely necessary to communicate to my daughter God's fatherly love and mercy. It surely wasn't the only thing, but it was the most important and God-like thing.

Similarly, I always want my family to see the Church as the Family of God, our true and lasting home. Even though we might stray, the Good Shepherd goes looking for us, and there's great rejoicing in heaven when He finds us and brings us back into the fold. If my family is truly to be a "domestic Church" or as Pope John Paul II called it, a "sanctuary of life," I felt it was imperative to extend an arm of assistance, welcome, and unconditional love to my daughter in her time of need.

Through the spring the entire family eagerly awaited the newest Suprenant. Meanwhile, there was subtle yet real strengthening of family relationships. Maureen became her labor coach and helped her get ready for childbirth and beyond. Finally, on June 13, the feast of St. Anthony, little Alexandra ("Alex") Marina Terese Suprenant was born. It didn't take much for this beautiful little child of God to steal her grandpa's heart.

Our daughter and Alex are a gift to the entire family. They share a room with my daughter Mary Kate, who loves being their "roommate." Alex has two doting uncles (Samuel, 5, and Raymond, 2) who consider themselves her bodyguards. Meanwhile, our daughter continues to grow and mature as a full-time Mom. She has been a big help to her ailing grandmother, and she has become an indispensable part of our homeschooling operation, as she has been Samuel's kindergarten teacher this year. But beyond all that, her face looks happier than it has for many years.

My prayer and wish for my daughter is that she and Alex will continue to live with us. We want to encourage her ongoing growth as a woman of God and as a mother in our home until that day, God willing, that our Lord calls her to the Sacrament of Marriage. Of course, all of that is her decision, not mine.

Leon Suprenant

Leon is the director of catechesis and program development for www.mycatholicfaithdelivered.com, an online, Catholic learning center. He has written many books and articles on the Catholic faith. He resides with his family in the Archdiocese of Kansas City in Kansas.

THE LITTLE THINGS

It's the little things that really matter—an impromptu game of marbles or discovering a family of ladybugs on the kitchen windowsill. Jungle animals imagined in drifting cloud formations. Quiet togetherness. Watering newly planted pansies. One boy's huge chocolate-brown eyes peering slyly over a splayed hand of Uno; the other's pensive azure-blue eyes expectantly taking in a thick, juicy, new novel. Steaming hot cocoa after wintry sledding, icy lemonade after a summer bike ride. Bare, little boy feet slapping dewy grass at dusk on early summer evenings, catching and releasing fireflies, whoops of excitement uncontainable.

Often, what counts most are the strings of unremarkable moments. It's also the deeply sublime. Sitting side by side on our sun-splattered deck, one son grapples with Latin adverbs; the other conquers place value. Embroiled in the nightly clamor of the Osages' fierce war cries on the 1870s American high prairie, the terror of the Ingalls' family becomes ours. Consumed by the awesome humility of Aslan, sacrificing himself at the stone table in the world beyond the wardrobe, we, like his sons of Adam and daughters of Eve, are awed by his sanctifying grace and selflessness. Transforming our yard into the banks of the Nile, we craft Egyptian pharaohs' stately crooks and become one with the ancients.

While immersed in any of these ventures we call school, which have become the rhythm of our lives, day-to-day demands are often left dangling. The question of "What's for dinner?" looms unanswered, actually unthought-of many days. The laundry pile waits; the carpet frequently remains simply un-vacuumed. I often think, as we step over the daily effects of a family of four, that, well, I need to balance life, school and home keeping a bit better. My husband maintains a grasp on this disquieting awakening of mine that "school" persistently tops my lists over "home," as I mournfully tell him many nights, "I got nothing d-o-n-e today!" He centers me and brings me back to what is real.

We are there for it all. We nurture; we provide the constancy that is the foundation of their growing independence. And aren't we blessed? Is this not the greatest gift? The magnitude of our vocation to homeschooling continually unfolds to my husband and to me. My soul sighs in witness of our sons' small acts of kindness or independence or maturity or academic prowess that gradually reveal themselves. It is unfathomable to me that *one day* my sons will drive; master calculus; interpret Homer; translate foreign languages; conduct experiments around concepts which baffle me; be taller than me; not want me around; get married; become Daddies, be contributing members of our society and of our Church. All in God's plan.

I pray that all this will come in time. I pray for it; but I don't want it.

One day our sons will not be 7 and 10, but rather 30, 40, 50.... And because of this, the small things are what matter. They will become the hinges in the lives of the men we are privileged by God to see unfolding, little by little, day by day.

Christine Capolino

Christine Capolino loves her life as a homeschooling Mom! Chris grew up in Queens, New York and currently resides on Long Island with her husband and their two lively, lovable boys. Before becoming a Mom, Chris taught for a dozen years and holds degrees in Education from St. John's University. She is proud to be a columnist at www.amazingcatechists.com and www.catholicmom.com.. Chris is currently writing a book around the beauty and wonder of her family's everyday life.

FROM RICHES TO RAGS

I started my job search as a college graduate with a computer science degree. I was agonizing over having to accept a job that would have moved my fiancé Scott and me across the country and away from our families when, out of the blue, a wonderful job opportunity presented itself in our home town. What a relief! I'd be a computer analyst with a large, international organization in a fast-paced, prestigious work environment that many would envy. I would be making almost double what most people could expect coming right out of college. Of course I took it and started immediately.

Working in the corporate world as a computer analyst in the mid-1980s was exciting. I utilized my major. I wore nice suits and pretty blouses. I rubbed elbows with smart and interesting people. This career enabled my husband Scott and me to buy our first home right away, as well as an expensive, sporty, bright red Camaro. I'm sure everyone thought we were living the "good life".

As our first two children came eighteen months apart, the demands at home and at work began to wear on me. I'd work, come home, work, go to bed, work and then do it again the next day. I had hardly any time with my children. After five years in the corporate world, I seriously began to question my priorities. Work was becoming increasingly demanding, and I felt an enormous maternal pull towards my little ones at home. I had a good babysitting arrangement but felt that the babysitter got the best part of my children's day. When my children's little arms wrapped around me at night I began to think that working wasn't all it was cracked up to be. I felt increasingly discontent. I felt gypped.

This feeling never went away. Each day wore me down more and more. I'd kiss the children good-bye with an aching in my heart that lasted all day until I was with them again at night. Then suddenly one day, I hit my breaking point. I was sitting in a staff meeting listening to my boss impose 16 hours a week of mandatory overtime on me and my colleagues. At the time, I was still nursing my eight-month-old son, expressing milk throughout the day at various intervals for him. I asked my boss if I would be able to go home at the end of the day to eat dinner with my family and nurse my baby. I was told that the baby would have to be brought in for me to nurse. I imagined this: after a twenty minute rendezvous with my little family, in which time I hastily nursed my baby, I would be asked to kiss his sweet little head goodbye, say goodnight to him, my husband, and my toddler daughter, and return to my office for the remainder of the evening. With my head spinning, I left that meeting feeling like I had no choice but to try to find a way out of this job that had once seemed like a dream come true. I wanted out, immediately.

When my husband came home from work that night, he found me sitting on the floor of the family room, crying. I had bills sprawled out all over the floor, and I was feverishly punching numbers into a calculator, trying to figure out a way to manage on his entry-level engineer's pay of $7.00 an hour. It was useless. There seemed no way for me to quit my job and for him to support our family of four, so I began to pray. *"Show me a way out, Lord!"* I begged. *"You have to understand how I need to be with my children... You know they need me... Show me a way!"*

Amazingly, within days my prayer was answered. It came in the form of a phone call from a family friend who said I had been on her mind. She was wondering if I wanted to do some part-time computer programming at home. This was the perfect "out" that I needed! I quit my corporate job and rushed home to my family. Honestly, I never looked back.

The life of a stay-at-home mom began to take shape. I said goodbye to my business suits, nylons, and high-heeled shoes and hello to comfortable blue jeans, tennis shoes, and tee-shirts, complete with spit-up stains on the shoulders and leaky milk spots on the front. The part-time work at home lasted about three years, during which time baby number three came along, and my husband's job began to generate an income on which we could live. We clipped coupons, shopped clearance racks, rummaged through garage sales, and drove used cars. I thought I was living the "good life" before, but I discovered that this simple life was truly the "good life!" Being home with my kids was so fulfilling that I wanted to delve deeper into my vocation as mother. It simply seemed natural to consider homeschooling. The thought of homeschooling began as a gentle tug that just wouldn't go away. When I felt God beginning to call me to this new vocation, I said, "Okay God, but I want my home- school to be Catholic and I'm going to need someone to help me get started." Since I knew no other Catholic homeschoolers and there was no such thing as the Internet on which to find the answers, I didn't even know where to start. Incredibly, though, the doors just opened for me. God took my two requests and fulfilled them. I simply "knew" what the perfect curriculum for our family would be when I ran across it (Seton). I easily found (during a time when few in our small town were homeschooling) a mom that became my mentor. I did not question God's direction; it was just clear. That's all I can say. It was His grace. I asked. I trusted. And He doled out in abundance.

I did not re-enroll my daughter in the parochial school where she attended first grade, but instead began what is now my thirteen-year-long adventure of homeschooling. After twenty-two years of marriage, we have successfully graduated our first born, and she is thriving at college. The way I figure it, I ought to be ready to retire by the time we get our five boys to that point.

This is my life now, and I don't regret the choice I made to stay home and raise and educate our children. Of course, we hear the occasional, "We'd probably _____ if Mom was still working." Fill in this blank with "have a swimming pool," "drive a sports car," "wear designer shoes," "go out to dinner regularly," etc. but that thought quickly dissipates. Those things aren't worth the trade of the happiness we've gleaned from my choice to stay home. We have learned that the riches in this life aren't shiny red Camaros, fancy clothes and corporate careers. The riches that matter are the things that we can't buy...a fruitful marriage, beautiful children, and a solid faith in God that He will direct us to the riches of Heaven. Yes, my life is a success. Thank God for His grace to go from "riches to rags."

Mary Stutzman

Mary has been married to Scott, her high-school sweetheart, for more than 25 years. She is mother to one daughter, Sarah, and five busy boys, Greg, Adam, Jacob, Matthew, and Philip. Besides homeschooling, she sings in the church choir, teaches CCD, and enjoys quilting in her free time.

MAKING THINGS HAPPEN

I really, really want a set of encyclopedias! I thought this over and over as we were about to embark on homeschooling. It was the beginning of summer and we'd start homeschooling in the fall. I was trying to pull everything together. This was in the mid-1990s, before Internet and websites and instant information, and I desperately and specifically wanted a World Book Encyclopedia set for my five children, aged seven and under.

When I was growing up, we kept a Collier's encyclopedia set in our living room, and not only was it a good resource for reports, but Mom would send us to it often in response to childhood questions. "What kind of dog is that?" one of us might ask, as we saw a new canine running through the neighborhood. "Let's look it up," she'd reply and point us towards the proud set of books standing in the corner. Sometimes I'd just grab a volume and curl up on the sofa, turning page after page, reading whatever was of interest to me. "D." "Diving." "M." "Minstrel" This opened up a new world of learning to us kids. Why, we even learned to spell 'encyclopedia' by the time we were seven or so. Yes, I wanted encyclopedias for my children, especially now that we'd be homeschooling.

When I checked out the prices on a new set I was flabbergasted. The regular edition (maroon cover) exceeded $600. The deluxe hunter green with gold binding was more than $800. That was at least eight weeks worth of groceries. There was no way we could afford that!

Shortly afterwards, I was at a dinner party with some colleagues of my husband and their wives. I began chatting with Norma, a school teacher. I was lamenting the cost of the reference books and she gave me an idea.

"You know, I earned a set way back when," she shared. "I don't know if World Book still does it that way, but if you sold a certain number of sets you used to be able to earn one for yourself. I might still have the phone number somewhere of a district representative."

That's all I needed to hear. The next day Norma provided me with the number and I found out that yes indeed the program was still in place. My mother volunteered to watch my little ones while I signed on to go door to door.

I got a selling kit, and familiarized myself with the product. Back then, the CD Rom was a big invention and seller for World Book. I learned to extol its praises but personally liked the hardcover version best. Although I hated cold-calling and never envisioned myself as a salesperson, I followed protocol and went through the neighborhoods, starting with people I knew.

"May I have a minute of your time?" I'd begin, holding my flexible brief case containing encyclopedia samples, testimonials and of course order forms. I really believed in the product. I wanted one so badly myself that I was willing to trudge house to house and ask for a moment of people's time, although it was much more like twenty.

I came up with a note card system to keep track of people I contacted, new leads and potential buyers. I looked through our church and neighborhood directories for names. I asked others for ideas. I padded out in the morning, waving goodbye to my little ones, which I hated to do. I forced myself to leave them playing with Grandma, telling myself it was hopefully just for a few weeks in the summer and reminding myself that this time with Grandma was quality time. My mom was a great encouragement, telling me how wonderful it was that I was doing this for our family and keeping the children busy with games and books. She even asked me for details about my day when I came back, collapsing on the sofa and lunging for the baby.

I simply wanted my encyclopedias and to be done with the deal. Therefore, I poured myself into this project and hyper-focused on it in order to finish. I went through the leads every night. I targeted potential buyers and followed up with every opportunity. At the end of four weeks, I received a phone call.

"Theresa, you are the top sales person in the district for July. You have earned the hunter green, gold bound set of encyclopedias, a little cash bonus and a halogen light as a prize." It was the voice of the World Book district manager, the lady in charge. She paused and then asked me, "Would you consider continuing to sell for us? You would have a great career doing this".

I was thrilled that I had reached my goal.

"Oh thank you!" I exclaimed, imagining the beautiful hard bound set on our den shelves. I could hardly contain my excitement. And then I quickly added, "No thank you!" to the thought of continuing to sell. I am positive I sounded too enthusiastic about that, but I couldn't turn in my sales material fast enough.

I was so proud when the encyclopedias were delivered to our home. The kids and I tore open the box and sat on the sofa right then and there, smelling the pages and looking things up. When the halogen light appeared on my doorstep a few days later, I excitedly presented it to my husband.

You might think this is a recollection about perseverance, of putting one's mind to something and going out and getting it. Well, it is, sort of. Homeschooling mothers will do things they don't particularly like to do if it means their families will benefit. But this story is also about more than that. If you look back carefully you will see the words above, "Mom would send us off to it," "Mom volunteered," "she encouraged"... It's almost like a little afterthought to notice and acknowledge her involvement, but she was actually the adhesive for my whole encyclopedia-selling project. Like the stitching on a dress, her help was critical although perhaps not initially fully noticed. Without her participation, this simply would not have happened. Mom knew that I would never have left my kids with a babysitter to pursue this encyclopedia selling. As the mother of 13 kids herself, she was certainly not sitting around looking for something to occupy her time, yet she made me feel like there was nothing that she'd rather do than come over and play with her grandbabies while I accomplished something for them.

As I look back carefully, I see the common thread of her gift of time sewn throughout my life: a phone call here to give encouragement, an offer there to help me catch up on laundry, a book found just for me that she thought was relevant.

"Go take a walk. I'll hold the baby."

"Go take a nap. I've got it covered."

Her handiwork is most noticed through the eyes of retrospection.

So, while lesson number one is to stick to a task if you really want something, lesson number two is to remember those who help to make it possible. I'm resolved to pass on more than just the love of education, and encyclopedias, that my mom cultivated in us. I'm also determined to pass along her genuine selflessness and spirit of encouragement. When the time comes I hope to assist my children in their own pursuits.

Thanks, Mom for teaching me how to make things happen both for myself ...and others.

Theresa A. Thomas

Chapter 11

LEARNING NEVER ENDS

"The good man leaves inheritance to his children's children." (Proverbs 13:22)

PASSING EXAMPLE

As part of our school day my children Madeline, age 11, Graham, age 9, and I once prayed the Rosary in front of the Planned Parenthood clinic. It was in January 2006 and a bit cold and windy, even for Arizona where we live. We were bundled up and the kids held out without complaining. I thought it would be good for them to see faith put into action but afterwards didn't think much about it.

A week later the kids finished up lunch and I got preoccupied with something in the kitchen. About twenty minutes after we were to start our afternoon schooling, I went looking for the children and found them in the backyard. I heard them laughing and talking, but couldn't see them. When I pulled back some bushes I found them sitting up on the back wall of our yard holding up posters to all the passing traffic. Many cars were honking and the kids were excited and motivated. When I glanced at the cardboard posters I saw that they were the same ones we had used at the clinic the week before. "God loves Babies" and "Thou Shalt Not Kill." The kids obviously decided to get more mileage out of them.

"What made you decide to do this?" I asked, a little surprised.

"We want to save more babies *now*," they enthusiastically answered.

And apparently, judging by the honking of the cars driving by, they were making an impact, now. I could only imagine what was to come!

Darlene Neilson

Darlene lives with her husband Gordon and children Madeline, Graham, Gregory, Diana and Matthew in Jacksonville, North Carolina.

I am always ready to learn, but I do not always like being taught. ~Sir Winston Churchill

FOR HEAVEN SNAKES!

My first year teaching at home was a challenge to say the least, but I was determined that we would embrace every learning activity that came our way. However, I eventually learned that a mother's willingness to embrace opportunities has limits.

I had gone from the previous year with two kids in the Catholic school and one in public school, (no room at the inn), a preschooler and one-year old, to starting my first year at home with four school-aged sons, my toddler daughter and newly pregnant. It was also our first year living in the country.

Even lying on the couch trying to manage my morning sickness, I discovered that I really could do this. We used text books but also made learning enjoyable. It seemed every subject presented itself with a way to have fun and get personally involved, especially when it came to science. It was typical to find the boys outside looking for leaves to match up with the ones identified in a science book or bird watching and catching and mounting insects. We hatched chicks and learned firsthand why it's not a good idea to help a chick escape an egg he has been unable to get out of himself for three days. (Trust me, you don't want to know the rest of the story.)

That first spring, after attending a group homeschool science class, fourth-grader Luke and second-grader Tyler, came home and caught and then froze a frog. I did not realize what had happened until I walked in on the defrosting process and heard the conversation.

Tyler: "Luke, it's a certain kind of frog that can freeze and come back alive."

Luke: "Yeah, I think you're right. This is the second one I've tried and it's not moving."

Later that week, my husband Mark heard of a rattlesnake round-up in a near-by town. We both thought it would be great fun for the boys to attend (and give the frogs a break). I stayed home with the new baby and toddler, but thoroughly enjoyed the boys' enthusiastic descriptions when they returned home. I loved hearing how the snakes were caught, decapitated, skinned and then fried and served up for eating. The boys thought it was so cool to be able to say they had eaten rattlesnake.

The event left such a big impression on my kids that by the following Monday, they were still talking about it, particularly our two little nature boys: Luke and Tyler.

"Mom, I watched how they skinned the snakes and I know I can do it," Luke reported.

"I do too," Tyler chimed in.

"That's nice," I chuckled. "If we ever run out of food, we can eat snake."

We mothers must take care when we use sarcasm with our children lest they misunderstand. My own boys took my remark as permission. Or at least, they figured I did not tell them *not* to skin snakes.

After our lessons were over and chores completed that day, I took advantage of a little quiet time to do some writing while the girls napped and the boys played outside. "Mom, we did it!" I heard a cry from the distance.

Seconds later, Luke and Tyler appeared before me, proudly holding up their trophies. One boy held up an eight-inch snakeskin and the other held up some white, slimy looking meat. (Rest assured, it was a garter and not a rattler.)

"Oh my goodness," I declared. "I did not expect you to actually go out and skin a snake."

"But you said we could," they both claimed in earnest and in unison.

But the big surprise was yet to come. "Will you cook it for us now?" Tyler asked. Both boys stood wide-eyed, waiting for my answer.

"Cook it?" I asked incredulously.

"Yes," explained Luke. "You just need to bread it and fry it like they did with the rattlesnakes."

I knew that they boy's adventure would not be complete if they could not say they ate the snake. So, like any good homeschooling mother would do, I breaded the slimy meat and cooked it up until it looked like a big, fat onion ring. The boys were more than satisfied and I considered it a good memory for them.

But I was wrong. Luke and Tyler had only just begun. Luke read books about curing snakeskins with salt. Soon he had quite a collection. (Sixteen years later we still have some of those skins.) And each time, we either cooked the meat or he wrapped it up to put it in the freezer for later. In case you are wondering, I never tasted the snake myself. The boys said it tasted like chicken, but I doubt it. They never really ate much of it. I suppose the bones got in the way since they had no idea how to filet the thing.

Our snake adventures finally came to an abrupt halt one day when Luke, Tyler and a neighbor boy caught the big daddy of them all. It was summer by then and windows were open, so I think everyone from miles around must have heard their loud shouts and excited screams. I ran outside to see what the commotion was about. The boys had caught a four-foot bull snake. No big game hunter could have been more excited. The neighbor boy's grandmother looked out her window from the hill above our house, laughing and waving. She was a kindred spirit, relishing the joy of watching three young boys embracing the country life.

The boys quickly skinned the snake, marveling at the large skin they had to cure now. But when they brought four-feet of slime into my kitchen to cook, I protested. "You don't really want to eat that, do you?" I questioned.

All three boys looked at me with surprise. But of course they wanted to eat it. This had been a big hunt and they were ready for the big feast.

I looked at the meat. Chicken it wasn't. "Okay," I relented. "I'm going to cook this up, for one reason—because I love you. But this is going to be the last time. I'm not cooking anymore snake after this."

The boys agreed readily. I breaded and put the meat into my big frying pan. It stiffened into a circle looking like an onion ring on steroids. I served it up onto a big plate. The thick, stiff meat did not readily lend itself to cutting. Each boy took a bite and expressed pleasure. I have no doubt that it could have tasted like dirt and they would have responded the same. It was the idea of what they had accomplished that they loved, certainly not the flavor of the serpent. After a few nibbles, each boy declared himself full and went onto the next adventure.

I kept my vow not to cook up another snake. Luke and Tyler, however, remember their snake hunting adventures with gusto. Although we moved into town, my children Teresa, age 14, John, 10, and Isaac, 8, love to catch snakes at a park we frequent near the Missouri River. I've refused to let them bring any home. (No, we are not preoccupied with snakes. My kids will catch anything that moves.)

I'm thinking of taking the kids to the rattlesnake round-up this year. I would like to see the event myself. However, there will be limits this time around. I often ask God to help me to stay as enthusiastic with the younger kids as I was with the older ones but I'm asking for a waiver from Heaven when it comes to snakes.

Patti Maguire Armstrong

FLOWERS ON THE HOUSETOPS

For one week, three buses of Catholic students from Mishawaka, Indiana were going to New Orleans, Louisiana in order to help rebuild the still-lingering damage from the tragic disaster Hurricane Katrina. When I heard about the opportunity, I immediately thought, *The South is pretty, right?* and signed on for the trip. Sister Marie, a Franciscan sister and theology teacher at the Catholic high school, was going to be one of the chaperones, so when I approached Mom and Dad, they were open to the idea. The fact that it was a service project clinched the deal.

Soon I found myself on a bumpy bus ride traveling south. We laughed, talked, and slept. On the way down we stopped at ETWN in Birmingham, AL, toured the grounds a little, and attended Mass. These experiences, as well as visiting the house of Martin Luther King Jr. and touring the Birmingham Civil Rights Institute definitely started to make me take the whole trip more seriously and see it is an opportunity for personal enrichment.

Upon arriving in the city of New Orleans, everyone's mood changed to a quiet yet enthusiastic awe. At least three times, we searched for a restaurant on our GPS so we could grab a bite before heading to the retreat center where we would be staying only to find an eating establishment in ruins. Hundreds upon hundreds of houses were still boarded up. Three years after the storm, people were still living under the overpass in tents. And yet, the people were healing, and moving on to rebuild not just their buildings but also their lives.

After driving through the city of New Orleans and getting just a brief 'sneak-peek', everybody was beyond excited to begin work the next day. My specific group was to renovate a local school, which had been flooded. The students were having classes in about thirty different trailers. We all woke up bright and early around 5:30 a.m., put on work clothes, grabbed tools, and headed out on the bus to the dilapidated school grounds.

Arriving at the school, we worked enthusiastically for about two hours outside, removing rocks and debris from the area. As the students passed from class to class, they smiled and waved, often personally stopping to hug us and thank us. The labor was backbreaking, but nobody minded. At one point in time, exhausted by the heat and constant lifting and digging, I ventured over to where the water was, a simple enough task, or so I had thought. In a split second, my right knee gave out and I toppled backwards.

I have had an odd knee problem for as long as I can remember; it will occasionally swell, dislocate, and lock up, making it excruciatingly painful for me to attempt to move it for anywhere from thirty seconds to about an hour. Eventually, it unlocks and pops back in, either by itself or with my urging, and the swelling goes down, leaving me with only mild discomfort for another hour or two. I would later find out that this bizarre aspect of my anatomy is caused by a combination of premature arthritis, hyper-extended knees, and a discrepancy in the angles from my hip to my knee to my ankle.

"It's okay. This has happened before." I grimaced and tried to reassure my concerned colleagues. "Give it a couple of minutes." The pain was sharp and I tried to move my knee back into position but was having no luck.

After I sat for thirty minutes with increasing pain, Sister Marie and another chaperone, Ms. Hinora, urged me to allow them to take me to the hospital but I didn't want to leave. "The most time it's ever taken (to pop back) is an hour." I insisted.

About an hour later, my knee was swelling more and I had no pain relief so we left for the emergency room. I looked out the window as I rode in the car, trying to hold my knee stable so it wouldn't hurt too badly when we inevitably hit bumps and jolts in the road. I noticed that the roofs of hundreds of houses were a pure radiant yellow. When we slowed down enough to look closer, it became apparent that it was not the roofs that were yellow, but the flowers that were overrunning the roofs. *The flowers were growing on the housetops.*

It was later explained to me that the waves from the ocean that Hurricane Katrina had caused deposited immense amounts of soil and sand on top of people's homes. When the water levels went down, the sand and soil stayed. The yellow wildflowers had then grown in what was left. It immediately became a powerful metaphor for me, reflecting the hope and spirit of the people of New Orleans.

We pulled into the hospital parking lot and I limped in with my chaperones. We waited in the emergency room for six hours before we realized it was a public hospital that could not help us. Again, I hobbled out, with help and we drove to the private hospital and got in within an hour. When the doctor called my name, I let out a huge sigh. Finally. I would be able to walk again.

Unfortunately, this was not the case. The doctor ordered a CAT scan and X-ray, despite me assuring him that neither of these would be of any help to him (they weren't) and then he refused to relocate my knee under the pretense that he did not want to damage anything. I was incredibly frustrated! My right knee and ankle were now roughly twice as large as those of my left, and the pain was getting worse. Now, every minor muscle twitch from anywhere in my body caused me to bite my tongue and sweat. He was adamant, though. "Come back in the morning." He said, handing me a prescription for oxycodone, which I gratefully accepted. "If nothing's changed, we'll see what we can do."

Sister Marie then informed me that a close friend of hers had offered the hospitality of her home for me. The retreat center where the rest of the group was staying had no air conditioning, and she simply had to insist. The hospitality that this complete stranger showed me was so overwhelming. She helped me prop up my knee with pillows and blankets, brought me food on the couch, and offered me every comfort that she had available throughout that excruciating night.

We showed up at the doctor's office the next morning. He injected me and popped my knee back into place in no time. Previously, the longest amount of time for which I had ever experienced a 'lock-up' was about an hour. This round had gone roughly thirty-eight hours. Because I was still in pain and the knee was weak, despite my newfound ability to actually move my right leg, I got crutches and a knee brace. I was unable to help with any physical labor projects much to my disappointment. I could only sit and watch.

I had gone to New Orleans to give, and ironically, I learned to receive. I felt, in some ways, as helpless as the people of New Orleans must have felt as an unexpected negative event changed their plans and their entire lives. The service trip was not a loss, though. Oftentimes, the unexpected happens and your course is changed beyond your control....but you move forward --with hope-- and find the flowers on the housetops.

Caroline Thomas

Caroline was homeschooled until ninth grade before attending the local Catholic high school. She is now a sophomore at the University of Dayton (OH) studying Psychology and Fine Art, and she hopes to pursue a career in social work and art therapy.

GUARDIAN ANGEL LESSON

Enchiladas sounded especially good for an autumn supper. I was midway in the process of adding the spicy ingredients that made this one of the family's favorite meals, when Katie, our then seven-year-old said, "Mommy, I liked reading about guardian angels today. Do you really think that they keep us from getting hurt?"

I answered her saying; "Our angels are assigned by God himself to guide us always toward good and away from evil. We should talk to our angels every day and ask them to help us know what we should be doing at all times."

Satisfied, Katie began to set the table. A few minutes later she came up to me as I stood at the stove, stirring the thickened sauce and started talking about guardian angels again. I didn't notice that she had set a glass plate on the burner that I had just removed the saucepan from. It was still on. Five-year-old Teddy had been listening to the discussion and had just come up beside Katie when suddenly, the plate exploded in hundreds of tiny shards of glass! Just as it happened, I thought of our angels. Katie screamed which frightened me that flying glass might have hurt her. But when I looked over at her, I realized her cries were of excitement. In her high-pitched little girl voice she sang out, "Mommy, our angels - they really did protect us!! See, none of us were hurt!!"

The three of us had stood within inches of that plate and yet, with shattered glass literally strewn from one end of the kitchen to the other, not one shard had touched us!

It's funny that we teach our kids the truths of our faith but we can still be astonished when we experience them ourselves. That was certainly a lesson for the day.

Nellie Edwards

LATE NIGHT CATECHISM

It's almost 8 o'clock, and I really want to get these kids to bed. I've got a business to run, and work to do, and I need the time this evening.

"Mom!" Sarah calls from the open back door, "Rachel says there isn't any God. What can I say?"

The rest of the neighborhood is on our driveway making chalk creations. "Come in here for a second, honey," I call.

She comes in the kitchen, and I search for something to say. *Holy Spirit, help!* I pray.

"Honey, you know you can tell Rachel that even if she doesn't believe in God, He still believes in her."

"But her parents told her, Mom! Her parents told her there is no God! How can they say that?" Sarah says, incredulous.

"I don't know, honey. I guess when parents don't believe in God, that's what they tell their children. Why don't you just go out there and be as nice to Rachel as you can," I say.

"Why?" she asks, just like a kid.

"Because I said so," I answer, just like a mom. Sometimes, I have to punt. I wasn't prepared for that question at that moment. But that is mothering on most days. It's a vocation of interruptions. I am thinking about mats and frames and glass, and suddenly, I have to wonder how parents can tell their children there is no God. The streetlight goes on, signaling them to come in for the night.

"Pajamas!" I call as they troop in, "Teeth! Wash the chalk off! Wait-wash first! Then pajamas--then go to the bathroom! And then I'll read to you!" I try to be as efficient with my words as I want to be with my work tonight.

I am an artist's assistant. My husband is the artist. I take all of his photographs and mount, mat and frame them. I keep the records (entering every customer into a database that now holds close to two thousand names), tracking the zip codes so that I can mail our schedule of art fairs to them just prior to each show. I also do the accounting, inventory, ordering and most phone calls. And I homeschool.

Some days I wonder if it's really possible to do it all. Some days I think how easy it would be and how freeing to send them off to school. Then I could frame all day instead of waiting until night, when I'm tired and wish I were reading instead. But then, I see my children watching me on the computer, and asking me how I get those numbers to add up, and I teach them how to balance a cash flow sheet. They know how much money in change we take to each show and they can tell me if we need a roll of quarters. One daughter can help inventory our small pictures and give me the list of what needs to be printed before the next show.

And every day, we're together, learning and growing, and most days, I am grateful for the job that keeps me home, close to my husband and children, and that has provided our family with a lifestyle that I wouldn't trade with anyone.

We travel during the school year, we work, eat and play together, and most days, I am glad I homeschool and work at home. I have always homeschooled, but not always for the good reasons I have now.

When my oldest was four, we decided to homeschool her because she was bright. They weren't going fast enough for her in preschool. So, I read all the *Home Education* back issues I could find in the library, and came up with my homeschooling philosophy. I would homeschool for the sake for my child's inner freedom. I wouldn't test her; I would allow her to discover the world at her own pace and in her own way. This philosophy went along with my liberal thinking at the time. My child would be free of the constraints of the "system" and grow without schooling.

That worked for a couple of years. I was attracted to unschooling. It fed my lazy nature and my desire to do child-led learning. Then, two things happened by the grace of God. First, I was introduced to the Mary Fabyan Windeatt books, the children's stories of the saints. Prior to this, I didn't know anything about the saints. The first book I read was about St. Martin De Porres and it was as if everything in me changed. I can still recall the wonderment I felt at that period of my life. I had been a "good enough" Catholic. I had known that something was missing, but still thought I was doing better than most. After all, I still went to Mass each and every Sunday. But try as I might, I couldn't seem to make any spiritual progress. When I went to confession, I confessed the same old sins over and over. I was stuck, and but I didn't know why.

Then I read about St. Martin, and I realized that "good enough" wasn't good enough. I was called to be a saint! And this book, this story answered some spiritual questions I had. Suddenly, I knew that I couldn't just go along, not caring that much about my faith. I had to do more. And this corresponded exactly with the second thing that happened. A friend invited me to her Bible Church's Women's Bible Study. I attended for about six months. At first, I thought I was being so ecumenical and open that I could attend this Bible study.

After a while, I would tell them what the Catholic Church said about certain Bible verses, and try to show them that there were deeper layers of meaning. They were spending hours each week just barely scratching the surface of the Bible. The words were taken literally, or skimmed over. At first they seemed to listen to me, but they did not like it when I mentioned my particular religion. I was told not to mention my church, and to just attend and get what I could out of it. I was a bit hurt, and after that, I began to notice the subtle anti-Catholic things I was hearing. Then I found out that a lot of these women were ex-Catholics, and then I wondered why. I wondered where the truth was; I wondered if their interpretation of the Bible could be the right one.

Then one day at the Bible study, it all came to a head. The leader was explaining a certain passage in St. Paul in a way I'd never heard before. I went home confused and puzzled. I looked up that passage and I could see that there wasn't a "plain" or an obvious meaning.

Maybe it did mean what she said, but somehow, I didn't think so. It seemed like a "protestant" interpretation, and I wondered if there was a "Catholic" interpretation, and why they would be different. And for the first time in my life, I wondered how, when the Bible wasn't clear, how you could come to know the true meaning? And I really credit God with giving me the understanding at that point that there was "a" truth. I somehow knew through His grace, that there couldn't be two conflicting ways of interpreting the Bible.

I connected to the Internet, and looked up Catholic Bible Study and Ecumenical Bible Study. I got one hit, a site called Catholic Convert. I started reading, and found out here was a guy (Steve Ray) who actually converted to the Catholic Church! This was a revelation to me. The Catholics I knew were all cradle Catholics or ex-Catholics. I had never heard of anyone converting to the Church; I actually didn't know it still happened!

Steve and I e-mailed. He had an article on his website about ecumenical Bible study (which is why the search engine had found his site) and he went into all the reasons that Catholics should attend only Catholic Bible studies. I understood, and started on a fantastic journey into the world of people understanding the Catholic faith a lot better than I did-the world of Catholic converts. Over the next few years, Catholic converts would teach me my faith.

After learning all I could about the Church, and where the Bible is from, and who had the authority to say what books were in it, and how there is a way to know the right interpretation, I knew at this point that if I wasn't already Catholic, I would have had to join the Catholic Church.

I can't call myself a convert, like Scott Hahn or Steve Ray. I can't call myself a revert, like Jeff Cavins. I had always been Catholic, had always practiced my faith. Still, I had a conversion from a cafeteria-style, good enough Catholic, to a "trying to be perfect" (Matt. 5:48) Catholic. So, my decision to homeschool my children also went through a conversion, and now, I homeschool to pass on the faith, to raise saints and to get my family into heaven.

So, back to my day. How do I homeschool while running a business? Like everyone else, I use the opportunities that come my way as teaching moments. We use all Catholic materials because I think that's important. There are some days where we use a lot of the curriculum materials, and on other days, when we're preparing for an art show, we teach in a less formal way. Somehow, it all works out, and there is always time for everything, even when it didn't look like it at first.

Since my conversion, I strive to overcome my lazy nature, rather than giving in to it. I work hard at giving as much of myself as I can. I try to see the sacrifices I make as helping me get to heaven, so that I won't resent the time away from "what I want to do."

Homeschooling isn't always easy. It's a sacrifice we make for our children and families. The time we give now is important, if we use that time wisely. We all have opportunities every day, and if you're like me, at the end of the day, we examine our conscience and find that we left many opportunities behind.

So, we strive to wake up tomorrow, and try a little harder, try to sacrifice a little more, try to become more and more like Jesus, like the saints. One day, a national magazine writer interviewed Mother Teresa. This writer said to Mother Teresa, "Oh, it must be so easy to do what you do, since you're a living saint and all."

Mother Teresa just smiled, turned to the writer and said, "I struggle every day."

I struggle every day, too. It's a little easier knowing the saints struggled as well. I try to be the best parent, I stop reading to answer questions, do a little impromptu catechism instruction, give an unplanned bath to the child who fell in the mud, and a thousand other vocational interruptions.

And, I struggle to be the best Catholic I can be. I try to live the Catholic life in a way that shines forth through me, my children, our family and our way of life. I try to stay calm and peaceful in the midst of the struggle of the day.

"Mommy?" I hear someone calling from the bedroom long after bedtime. I go to my daughter's room.

"Yes, love?" I whisper.

"Can I just talk to God tonight, instead of saying the Our Father and stuff?" she wonders, sleepily.

"Yes, love," I say with an inner smile, "you can just talk to God. He will love that. Goodnight, sweetie."

"'Night, Mom," she answers.

And the catechism lesson is over for another day.

Nancy Carpentier Brown

GIFT AT MASS

At Mass, I glanced over at the three children next to me. My six-year-old was making shadow pictures on the pew. My twelve-year-old was doing a careful examination of each of her fingernails, while my fifteen-year-old was—I really wasn't sure where he was—but his glazed-over eyes told me he wasn't at Mass.

I sighed deeply: such is life. We have been attending Mass with our children since they were born. Prior to relocating for my husband's work, we were even blessed with a schedule and neighborhood church that allowed us, as a family, to attend daily Mass for almost four years. Recently I was noticing that my children—especially those mentioned above—had developed a "familiarity breeds contempt" view of Sunday Mass.

This is not the case every Sunday. My oldest son is an excellent server, and enjoys being the priest's "go-to guy" for a role in which his gaze rarely leaves the altar and the tasks at hand. I've noticed the rest of the children are more content and attentive on the second Sunday of every month (except in July and August.) That is our parish's donut Sunday schedule when everyone is invited to meet and greet over coffee, juice and donuts. I have used the bribery effect that donuts (and other tasty treats) can have on their behavior—not specifically at Mass but at other public place—so that they expect this same reminder at Mass.

For every family there is a rule or expectation of behavior at Mass. For some families younger ones may be allowed small snacks, books or toys. Some families allow this same type of distraction for children who will then be receiving Christ in Communion. Other families bring nothing and manage to get through only a little worse for wear. For our family, I will not allow anyone over the age of four to bring any sort of distraction, no matter how "holy" it may be. This rule isn't a problem, but what about distractions that come from inside of the child? What could I do to help my older ones be more attentive at Mass?

Over the next week or so, I prayed about the problem and during one particularly difficult Mass, in what was surely an inspiration from the Holy Spirit, I had the idea to try to make my children more "present" at Mass by trying to see themselves as a "present" to Jesus. Just as Jesus gives the gift of Himself at every celebration, couldn't my children give themselves as a gift back to Him?

At home, I wrote down my ideas and compiled the tools of my lesson and waited for a good opportunity to spring this idea on them. On a lazy afternoon, while the youngest ones were in bed for naps, I gathered the usual suspects around the dining-room table where several empty gift boxes, wrapping paper, ribbon, small pieces of paper, markers, tape and scissors were waiting.

The lesson was simple. We talked about the two meanings of the word "present," the presents they love to receive at Christmas and on their birthdays, and the aspect of being present at an event such as Mass. We talked about whether they thought they were always being their best at Mass and, by God's grace, they all admitted they weren't. We talked about the reasons we go to Mass and Who we are visiting. If we believe we are visiting with the King of the Universe, why aren't our actions always proper, polite and kind?

With a humble admission of my own guilt in this matter, we discussed how we all get distracted by each other, our own thoughts, and even the people around us. I spoke about the fact that time playing with our own thumbs, or talking with our sister about our favorite movie took time away from Jesus. We then began to brainstorm about how we should act. The words "quiet," "still," "hands and feet quiet," "eyes on the priest," "prayerful," and even "no squishing each other,"(from my six-year-old) were put on a list.

These words and actions, I told them, would become a gift they would bring to Jesus. They would bring quiet feet, still hands, prayerful hearts and more to Jesus when we went to Mass. They each wrote these words and others they came up with on the pieces of paper. We said a prayer together asking Jesus and our guardian angels to help us, all of us, be better behaved at Mass. We then placed them into the gift boxes, wrapped them up with paper and decorated each gift with ribbons and stickers. We then talked about a typical Mass.

With the gifts in our hands, we started talking about the Mass and how we would become distracted. My daughter remembered her habit of examining her lovely long fingernails. Upon this remembrance, she had to open her present, take out the card that read quiet hands and then attempt to re-wrap the present. We went around the table with each mentioning a distraction they knew they were guilty of, including Mom. I was reminded of how I would focus on the meal I would be fixing later that day instead of the Last Supper I was remembering that moment. We did this several times and I allowed the child to mention things to each other and to me. By the end of the time, our boxes were almost empty of cards and our gifts to Jesus, the beautifully wrapped presents we had started with, were a disaster. As we surveyed the mess, we were struck into silence and more than a bit of sorrow.

How easily the present of ourselves to Jesus at Mass had become a pile of torn paper, crumpled ribbon and abandoned ideas. My daughter said this wasn't a gift worthy of anyone, much less Jesus, while my oldest son hung his head, embarrassed to let us see the tears in his eyes. Immediately, we began to think again on how to keep our hearts and minds on Jesus, the reason we were there. How could we stay focused during Mass?

Using a children's book on the Mass, we started at the beginning, talking about each part and if it was a struggle to pay attention then. We discussed what each part meant and the purpose behind what we did and what the priest did. They all agreed it didn't get hard until the Liturgy of the Word where is it was difficult to listen to sometimes unfamiliar readings. Our resolution was to go over the readings before Mass. The words would then be more familiar and they would listen to see if they could remember what we read and what was being said. The older children said they enjoyed reading along and resolved to get a missal before each Mass.

The homily was the next sticky point, and I had to admit that I, too, sometimes had trouble staying focused. We knew that due to many factors, including their age and maturity and the skills of the homilist, they often just couldn't keep their minds from wandering. We decided that while we couldn't stop the wandering, we would make efforts to keep our minds in the church. No longer would my sons take mental trips back to the house to play computer games; my daughter wouldn't travel to a sunny beach for a vacation, and I would stay out of my kitchen cupboards. We resolved that if our eyes and attention wandered we would try to keep them in the church were they could dwell on our church's beautiful statue of Mary, on the tabernacle to make a quick visit to Jesus, or on one of the carved Stations of the Cross on the walls. This resolution wasn't perfect, we knew, but while we were working on our muscles of self-discipline, checking what Mary was wearing was better than checking out what the woman in the pew ahead of us was wearing.

During the Liturgy of the Eucharist, the key was keeping our eyes on the altar, where before our very eyes a miracle was going to happen. Through the power of God mere bread and wine was going to become the Body, Blood, Soul and Divinity of Jesus Christ. Small, short prayers help us to remain focused on the miracle. By repeating Jesus' name or "Jesus have pity on me, a sinner" or any of the many other short prayers, we can keep our eyes and hearts on the altar. Looking back over the children's missal, we came up with appropriate aspirations for each period of silence. We decided what would be important for them to say during the raising of the cup and the Elevation of the Host. We talked about whom we would remember during this most powerful of prayers. Finally, we resolved that we would remember to place ourselves on the paten with the host as a true gift to Jesus.

I then admitted that a problem for me was being distracted by those receiving Communion. I told my children that many times I find myself giving attention to the outfits and shoes of those receiving and would even make judgments on the state of their souls! I asked them what I should do. Their brilliant idea was that instead of judging those people, I should pray for them. This bought my own words back to me, because I remind them to pray whenever they have problems with friends or family members. We all agreed than instead of seeing the Communion line as a fashion show, we would see it as a line of fellow Catholics who need our prayers.

The last part of our lesson was going over the family's sign language, those silent signals given to the children to remind them of the manners and actions expected in any public place. We use the familiar finger over the lips for silence, but also tap a finger near the eyes to remind them of where their eyes should be. We point a finger into each palm of the hand (actually sign language for "Jesus") to remind them to keep their hands still. Finally, we point to their hearts when we want to remind them to love their siblings and for Jesus, and to stop squishing or teasing.

The lesson was complete, and as a final gift to Jesus we took a set of reminder cards, put them in a nicely-wrapped box and placed it on the mantle, next to a statue of Mary, His mother. It remains there today and on Sunday when we walk past we remind ourselves of how we want to act, the gift we want ourselves to be.

That day, as I was putting the supplies away, I was struck by my own failures to keep my mind and heart on Jesus at Mass. I also realized that there were holes in the children's understanding of what Mass is and should be. I had assumed they knew more than they did. It's not that they weren't taught. Rather, they simply had to be reminded. My husband and I are their primary educators in the faith and all other subjects. However, while we were good with using repetition as a skill in math and spelling, we had forgotten its value in every subject including faith lessons. I made a resolution to myself, and later shared it with my husband, that we needed to take a few minutes each week to remind them of what we expected and what they could anticipate. I also admitted that my example had not been what it should have been. My children were only doing what they had seen me do time and again.

I resolved to take myself to confession. In the end, what had begun as a lesson for the children had, as so often happens, become a real lesson for me.

© 2006 *Catholic Exchange*

Rachel Watkins

CHASING BUTTERFLIES ALL THE WAY TO GUATEMALA

Creativity has always been an ally and an enemy for me, and in a formal school setting, it netted me plenty of tickets to the principal's office, where my principal would stare at my rap sheet, not sure if I actually broke any written rules, but certain that it was his responsibility to harness me in. When I was being homeschooled, that creativity was boundless. My parents decided to take me out of school in the fourth grade and it eventually almost got me arrested for transporting endangered butterflies across international borders.

But first, let's back up a bit. For about three years of my life, I was buggy for bugs. I captured them, read about them, categorized them on pin-boards, and experimented on them (I just needed to know if after being frozen, an electric fence could bring you back to life, sadly, it could not.) I believed in those years that I would one day become an entomologist.

In a conventional academic setting, I can't imagine our six legged friends filling more than a chapter of most science classes. For me, they filled an entire chapter of my life. I would rush through my other subjects and promptly be out the door with my butterfly net and killing jar. There was a microscopic world out there, just waiting to be discovered. When my mom took me to the library, I brought home stacks of college level books on insects.

In hindsight, I wonder what the librarians who checked out the books for me thought? Here I was at eleven and twelve, walking out the door with titles like, *A Theoretical Framework for Understanding the Seasonal Behavior Patterns of Leptocoris Trivittatus.*

So I liked bugs, and I devoured everything about them. When I read that some cultures eat them, I *literally* devoured them. My recipes typically triggered my gag reflex, but that might have just been because I was too busy with bugs to study the culinary arts.

When I was thirteen, a mission group from my church was going to Guatemala to build houses for the poorest of the poor. I was eager to help people, and it sounds shallow to admit now, but when my parents gave me permission to go on the trip, I was thinking more about all the exotic species of insects I could collect down there. Such was the extent of my interest (obsession?).

Soon, those colorful pictures of Central American species, which previously only been in my books, could be mine.

With a suitcase full of insect-collecting equipment and a Spanish phrase book, I boarded a plane. I was a thirteen-year-old in an otherwise all-adult mission group, except for my fifteen-year-old brother, Aaron, who was also along on the trip.

As a side note, my parents, albeit a bit crazy themselves, were not irresponsible in sending their sons off to the Third World without them; although, my big, Catholic family would have still been able to fill up the front Church pew on Sundays if they lost us. They were friends with Patrick Atkinson, the founder of The GOD'S CHILD Project (GCP)—the organization where the volunteer group was headed. They spoke with him, and it was arranged for us to stay at his house. He might have backed out of the arrangement if he had known I would be overturning every rock in his yard in search of beetle larva.

While everyone else in the mission group was absorbing the new world they found in Guatemala, I was absorbing two—the macro one that consisted of a foreign culture and language, and the micro one beneath everyone's feet. People started catching on. Children in the GCP's Dreamer Center School watched *el Hombre Insecto* pinching bugs from the foliage, and they started catching insects and bringing them to an ecstatic me. My Guatemalan collection, thanks to the help of the schoolchildren, grew and my pride swelled.

My time in Guatemala flew at the speed of a Monarch, and too soon, the time came to board a plane home. My luggage was filled with Ziploc plastic bags containing soon-to-be categorized insects. I was also carrying some bugs I had not tried to collect. For the flight home, I was feverish and my babbling stomach caused me to frequently run to the restroom (A lab test back home would later confirm that I had worms). *Disgusting, worms are not even insects. They are not even closely related to them!*

When the customs official asked to search my bag, I begrudgingly put it on the aluminum counter. His gloved hands began pulling out a gambit of suspicious materials. Professional entomologists often carry chemicals (I used rubbing alcohol) for killing insects, syringes for safely injecting these chemicals into jars, and of course, they often carry insects. This would be permissible for a researcher with the proper credentials. But finding these things in the bag of a thirteen-year-old boy is not something that Customs and Boarder Control likely encounters very often.

As I held my bubbling stomach, the agent waved his supervisor over, and they turned over the contents of my bag to look at the strange items from different angles as they puzzled over which laws I was breaking.

"They're for insects," I explained.

"For insects?" the agent repeated interrogatively.

"Yes," I retorted, indicating a black plastic bag that held my treasures. They agent raised his eyebrows and opened the bag to find my dozens of plastic bags filled with dead insects. He looked disgusted, but when he got to the butterflies, he become genuinely alarmed.

"You know it's illegal to take endangered species, dead or alive, out of a country," he said in an official tone.

"Yes," I said, beginning to worry that I could lose what were at that time my most valuable possessions, "but none of these are endangered." Secretly, I wished I *did have* some endangered species. What a trophy those would make! I elaborated, "You can look them up if you want, but none of these are endangered. Trust me; I would know if they were."

The agent looked completely dumbfounded. Surely, they had not covered this situation in his training. In the end, despite the fact that he said my bag was one of the "most suspicious bags he had ever seen without making an arrest," he let me and my insects fly home. Soon each insect was proudly pinned to a tag boards inside wooden cases that my dad and I made for them. I think those cases are still in my parent's attic.

The things we are certain of in childhood often don't make it to adulthood. While I still have an impressive store of unnecessary insect knowledge, my interest in them has long since faded. I still find them fascinating, as I find most things in this wondrous world, but it was not something I studied in college. But when homeschooling allowed me to spend hours a day studying insects, I was actually learning something far more valuable than the fact that cicadas spend seventeen years in the larval stage. I was learning how to learn, learning how to teach myself the things I wanted to know, without needing any teacher other than myself to acquire knowledge.

With only a library card and an observing eye, I discovered that I could learn about anything I wanted. There are no bits of knowledge off limits to anyone. All that is needed is the desire and the commitment. With these two things the vast, sometimes daunting world shrinks to a more manageable size.

Outside of homeschooling, it is unlikely my thirst for knowledge would have been as quenched. Taking three weeks off from school to go to Guatemala would likely not have been an option. And even though my path did not end up being laden with beetles and butterflies, the opportunity that homeschooling afforded did lead me to where I happily am today.

Through the many twists and turns on life's enigmatic road, more than a decade later, I ended up back in Guatemala starting my third year as a staff member of GCP. Now, instead of filling up jars, I am part of an organization that fills lives of poor boys and girls with the sort of things that will help them, "break the bitter chains of poverty through education and formation" (The GCP mission statement). I even found myself with a Guatemalan girlfriend, and when she cringes at a moth fluttering above her head, I tell her "Oh don't worry, that's just *Pachispinx Modesta*, it can't hurt you, it's actually a fascinating species..."

If one day I have kids of my own, I plan on teaching them how to catch grasshoppers, like my mom taught me (whenever I was in the outfield in Little League Baseball, my mom would find grasshoppers jumping out of my uniform's pockets onto the laundry room floor). Even if they hate bugs (heaven forbid it!), I hope they have the same opportunity that I did—to freely pursue their passions as far as their desires directs them. Homeschooling did that for me, and it will certainly be something I will consider as an option for them. I'll just have to hope and pray that lion taming or skydiving is not their passion.

Luke Maguire Armstrong

Luke Maguire Armstrong lives in Antigua, Guatemala where he directs The GOD'S CHILD Project's Guatemalan programs. His booki Poems for the Dolphins to Click Home About is available on Amazon.com. His is the co-author of Amazing Grace for Survivors and The Expeditioner's Guide To The World: Stories Of Intrepid Awesomeness From The Open Road. Follow him on Twitter at twitter.com/lukespartacus.

UNKNOWN SUBJECTS

It's been almost thirty years since I was homeschooled in sixth grade.

Since that time, compared to most human endeavors, homeschooling has answered its critics so resoundingly that it has surprised even its ardent supporters. When my mother was promoting homeschooling thirty years ago, she couldn't have reasonably expected the level of success that homeschooling has achieved. It has gone from being a fringe activity to a mainstream one. During this time, I don't know if I've heard *all* the objections to homeschooling, but I'm confident I've heard *most* of them.

Among these objection questions:

> *"How will homeschooled children make friends?"*

> *"How will homeschooled children get in sports programs?"*

> *"How will homeschooled children get into college?"*

> *Last but not least, my personal favorite: "How will homeschooled children learn multiculturalism?" (I lie awake nights worrying about this one.)*

During the past generation and a half, most objections to homeschooling have been asked and answered.

One objection, however, has proven especially resilient, namely:

> *"How can a parent teach a child a subject that he does not know himself?"*

I'll call this the "Unknown Subjects Argument."

When I first heard this argument as a teenager, it sounded like it made sense. It has a sort of metaphysical logic to it, i.e., "You can't give what you don't have." I figured that some children need someone smarter than their moms or dads to teach them academic subjects. (Of course, I didn't think this applied to me; I didn't know any people smarter than my Mom or Dad. I still don't.)

As the years have gone by, I have realized that the Unknown Subjects Argument doesn't wash. The students *do* surpass the masters, and they do it regularly.

Even my young children disprove the theory. For instance, last November, I took my twelve-year-old son Demetrius to the National Aquarium in Baltimore and we toured the vast center, observing the fascinating sea life that God made on the Fifth Day. A few weeks ago, it dawned on me that Demetrius must have been more observant than I was. One night, after Demetrius and I finished cleaning the dining room together, we scampered into the living room and turned on *Jeopardy*, just in time for the second round. I might have to confess the sin of pride for this, but I like to impress my children with how many questions I answer correctly. However, that night, a funny thing happened. The category of "Sea Creatures" was highlighted, and I was stumped on every question. Demetrius wasn't. In fact, he started running the category. "What is a white shark?" he answered. "What is a sea dragon?" he answered. The kid knows a lot about sea creatures. This got us into a conversation about the mammals, fish, and marine biology. In fact, he informed me recently that he was thinking about being a marine biologist when he grows up.

If the Unknown Subject Argument were true, Demetrius' knowledge of marine biology would have been obstructed by the glass ceiling of my parental knowledge, but he has obviously surpassed my limitations. Because truth be told, the closest I've ever come to studying marine biology was a few Lents ago, when I ordered the #4 Fish and Chips combo meal at Long John Silver's.

In reality, there is no glass ceiling that parents pass on to their children. Pope Pius XI recognized this fact, writing: "For the most wise God would have failed to make sufficient provision for children that had been born, and so for the whole human race, if He had not given to those to whom He had entrusted the power and right to beget them, the power also and the right to educate them."

"The power to educate them." Maybe we fathers ought to spend a little time contemplating this idea: that *we have the power to educate our children.* One of the things that the Unknown Subject Argument fails to take into account is that educational methods have increased exponentially in the past thirty years. With modern technology, such as educational software, videotapes, CDs, DVDs, Internet sites, underwater web cams, online encyclopedias, videogames that teach children about sea life, not to mention books, magazines, and trips to aquariums, I have every reason to believe that Demetrius can use these tools to become a great marine biologist. He's already been doing a lot of this research on his own. Most importantly, he has a natural curiosity that drives his learning ability. The only glass ceiling in Demetrius' future is one on an aquarium tank.

This leads me to believe that the greatest educational gift we fathers can give our children is not to teach them; it's to *teach them how to teach themselves.*

I know very little about astronomy, nuclear physics, or computer engineering, but I believe that my children could learn any or all of these subjects at an "A" level. I have no reason to believe otherwise. Moreover, this isn't just theoretical on my part. The evidence illustrates that many homeschooled children have gone on to establish successful careers in fields that their parents knew very little about. The Unknown Subjects Argument survives in theory, but fails in practice. Theoretically, it can't happen, but in reality, it happens every day

John Clark

John is as investment advisor representative and serves as the President and CEO of Paladin Financial Group. John earned a B.A. from Christendom College and is recognized as one of the foremost experts in the field of investment ethics. He has written and spoken extensively on ethical investing. He is also a sought-after motivational speaker for Catholic homeschooling conferences, and writes a regular column in the Seton Home Study School newsletter. John resides in Front Royal, Virginia with his wife and nine children.

THE LAST WORD WITH DR. RAY GUARENDI

We would like to thank Dr. Ray Guarendi for allowing us to share with you the transcripts from Relevant Radio: On Call with Dr Ray and Friends aired 2nd March 09. Dr Ray is a clinical psychologist. He and his wife have ten adopted children who are homeschooled.

I don't know where this number comes from. It says, "Homeschooling goes BOOM! In America, (there's a) 74% increase in families teaching their own children" since...oh since 1999.

"Homeschooling movement is sweeping the nation". This is from World Net Daily. "Supposed estimate is (that) one and a half million children are learning at home"...If I am recalling correctly, the (number of) children who are in school... is around fifty-five sixty million; so one and a half million is what, two to three percent?

"Department of Education has reported that homeschooling has risen by 36% in just the last five years." The National Center for Educational Statistics statistician Gail Mulligan told USA Today "There is no reason to believe it would not keep going up".

Now I am not so sure whether I agree with that, because (homeschooling) can only go as far as the ceiling of stay at home moms. I think the number of stay at home moms, out of moms in total is 20%, 25% or somewhere near (that).

A 2007 survey asked parents why they chose to homeschool. Here are the most popular reasons:

Concern about the school environment, including reasons such as safety, drugs, negative peer pressure: 88%."

I am sure that many of you would speculate (that) the number one reason (they would homeschool) would be for moral or religious. The way the questions are phrased, negative peer pressure might come underneath that moral or religious rubric.

The second most common reason is "a desire to provide religious or moral instruction: 83%."

So there, that is for most folks, right up there in their motives for homeschooling.

- Dissatisfaction with the academic instruction at other schools: 73%
- Parents having a non-traditional approach to children's education or un-schoolers who consider typical curriculums and standardized testing as counterproductive to quality education: 65%.
- Other reasons such as family time, finances, travel distance: 32%.
- Child has special needs: 21%
- Physical or mental health problem: 11%
- Parents who said that they homeschooled to provide religious or moral instruction increased from 2003 to 2007

What that basically means is that more people are homeschooling because they feel that they can provide the kind of moral religious education (they want without) working so hard against the peer culture and the school culture. It used to be just the peer culture but unfortunately a lot of what is going on in the schools under the auspices of the schools is antithetical to the kind of moral worldview that many parents want their children to have.

Above all other responses, parents cited providing religious and moral instruction as the most important factor in the decision to teach their children at home. 36% said that's the most important factor. (The) second most important (is) concern about the school environment

I've got to believe there's overlap there. If you're concerned about the school environment, you're not necessarily just concerned about drugs or violence. Much more commonly, it's the peer culture with its attitudes, its language, its subjects of talk, its view of sexuality; its overall jaded material worldliness.

(The) third (most important factor in the decision to teach at home is) dissatisfaction with academic instruction 17%.

Research has shown the positive effects of homeschooling through the years. Brian Ray, President of the National Homeschool Research Institute, reveals that homeschooled children fair as well or better than private and public school students in terms of social, emotional and psychological development". That is true. The next time somebody says to you, "What about socialization?" you can have twenty different answers to that. But if you want to make it quick you just look and say 'Well, the research says they're better socialized.'

'WHAT?' (they might respond.)

"Argue with the research," (you might respond.)

And that's true; the research does say that... homeschoolers are more active civically (than their traditionally schooled counterparts). They tend to have... more involvement in their communities. They tend to ...score better academically...They tend to have better self-images; yeah that's right even the homeschoolers have better self-images. How could they do that without all those self-image courses? You know they must have those self-image courses. You homeschooling moms you better incorporate some self image courses in your curriculum. Homeschoolers earn higher marks than peers who attend public schools.

The home educated (children) in grades K to 12 have scored, on average, at the 65th to 80th percentile on standardized academic achievement tests in the United States and Canada compared to the public school average of 50th percentile.

How could that be? How could these untrained mothers, these non-professional educators, actually teach their children so that they outperform their peers? It's not possible!

Apparently it is. There are three studies, which demonstrate that demographics, income and education level of homeschooling parents are generally irrelevant with regard to quality of education. On average, homeschoolers in low-income families with less formal education STILL score higher than state school averages.

Yes, there has been a wonderful study done where they compared moms who are certified teachers (with) moms who are college graduates (with) moms with some college (with) moms (who are) high school graduates (with) mums (who are not) high school graduates. Do you know what they found? NO DIFFERENCE in the kid's achievement scores. The only place where there seemed to be a little bit of a blip was in mathematics taught by non high school graduate moms... But other than that the component seems to be not the mother's academic level but the mother's motives, the mother's heart, the mother's commitment, the mother's sacrifice. Doesn't that just beat all?

Relationship –who'da thought it?

ABOUT THERESA A. THOMAS

Theresa A. Thomas grew up the oldest of 13 children and graduated from Saint Mary's College, Notre Dame, IN. She is the wife of David, and homeschooling mother of nine children, ages five to 22. She is a columnist ("Everyday Catholic") for *Today's Catholic News*, a regular contributor to *The Integrated Catholic Life* e-Magazine, and freelance writer and speaker. She was a story contributor to several books in the *Amazing Grace* (Ascension Press) series, and her work has appeared in numerous national and local publications. Theresa treasures her vocation as wife and mother, and lives with her family on 10 acres in northern Indiana. She enjoys helping her husband grow organic vegetables...and kids.

To invite Patti Maguire Armstrong and/or Theresa A. Thomas to speak at your event, visit www.RaisingCatholicKids.com; email pattiarmstrong@mac.com or TheresaThomasEveryDayCatholic@gmail.com; or contact the publisher at 248-917-3865

ABOUT PATTI MAGUIRE ARMSTRONG

Patti Armstrong met her husband Mark in the Marshall Islands, Micronesia where they were both Peace Corps volunteers. They live in North Dakota and are the parents of ten children, eight boys and two girls, including two adopted orphans from Kenya. Patti has degrees in social work and psychology and a master's in public administration. She worked in these fields before staying home full-time to raise her children. Writing began as her hobby, here and there between kids' naps. As a freelance writer, Patti wrote for both secular and religious newspapers and magazines. She has authored 9 books, including: *Dear God, I don't get it!* (Bezalel Books), *Catholic Truths for Our Children* (Scepter Publishers) as a guide to help parents pass on their Catholic faith, and served as the managing editor and co-author of the Catholic best-selling *Amazing Grace* book series (Ascension Press). Patti has been a guest on EWTN Television's "Live" program with Father Mitch Pacwa and twice on Doug Keck's "Bookmark" program and on Catholic Radio programs around the country. She contributes articles to the Integrated Catholic Life and Catholic Exchange e-Magazines. Her website is www.RaisingCatholicKids.com

SPECIAL THANKS

Sarah Storick lives in central North Dakota with her family. She is the oldest of seven children, having five sisters and one brother. She is 14 years old and will be entering her tenth year of homeschooling this Fall. Sarah enjoys drawing, writing stories to entertain her siblings, photography and crafts.

Melissa Thomas lives in northern Indiana with her eight brothers and sisters. She is 15 years old and was homeschooled for nine years. Melissa enjoys drawing, writing stories, singing, and performing on Marian High School's dance team. She particularly loves chronicling humorous situations in everyday life through cartoons, and hopes someday to be a Disney animator.

Joan Steckelberg—cartoonist and photographer—has been married 23 years to Lyle. They live with their eight children, six rabbits and two dogs.

To contributors who provided photos for their stories. We know that the original color pictures you gave us more completely captured the essence of your story but hope you'll appreciate our efforts to make the picture black and white and share with the readers—we know they'll be gracious in accepting our efforts to share these little pieces of your life!

Thanks and acknowledgement goes to Prestige Photographics in Mishawaka, IN, Valentinos Photographics in Granger for the individual and family photos, as well as to the contributors for supplying the photos in their stories.

Bezalel Books

for your home, school, or parish

All titles available for bulk purchase by contacting us at

248.917.3865 or visit www.BezalelBooks.com

Religious Education and Catholic Living

1. *Our Jewish Roots: A Catholic Woman's Guide to Fulfillment Today by Connecting with Her Past* by Cheryl Dickow
2. *The Rosary Workout* by Peggy Bowes
3. *Becoming a Creation Steward: A Catholic Ethic for the Environment* by Dr. Thomas Collingwood
4. *Heart to Heart: Ignatian Spirituality* by Dr. Kuenga Chung
5. *The Way of the Cross for Children* by Kathryn Mulderink, OCDS
6. *Walk New: A Lenten Resource* by Kathryn Mulderink, OCDS
7. *Top Ten Ways to Build a Wonderful Marriage* by Deacon Patrick Hays

Children's Books (4 – 8 year olds)

1. *Joseph's Hands* by Harriet Sabatini is an excellent vocation awareness book
2. *Where Do Priests Come From?* by Elizabeth Ficocelli is an excellent vocation awareness book
3. *Little Rainbow Rosary* by Rose Maria Dennis
4. *Isabel's Sister* by Harriet Sabatini
5. *Lonny the Lizard* by Joan L. Kelly
6. *When Kids Dream and Trucks Fly* by Rosemary McDunn has a workbook section in back
7. *Where the Leprechauns Hide* by Charlene Hoyt
8. *Agatha Bagatha, very bad cat* by Jeanne Carr
9. *The Way of the Cross for Children* by Kathryn Mulderink

Young Readers (9 – 13 year olds)

1. *All Things Guy: A Guide to Becoming a Man that Matters* by Teresa Tomeo and Cheryl Dickow
2. *My Big Feet* by Joan L. Kelly
3. *The Green Coat: A Tale from the Dust Bowl Years* by Rosemary McDunn has a vocabulary and critical thinking section in back

4. *Dear God, I don't get it* by Patti Maguire Armstrong has a vocabulary and critical thinking section in back
5. The "*Hiding the Stranger* series by Joan L. Kelly
   a. *Hiding the Stranger in Hickory Valley*
   b. *Hiding the Stranger of Baker Street*
   c. *Hiding the Stranger: The Journey Home*

Teen Readers

1. *The Story of Peace* by Miriam Ezeh
2. *Daily Direction for Teenz* by Catherine Wasson Brown
3. *All Things Girl: Truth for Teens* by Teresa Tomeo and Cheryl Dickow
4. *The Way of the Cross for Teens* by Kathryn Mulderink
5. *Joey's Journey* by Brad Thomas
6. *The Green Coat: A Tale from the Dust Bowl Years* by Rosemary McDunn previously named #1 in historical fiction

Adult Inspirational, Group Study or Book Club Selections

1. *Elizabeth: A Holy Land Pilgrimage* fiction by Cheryl Dickow has book club questions in back
2. *Our Jewish Roots: A Catholic Woman's Guide to Fulfillment Today by Connecting with Her Past* non-fiction by Cheryl Dickow has group questions in back and downloadable pdf files on www.BezalelBooks.com under the "Our Jewish Roots" tab
3. *Mary: A Study of Papal Encyclicals on Mary* by Cheryl Dickow is a study with questions and prompts of 12 different Papal encyclicals over the past 100 years.
4. *The Seven Essential Goals of a Godly Woman* by Cheryl Dickow
5. *Newsflash: My Surprising Journey from Secular Anchor to Media Evangelist* by Teresa Tomeo has book club questions in back
6. *Joey's Journey* by Brad Thomas
7. *Broken and Blessed* by Catherine Adamkiewicz
8. *The Story of Peace* by Miriam Ezeh
9. *Loved to Life* by Janet Melia

A Few Pages for You!

We invite you to use these last few pages of the book to record your own "homeschool heart" stories or to have your children write or draw something.

And please know that you, a reader of our book and someone with a "homeschool heart," will always remain in our prayers...

LaVergne, TN USA
06 October 2010
199781LV00007B/80/P